POSTCARD HISTORY SERIES

Van Wert County

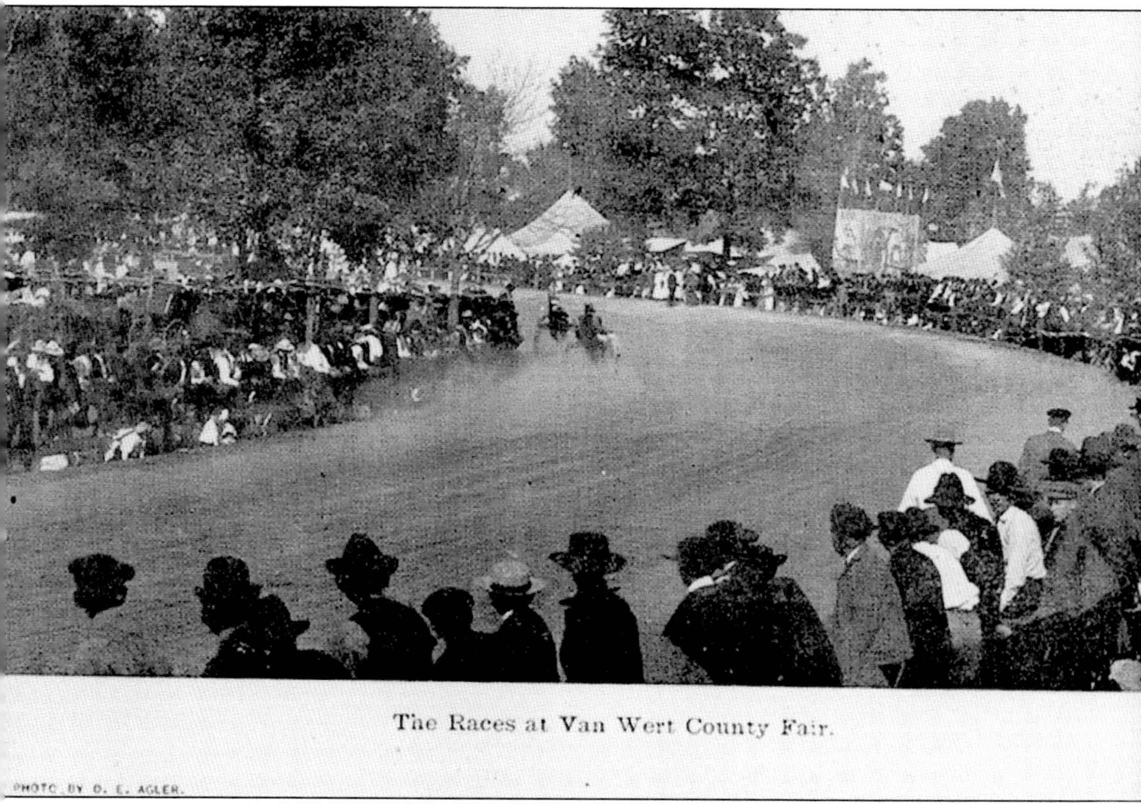

People could get no closer to the excitement at the Van Wert County Fair than an inside track seat on the grass. This D. E. Agler photograph card, postmarked 1901, was used to promote the fair for at least a decade. (Author's collection.)

On the front cover: The Hotel Van Wert was located at the corner of Washington and Jackson Streets in Van Wert. One of the women is listed as Nettie Embody in this *c.* 1912 postcard, but her position in the photograph is not given. (Ken Cripe collection.)

On the back cover: Of all the amazing sights at the Van Wert County Fair, the giant hot air balloon was the most wondrous. "Magnificent," declared one promotional postcard. "Two marvelous airship flights will be made each day of the fair by Strobel, the fearless navigator of the air." (Ken Cripe collection.)

POSTCARD HISTORY SERIES

Van Wert County

Cheryl Bauer

ARCADIA

ISBN 0-7385-4028-5

Published by Arcadia Publishing
Charleston SC, Chicago IL, Portsmouth NH, San Francisco CA

Printed in the United States of America

Library of Congress Catalog Card Number: 2005936751

For all general information contact Arcadia Publishing at:
Telephone 843-853-2070
Fax 843-853-0044
E-mail sales@arcadiapublishing.com
For customer service and orders:
Toll-Free 1-888-313-2665

Visit us on the Internet at http://www.arcadiapublishing.com

This book is dedicated to my mother, Ruth Bauer,
who has taught me so much.

Contents

Acknowledgments

Many of the fascinating postcards in this book would never be seen by the public without the generosity of Kenneth D. Cripe, who shared his large collection of Van Wert postcards. My thanks to Ken for his patience, helpfulness, and sense of humor.

My husband Randy McNutt spent hours scanning postcards to get the sharpest images possible, often a difficult task. As always, Randy was my advisor, editor, and proofreader on this project.

A special thanks is due to the Van Wert County Historical Society and Museum for lending some additional postcards for the book, and for providing a meeting place where Randy and I could scan Ken's cards.

Sincere thanks to the people who offered information, assistance, and encouragement for the project, including Marilyn Bebout, Martha Bigham, Cherrie Evans, Laura Gorman, Charlotte Harting, Frank Loomis, Darlene Meyers, Paul Oechsle, Helen Prill, Elizabeth Pruden, Jeanne Zeigler, the staff of the Brumback Library, and Valerie Elliott and the staff of the Smith Regional Library in Oxford, Ohio.

Finally, thanks go to Melissa Basilone and John Pearson of Arcadia Publishing for making this book possible.

INTRODUCTION

Van Wert County was as optimistic as any place in America during the golden age of picture postcards in the first two decades of the 20th century. People eagerly showed off their towns, homes, businesses, churches, and schools to postcard photographers. By then, photography had become common enough that photographers could quickly shoot something, develop large amounts of film, and even play tricks on the viewer with retouched photographs and views enhanced by artists.

The picture postcard craze was also fostered by the Private Mailing Card Act of 1898 that allowed for inexpensive (one cent) mailing of cards. The picture side allowed the sender to share a favorite view and the correspondence side provided a quick way to convey a message to loved ones or business associates. Some businesses included a photograph or comic illustration to embellish their advertising postcards.

The cards in this book date from 1873 to the mid-1950s. Convoy, Delphos, Middle Point, Scott, Van Wert, Venedocia, Willshire, and Wren are represented here. The search for postcards from other Van Wert County communities continues.

This project began with a collection of cards I accumulated over 25 years of browsing at flea markets and antiques shows. Having grown up in Tully Township, I started with Convoy cards and branched out from there. When the possibility of a book arose, I was introduced to Ken Cripe, a retired WERT Radio broadcaster and consummate collector of Van Wert postcards.

Ken's collection, gathered over 30 years and still growing, contains many rare and fascinating cards. I am especially indebted to Ken for his cards of the Van Wert County Fair and the Peony Festival, both of which earned their own chapters. Several postcards from the Van Wert County Historical Society round out the book.

A few general observations can be drawn about life in Van Wert County by looking through these postcards. People worked hard: on the farm, in corner shops, on delivery routes, in factories, and on the railroads that linked thriving villages around a busy county seat. Folks also liked to enjoy themselves by participating in parades, attending the fair, getting together with relatives and friends, and going out to movies and the theater.

Through the years, people have appreciated their rich history. The county was named for Isaac Van Wart, one of a trio of patriots who foiled a treasonous plot by Gen. Benedict Arnold and British spy Maj. John Andre in 1779, during the War for Independence. An infamous clerical error changed the spelling of the county's name.

Capt. James Riley became the county's first white settler in 1821, purchasing seven tracts of land near the banks of St. Marys River. Prior to that, many Native American people lived here, including members of the Pottawatomie, Wyandot, Delaware, Shawnee, and Miami nations. The U.S. government set aside 1,280 acres as a reservation for Jean Baptist Richardville, a nephew of the famous Chief Little Turtle, but when Richardville's people moved on, the land was opened for white settlers. Riley, an adventurer and sailor, named the county's first town for William Willshire, a British official in Africa who ransomed him after he was shipwrecked and enslaved there in 1815.

From Willshire's settlement to 1854, when the first train rumbled through Van Wert, growth occurred rapidly. Residents drained swampy land, opened stores, organized churches, and started farms and grain elevators.

Some loss was inevitable. Native Americans who had once established towns and seasonal camps drifted away, hoping to maintain their independence in other regions. The great woods of oak, sycamore, walnut, maple, and ash that once covered the area were harvested to build the county and create a short-lived timber industry.

Transportation, a popular subject of picture postcards, helped shape the county. Delphos grew as a result of commerce on the Miami-Erie Canal, and as the 19th century progressed, the county's other communities developed along train tracks and depots. When traction cars arrived in the early 1900s, the Fort Wayne-Van Wert and Lima Traction Company helped bring the city and the country together through the interurban electric rail system.

By the 1920s, the increasing availability of automobiles—thanks in part to Ohio City's John W. Lambert—and sprawling highway networks made transporting people and products even easier. U.S. 30, later a section of the national Lincoln Highway, accommodated east-west travel, and U.S. 224 and U.S. 127 provided north-south routes.

During this time of growth, postcards provided memorable views of Van Wert County, but for us they cannot tell the county's entire history. That job is best left to the books listed in the bibliography. Their researchers, editors, and writers have captured stories of the men and women who made Van Wert County such a good place to live, work, and visit.

One

AGRICULTURE

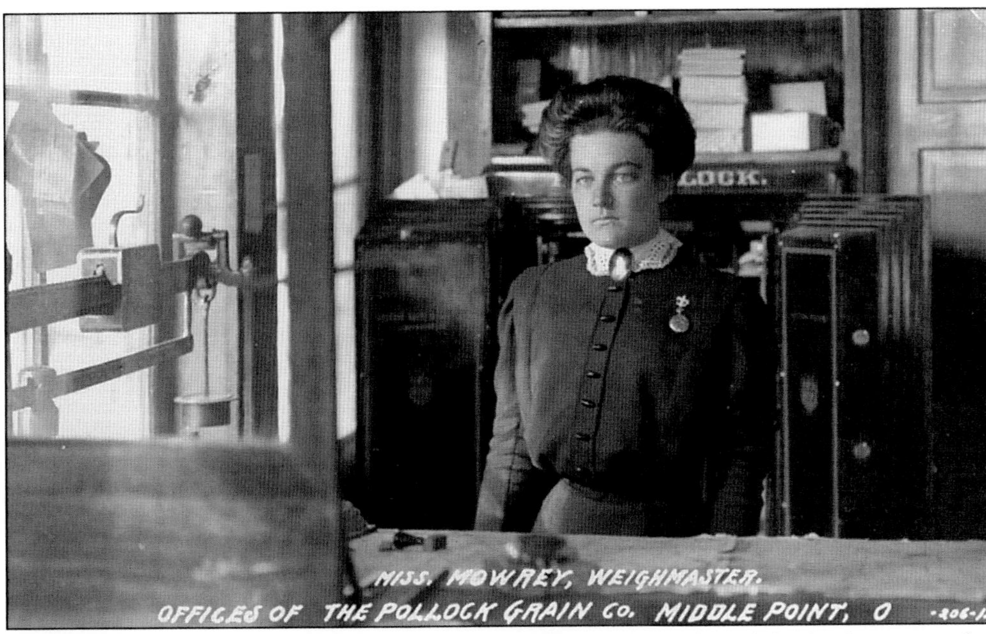

Weigh masters at rural grain elevators had to be intelligent, thorough, and absolutely trustworthy. A woman named Miss Mowrey performed the job at Pollock Grain Company in Middle Point at the beginning of the 20th century. The building of the railroad through Middle Point made the village an agricultural center. An advertisement for Pollock's identified the business as a buyer and shipper of grain, hay, and straw in car lots, and proclaimed the region "the Egypt of America," referring to the land's fertility. (Author's collection.)

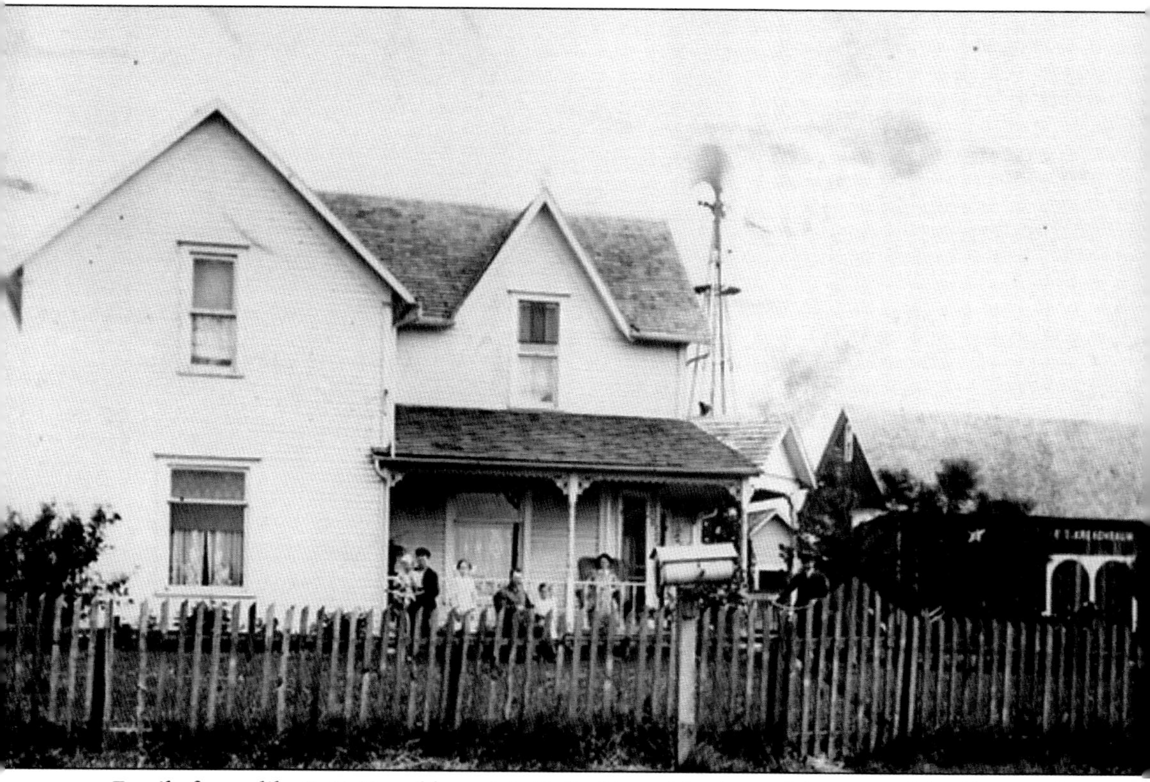

Family farms, like E. E. Kreachbaum's in Tully Township, formed the county's backbone. Three generations pose on the porch while a young man is perched on his bicycle behind the gate. "This is where we bunk," E. E. Kreachbaum wrote in a birthday greeting to his brother Charles in Columbus on August 28, 1911. By the beginning of the 20th century, a total of 202,071 acres in the county were dedicated to agriculture with almost half of them under cultivation. Tully Township's population in 1910 was 1,383 people, representing 451 families, most of whom were engaged in farming. The largest landholder in the county in 1910 was George H. Marsh, who owned 1,260 acres in Ridge Township. (Author's collection.)

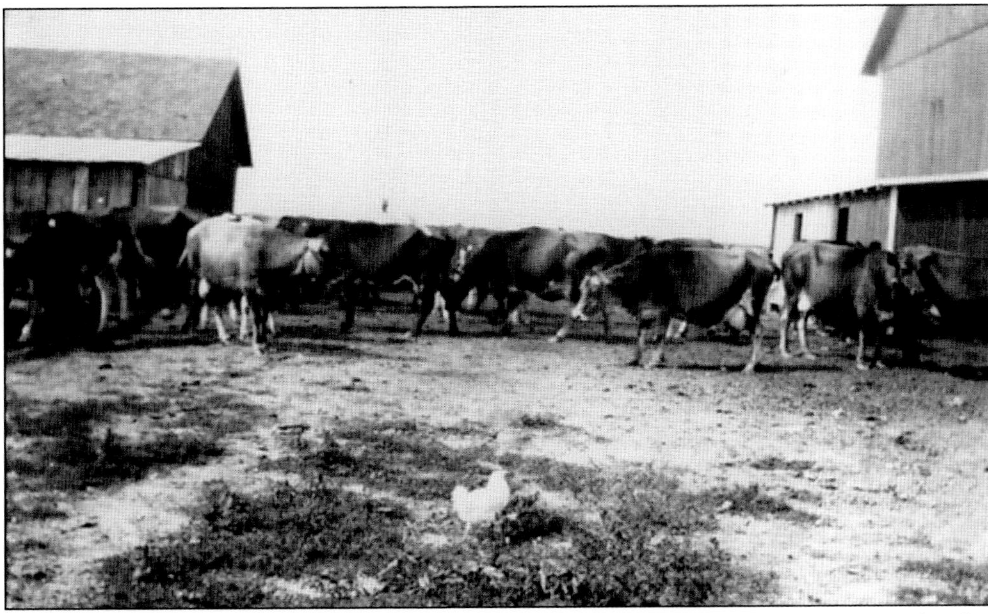

During the first two decades of the 20th century, picture postcards became so popular that farmers, including Frederick J. Bauer of Tully Township, had their livestock photographed. Guernseys, Jerseys, Ayrshires, and Holsteins were favored breeds. Dairymen like Bauer, with small to medium size herds, sold directly to customers. Bauer, the author's grandfather, is just visible on the left, standing behind the cows. (Author's collection.)

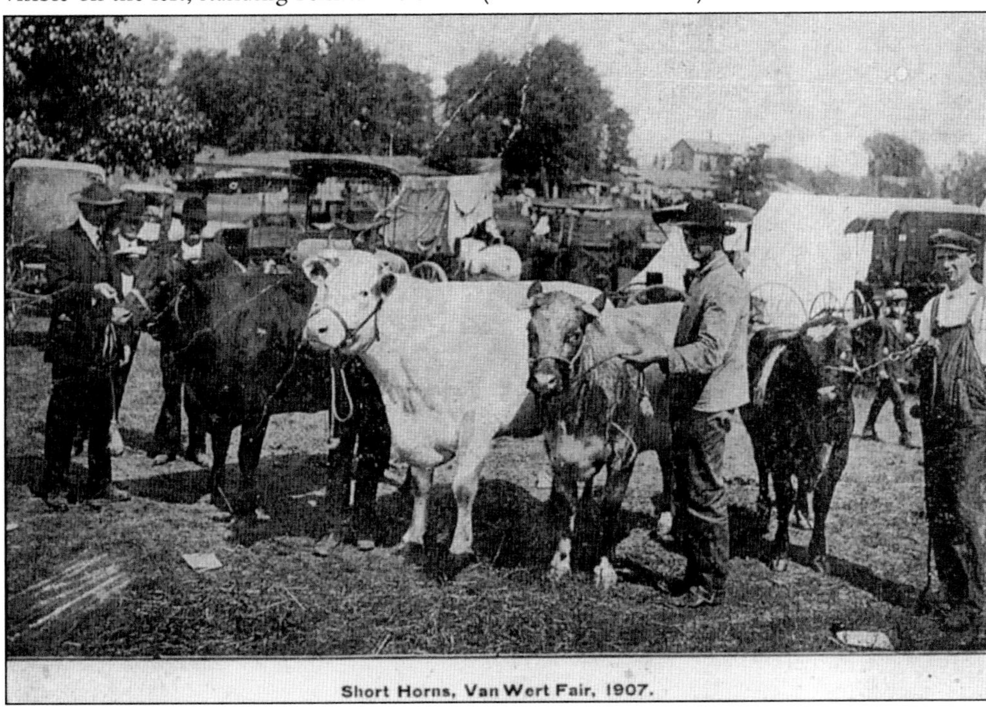

By the early 1900s, most breeders and farmers preferred short horn cattle. This advertisement for the 1908 county fair displays a sample of the cattle that had been exhibited the previous year. The advertisement hoped to entice more farmers to enter their cattle into the fair. (Ken Cripe collection.)

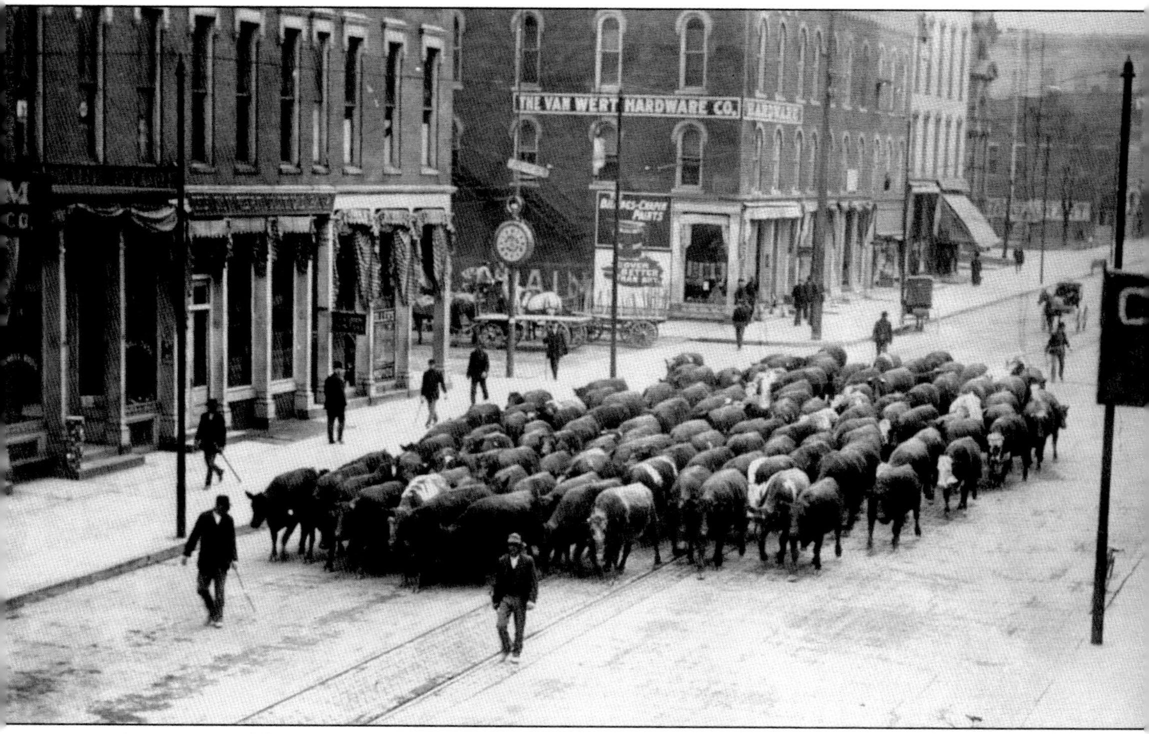

Carriages and buggies are seen pulled over in Van Wert in 1906 to make way for a cattle drive down Main Street as steers from Marsh Farm were driven to the slaughterhouse. George H. Marsh, one of the county's most prosperous and benevolent citizens, left 1,400 acres on the edge of town and over $4 million to establish the Marsh Foundation for boys in need in the 1920s. George H. Marsh, the son of George Marsh who first helped survey the county, made his fortune through his Eagle Stave Factory. He believed that hard work and education created success, and mandated that the Marsh Foundation provide academic and vocational training for its students. Agriculture was one of the vocations the young men could learn there. For decades the farm produced its own cattle, hogs, and chickens. (Ken Cripe collection.)

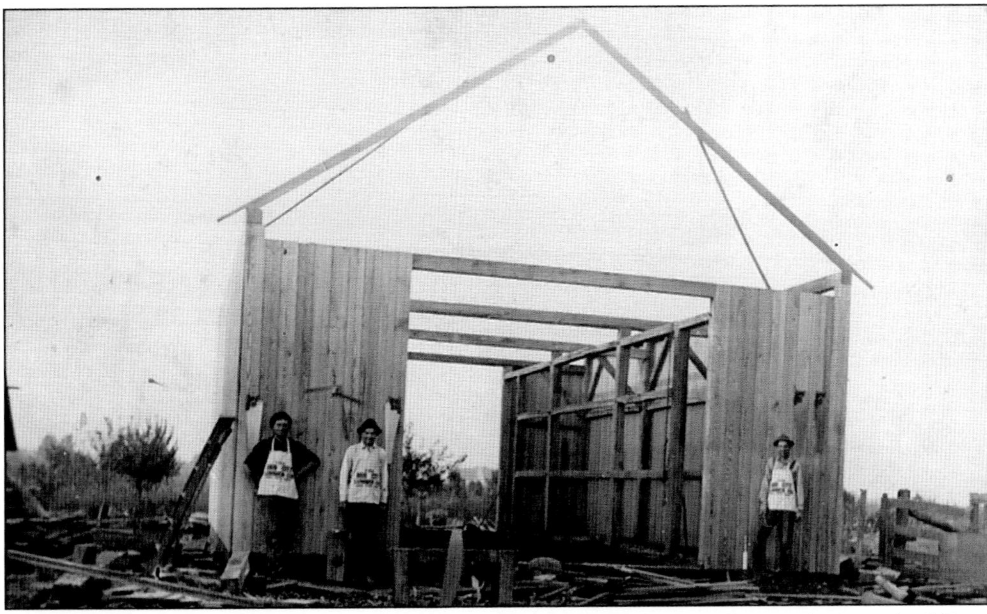

As agriculture continued to thrive in the early 1900s, a building boom of barns, sheds, outbuildings, and silos took place across the county. These carpenters wore aprons advertising the Ohio City Lumber Company, which prominently advertised fence posts and hay tools along with a complete line of lumber, glass, cement, and builders' hardware. (Author's collection.)

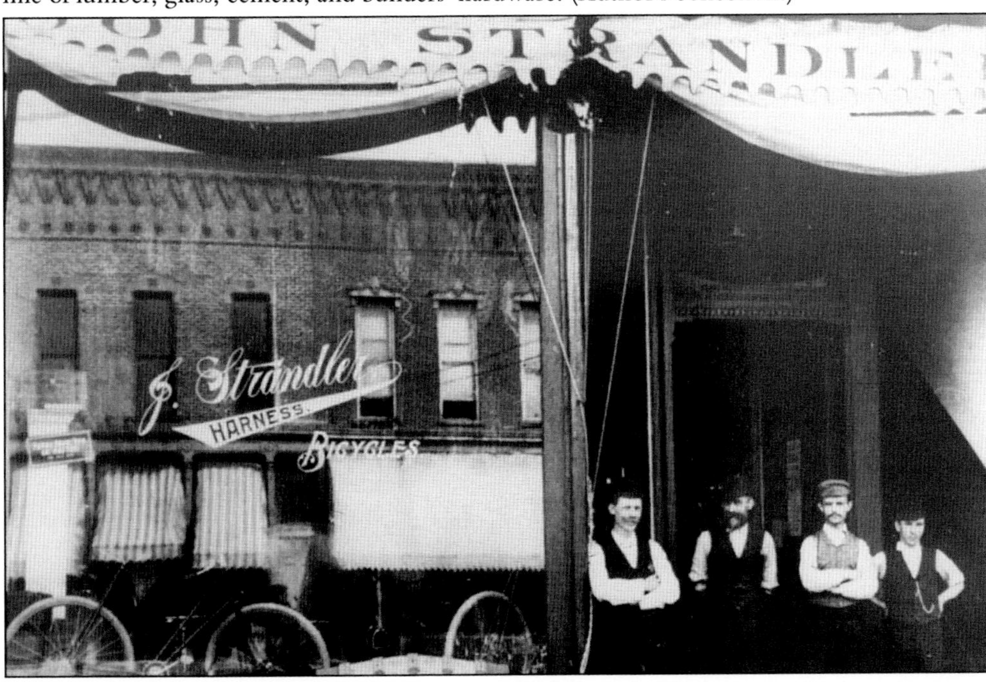

John Strandler's harness shop in Van Wert profited from the increase in farming. He began manufacturing harness in a West Main shop in 1867. He joined with harness maker B. F. Shoop in 1870, eventually buying him out. Strandler was so successful selling bicycles, harnesses, and related items that he funded the YMCA in 1916. The men in this early-1900s card are not identified. (Ken Cripe collection.)

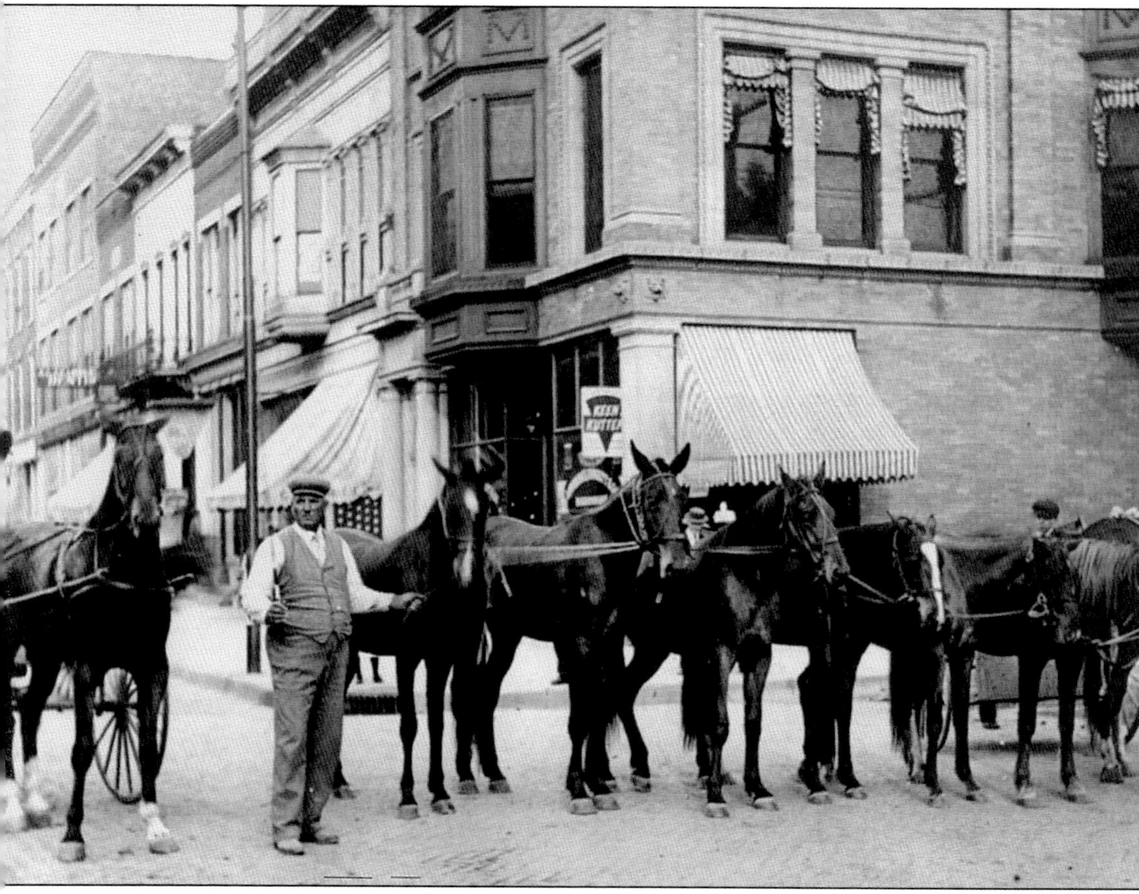

This unidentified man holds a fine team of horses at the corner of Main and Jefferson in Van Wert in the early 1900s. The photograph was taken from Third Ward Park, which was originally used as the town commons for horses and livestock. Van Wert's earliest residents typically kept a flock of chickens, a couple of pigs, a horse, and two or three cows. The cows were turned out to the commons each day to graze, each wearing a bell. "If you knew the particular pitch or tune of your cow's bell, you had little trouble rounding her up at milking time," wrote Ada Young Longsworth of her youth in Van Wert. A century before this photograph was taken, members of the Pottawatomie tribe lived there near the middle fork of the Little Auglaize River, later renamed Town Creek. Native Americans lived in bark huts, and hunted deer, bear, and raccoon. The arrival of the whites heralded a change to an agrarian culture. (Ken Cripe collection.)

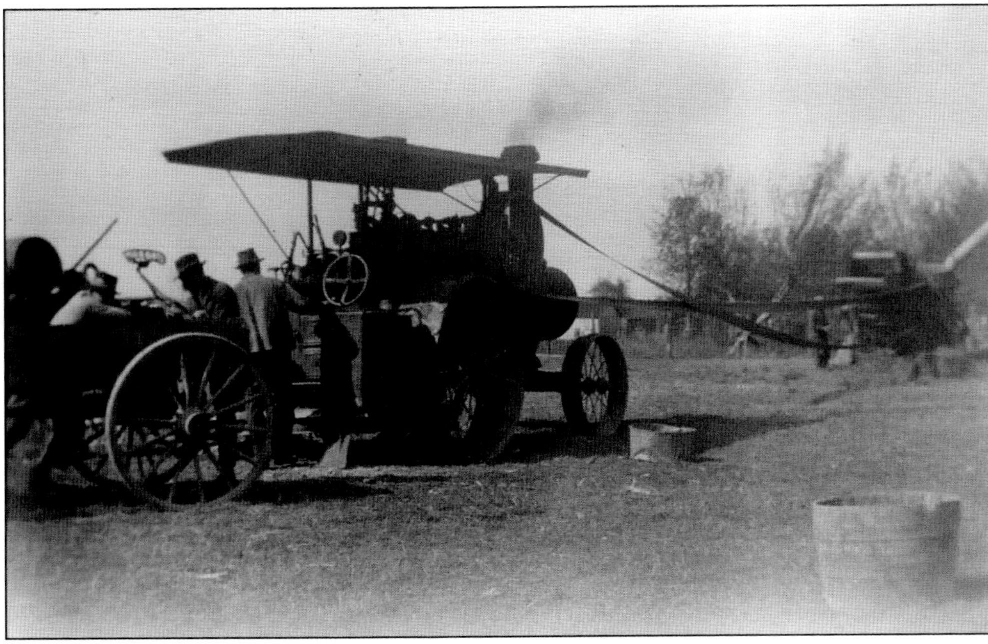

Threshing scenes like this were repeated thousands of times in the county. The steam traction engine on the left powered the threshing machine. Steam powered implements and equipment were in wide use by the 1890s. Farmers formed threshing rings to harvest each other's grain while their wives prepared legendary hearty dinners. This undated card does not specify where in Van Wert County the demonstration took place. (Ken Cripe collection.)

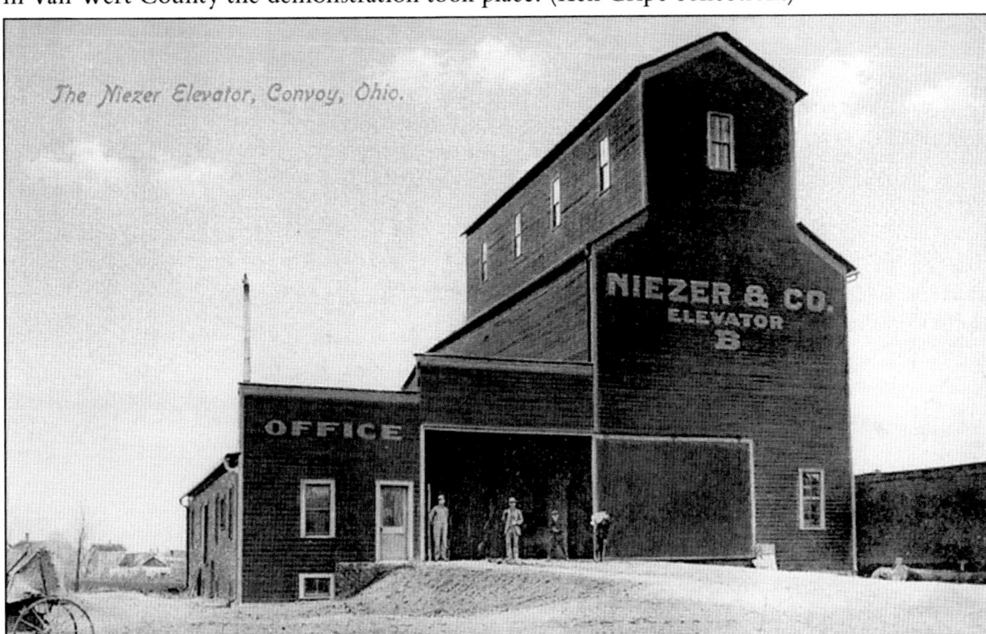

The Niezer elevator in Convoy sat close to the rails of the Ohio and Indiana Railroad, later the Pennsylvania Railroad. Niezer's and the Long and Long Elevator served hundreds of Convoy area farmers in the early 1900s. The Niezer elevator was sold for $16,000 in 1915 to a group of farmers who formed the Convoy Equity Exchange Company under a state charter. (Author's collection.)

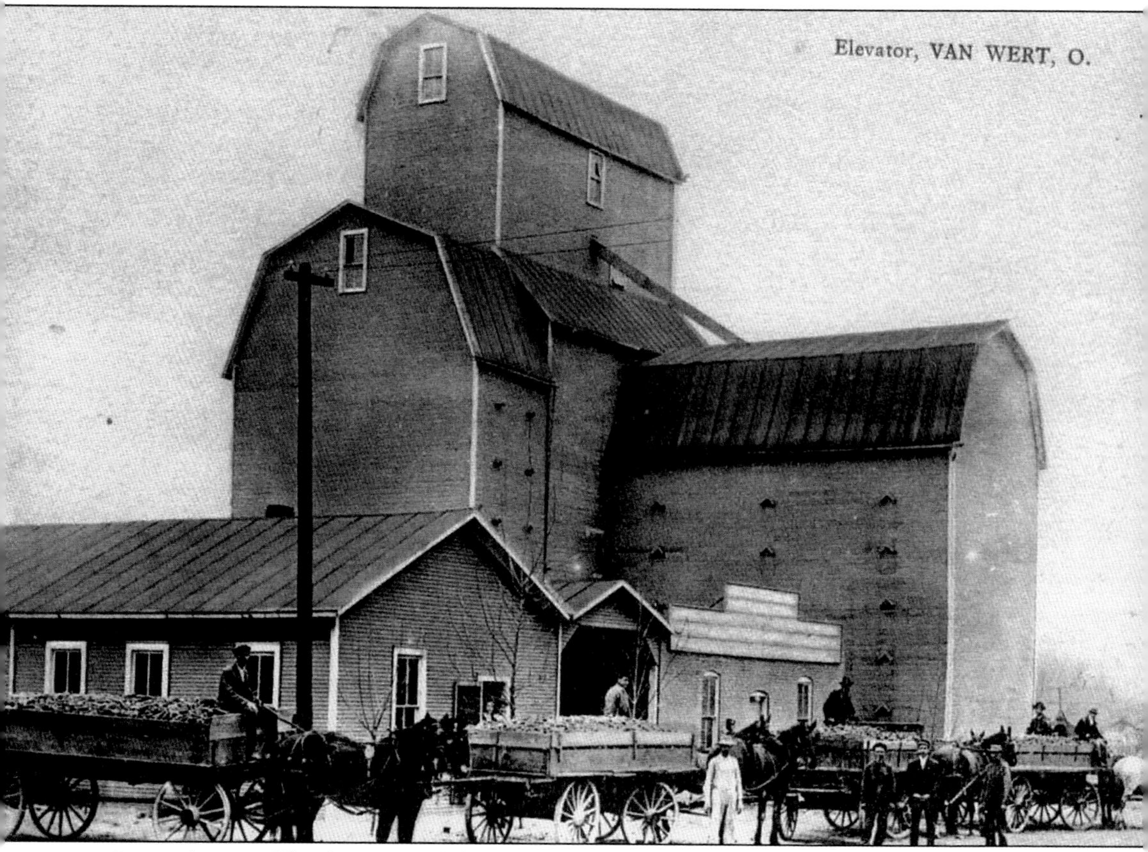

Large elevators like this one and the coming of the railroads in Van Wert heralded the county's future as an agricultural leader. An early boost for farmers was the Van Wert Agricultural Society, which started in 1838. Railroad tracks were completed from Crestline to Van Wert in 1853. The first train passed through Van Wert in 1854, and tracks to Fort Wayne, Indiana, were completed in 1855. Local residents purchased $50,000 worth of Pennsylvania Railroad stock to insure that the railroad would run throughout the county. In addition to transporting farm goods to market, the railroads helped farmers in another way. Farmers often waited at the depot to sell eggs, cheese, and produce to train passengers. The Ohio State Grange was formed in 1872 to help farmers succeed in the postwar economy, and chapters soon sprang up throughout the county. (Ken Cripe collection.)

Two

At the Fair

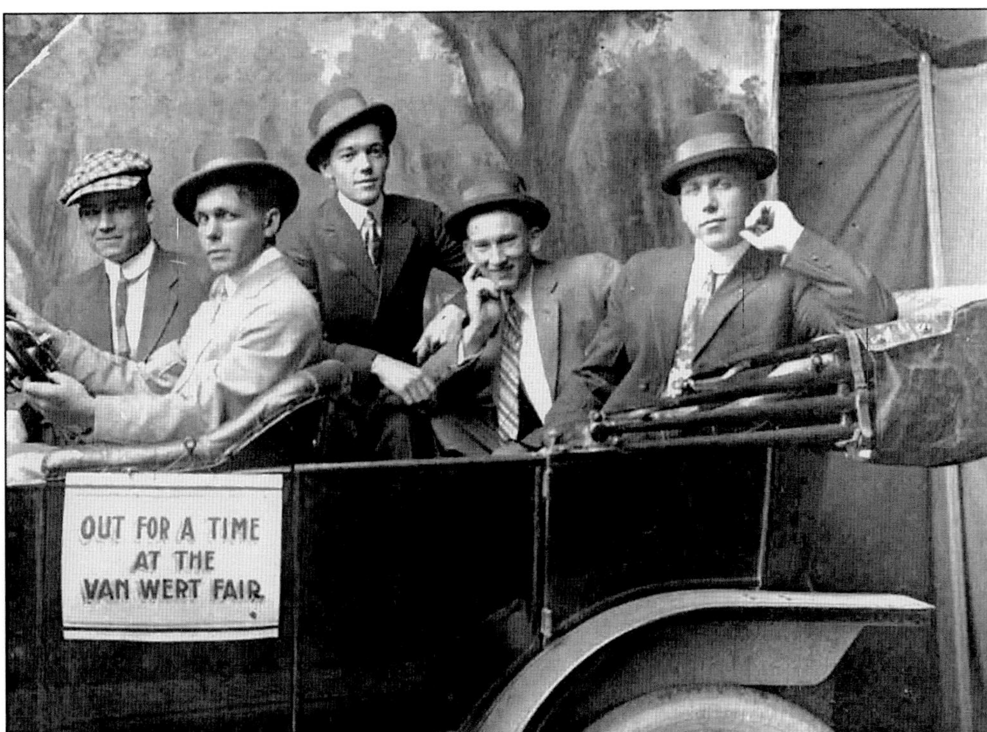

Since 1856, the Van Wert County Fair has offered fairgoers a good time. Souvenir photographs were popular in the early 1900s as visitors posed for a photographer in the Arts Hall. Cletus Munday is behind the wheel in this *c.* 1918 postcard. Standing behind him is ? Nickles (left) and ? Emmett. The gentlemen in the back seat are unidentified. (Ken Cripe collection.)

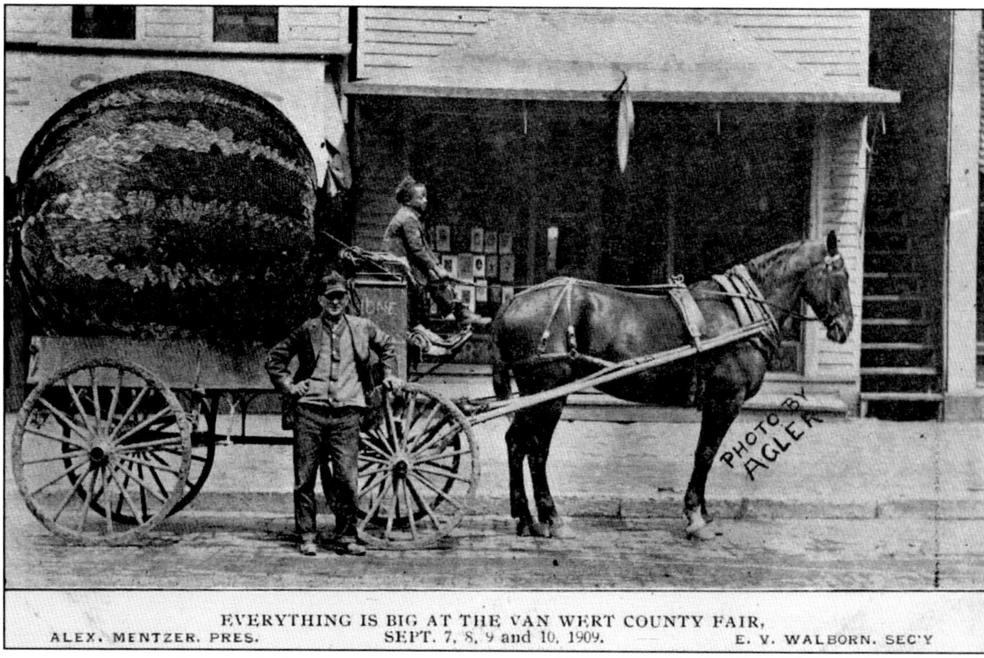

Exaggeration cards provided a humorous way of attracting the public's attention. The exaggeration cards shown here and on the following page were intended to promote the 1909 fair and entice people to enter their best produce, livestock, and handiwork. The people in the pictures are all unidentified. (Ken Cripe collection.)

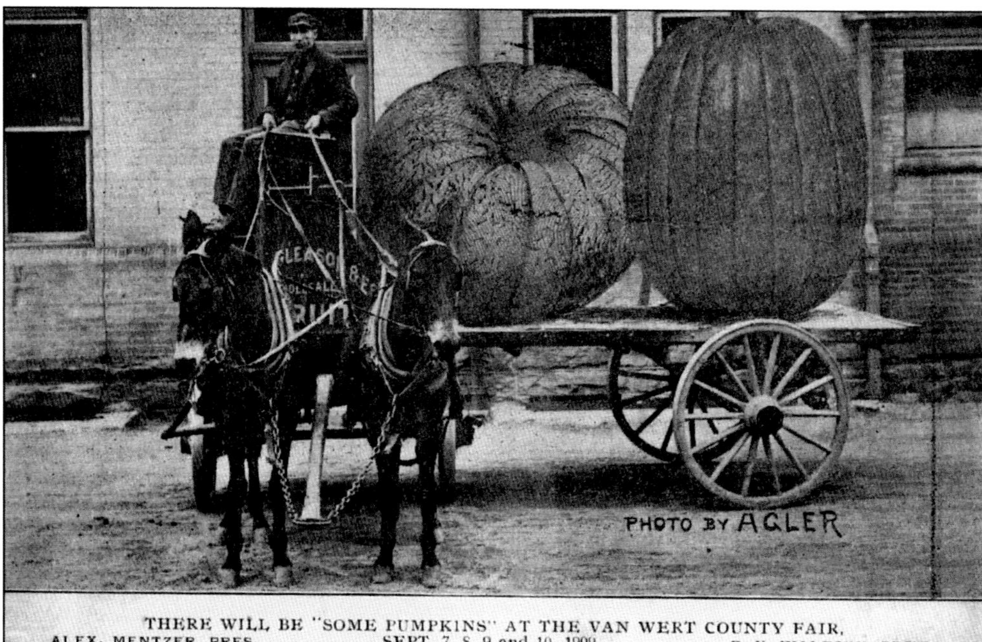

In 1871, the fair moved from October, prime pumpkin time, to September. Over the years, the fair has been held from three to seven days; in 1909, it ran four days. A small, one-day event in 1855 set the stage for the county agricultural society to establish an annual fair in 1856. (Ken Cripe collection.)

A more genteel reminder was mailed out in 1922. The classical style muses display some of the bounty to be exhibited. The "big fair" was named the best in Ohio in 1938, an honor that many fair supporters feel should be an ongoing title. (Ken Cripe collection.)

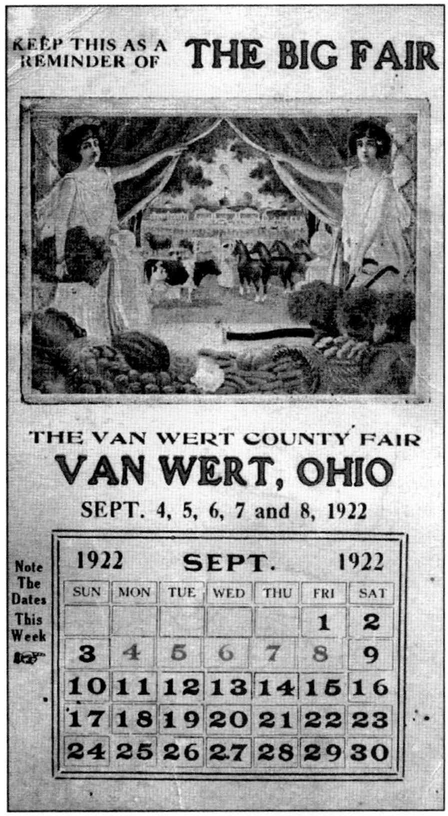

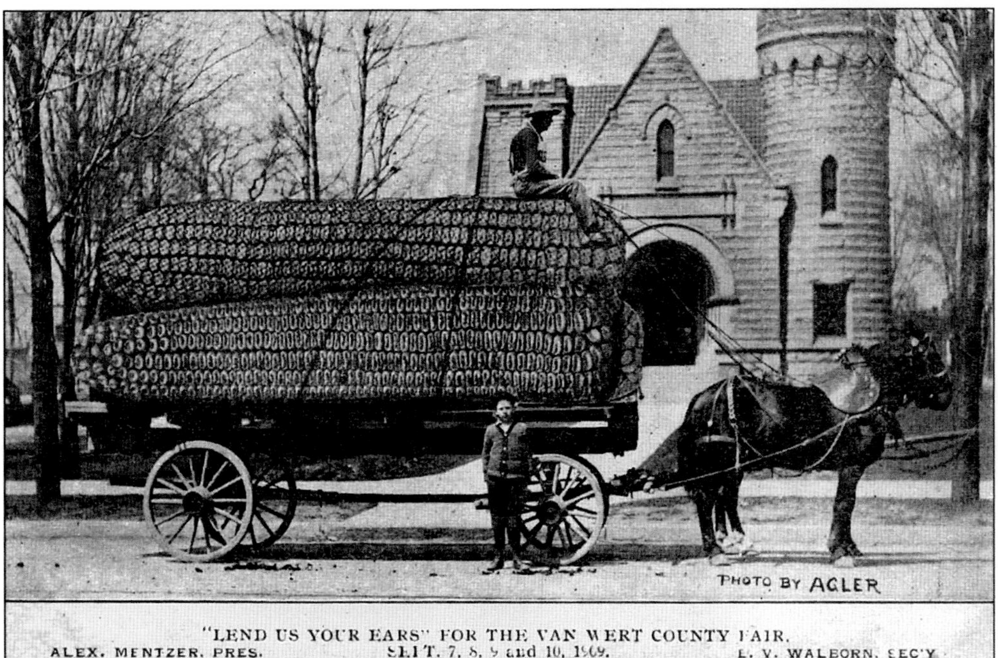

The creator of this postcard used some literary humor in paraphrasing Julius Caesar for a scene set in front of the Brumback Library. (Ken Cripe collection.)

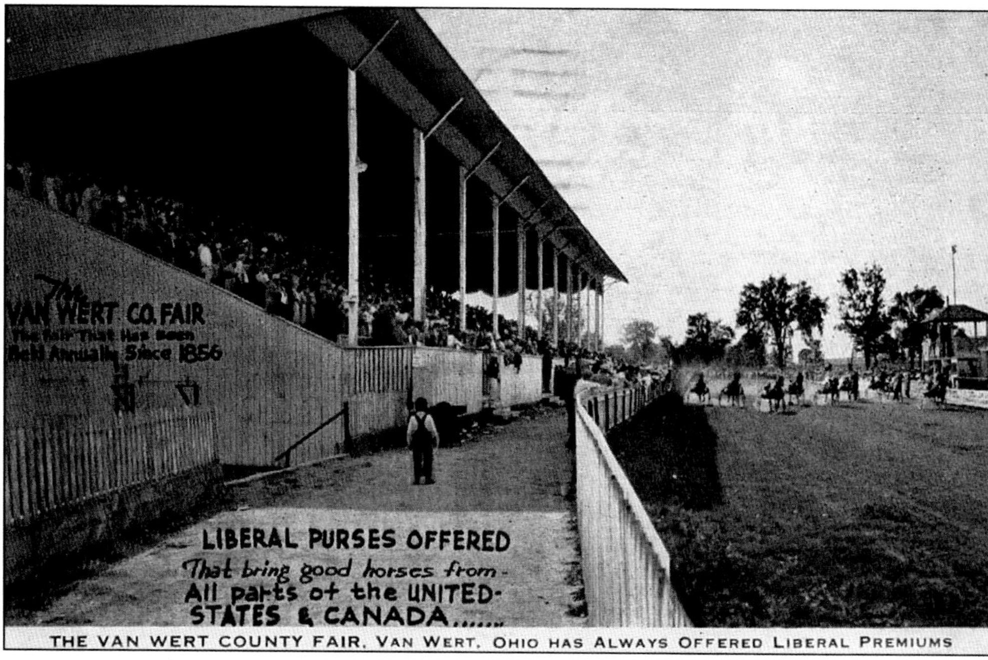

Harness racing has always been a popular fair event, even during World War II, as this 1943 photograph of a packed grandstand shows. Horses and drivers from across the country and Canada came to the fair to thrill the crowds. The fair proved more popular than ever during the war years with an opening day record crowd of 75,000 in 1945. (Ken Cripe collection.)

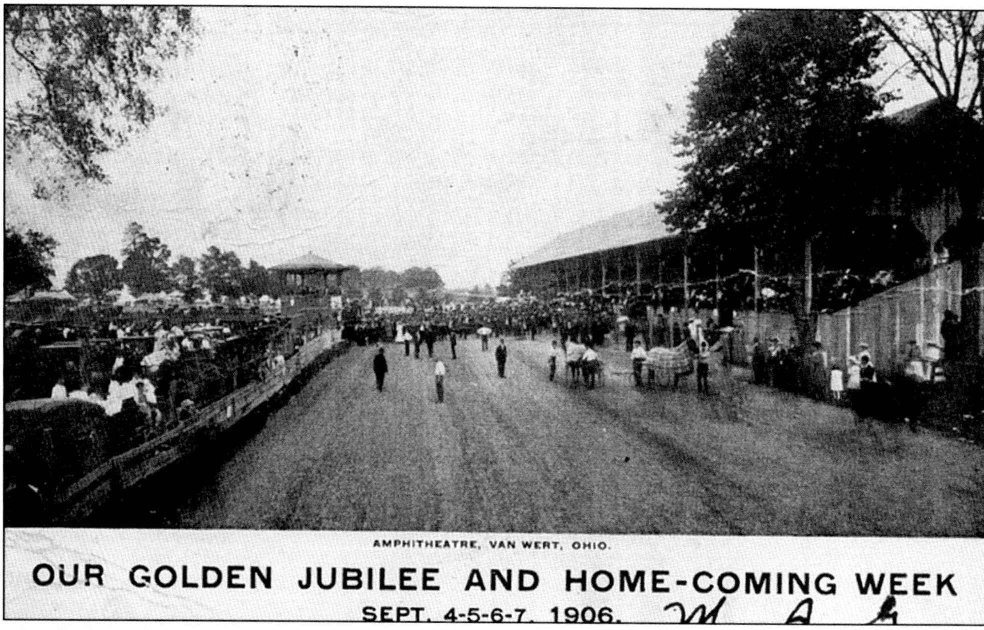

The fair's 50th anniversary in September 1906 was highly anticipated. This reminder card was mailed to Mira Ryant in Galena in March 1906. A Reunion Day program on September 5 featured registration of all former fair attendees, a public dinner, homecoming program with songs and speeches, a variety of races, and performances by Bronco John's Famous Wild West Cowboys. (Author's collection.)

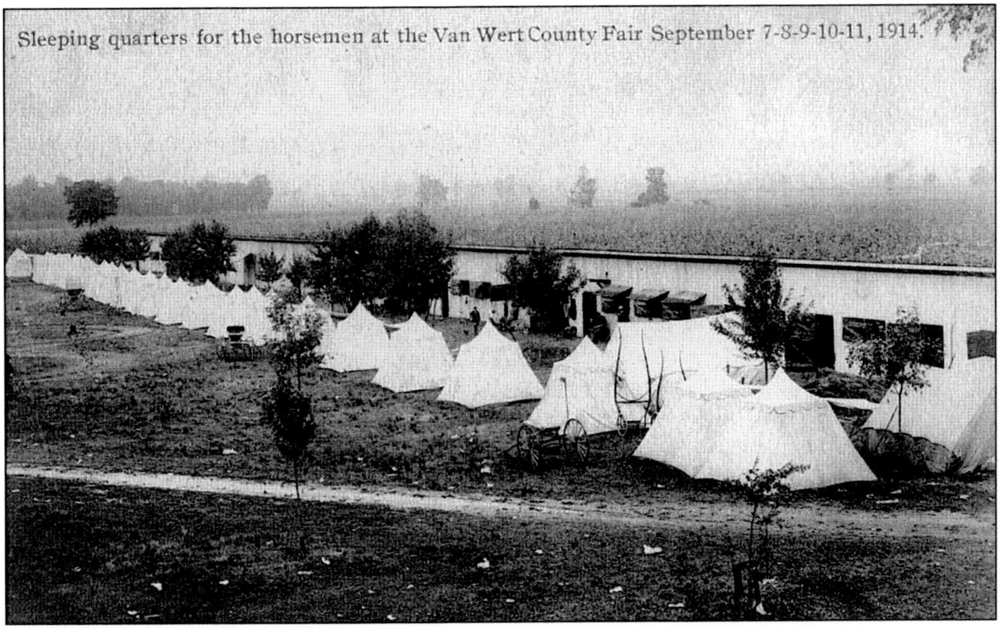

Tents for the horsemen stood next to the horse barn so drivers could keep an eye on their horses and rigs. Serious events over the years have included trotting, pacing, and running races in addition to fun events such as ladies' road races and races for farm teams. This postcard is from 1914. (Ken Cripe collection.)

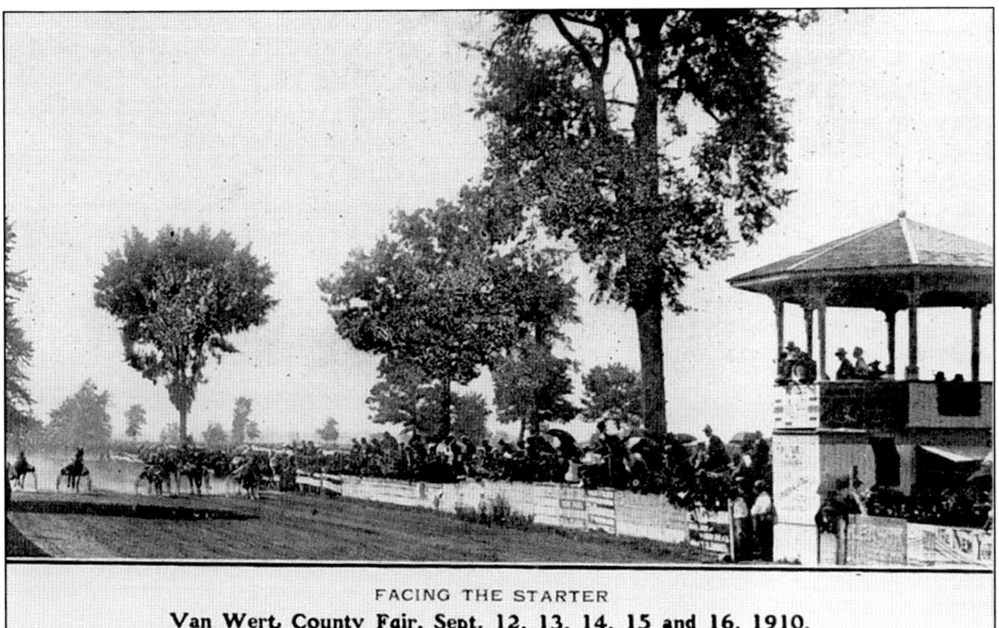

This photograph, taken prior to 1910, shows that a fence had been built to protect spectators in the infield. Earlier cards show spectators sitting on the ground, just feet away from the action. Advertisements for local businesses fill part of the fence. "Why not begin now to prepare an exhibit?" the agricultural society asked on the card's back. (Author's collection.)

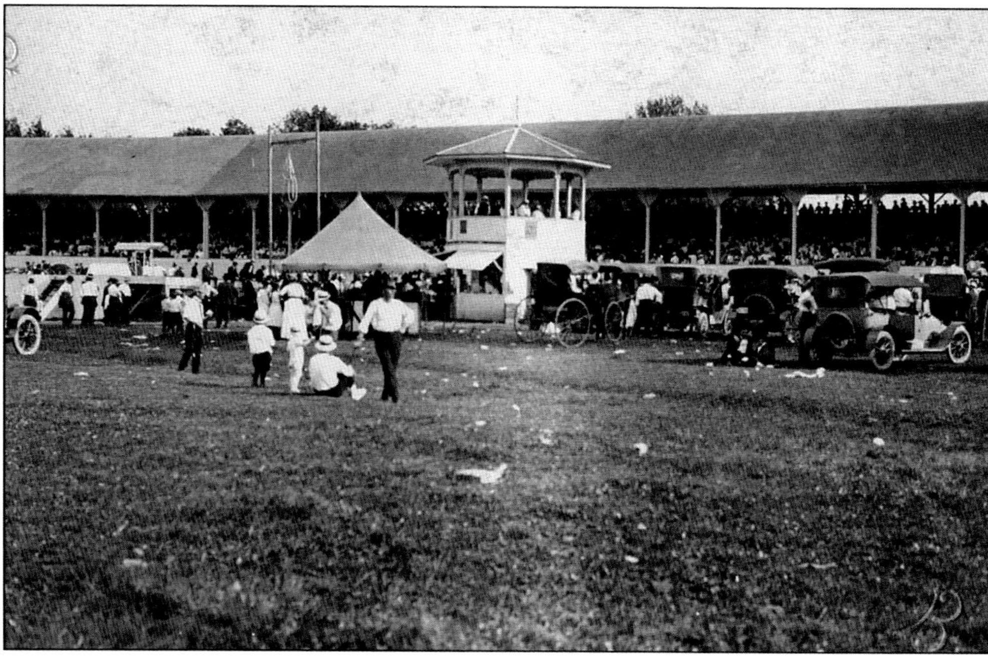

Spectators line up with their cars in the infield in this 1915 photograph. The grandstand is packed, with people standing at the very top of the seats. Built in 1903 for $2,900, the grandstand could seat 2,500 people. (Ken Cripe collection.)

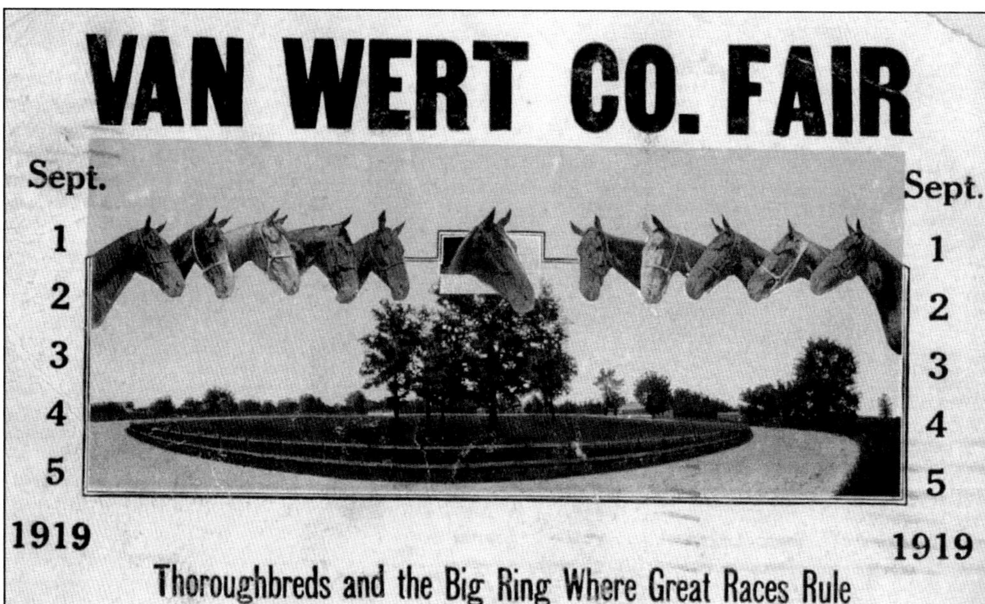

A line-up of thoroughbreds made an appealing 1919 postcard. Veterans of the Civil War, Spanish-American War, and World War I were admitted free to the fair and grandstand events on September 2 that year in honor of their service. (Ken Cripe collection.)

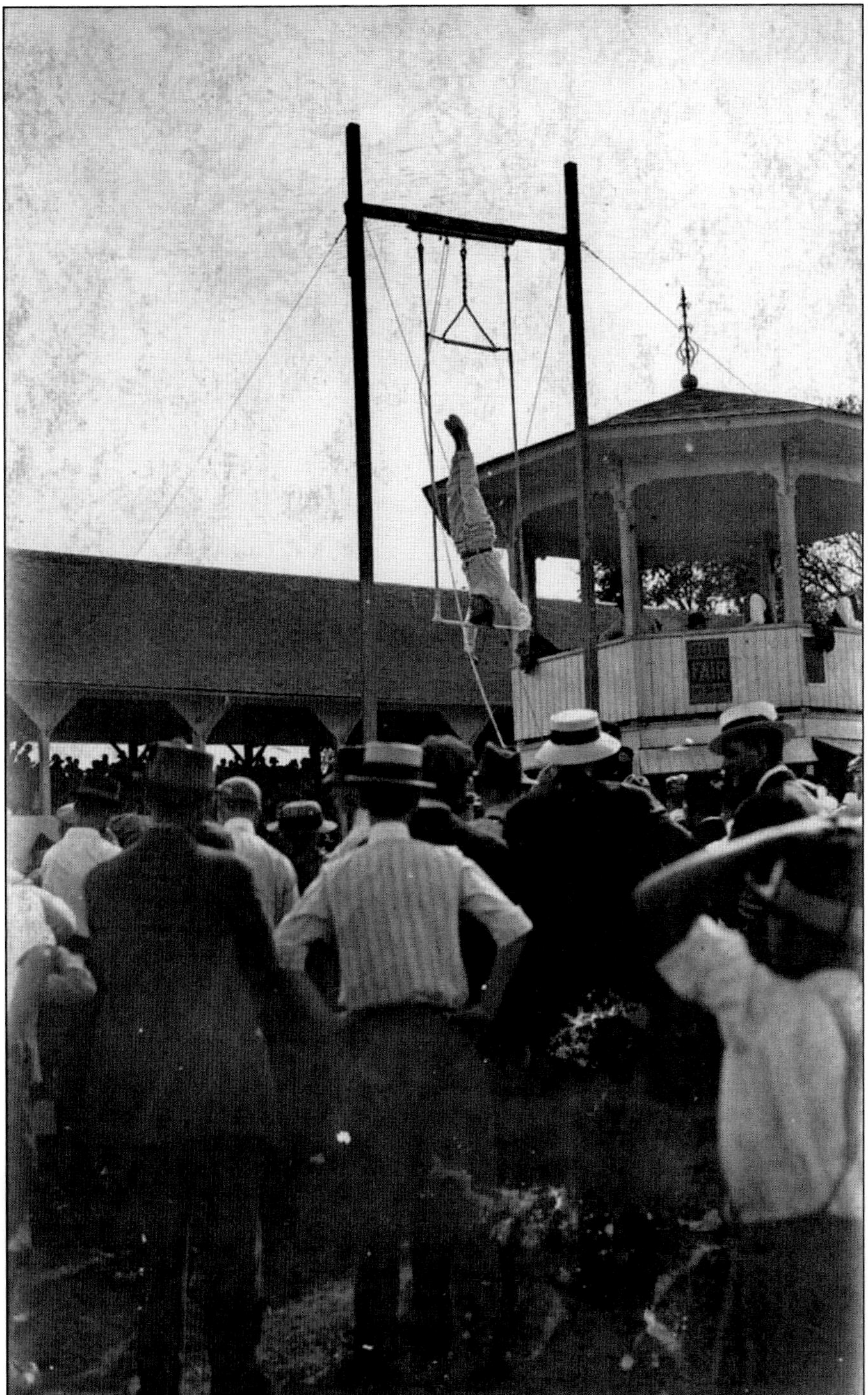

The racetrack and grandstand provided a prime staging area for many attractions. An aerialist captured the crowd's attention in this 1915 postcard. Over the years, patrons in the grandstand watched weddings, the community Golden Wedding Celebration, rodeos, band concerts, boxing matches, livestock judging, and parades. (Ken Cripe collection.)

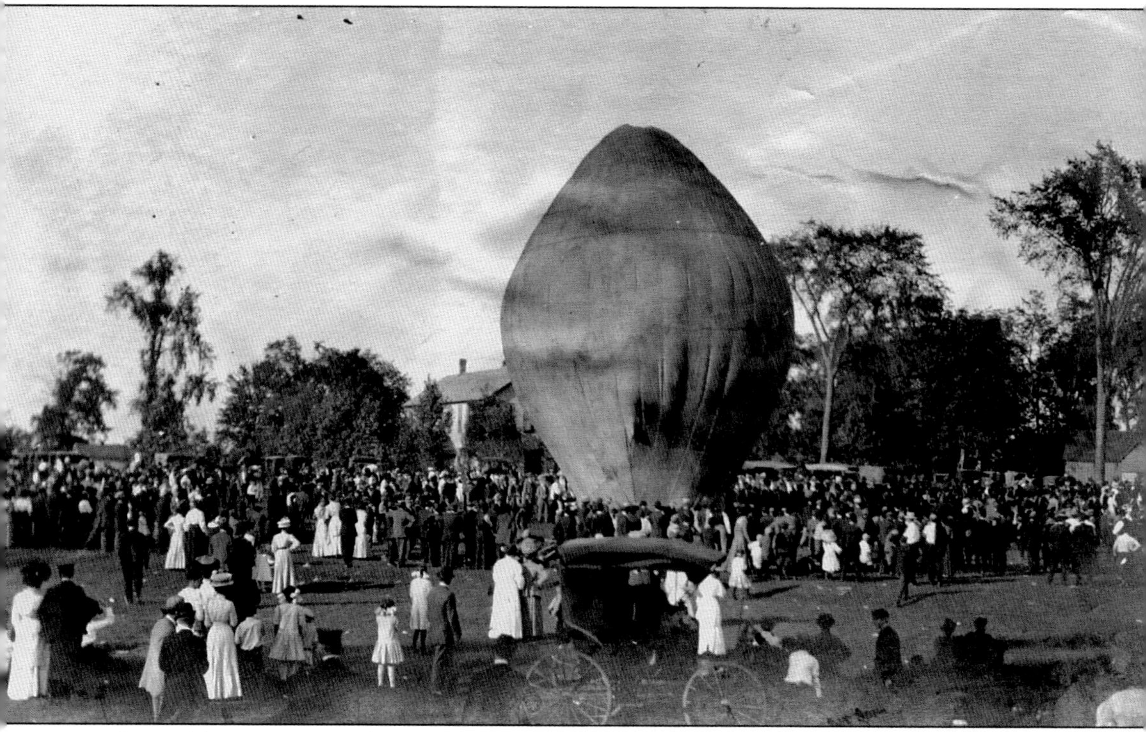

One of the most unusual attractions at the fair was the hot air balloon. A balloon ascension is noted in the 1896 fair records. The balloon was often exhibited in the racetrack infield. At one time, fairgoers could pay to take a ride in the balloon. (Ken Cripe collection.)

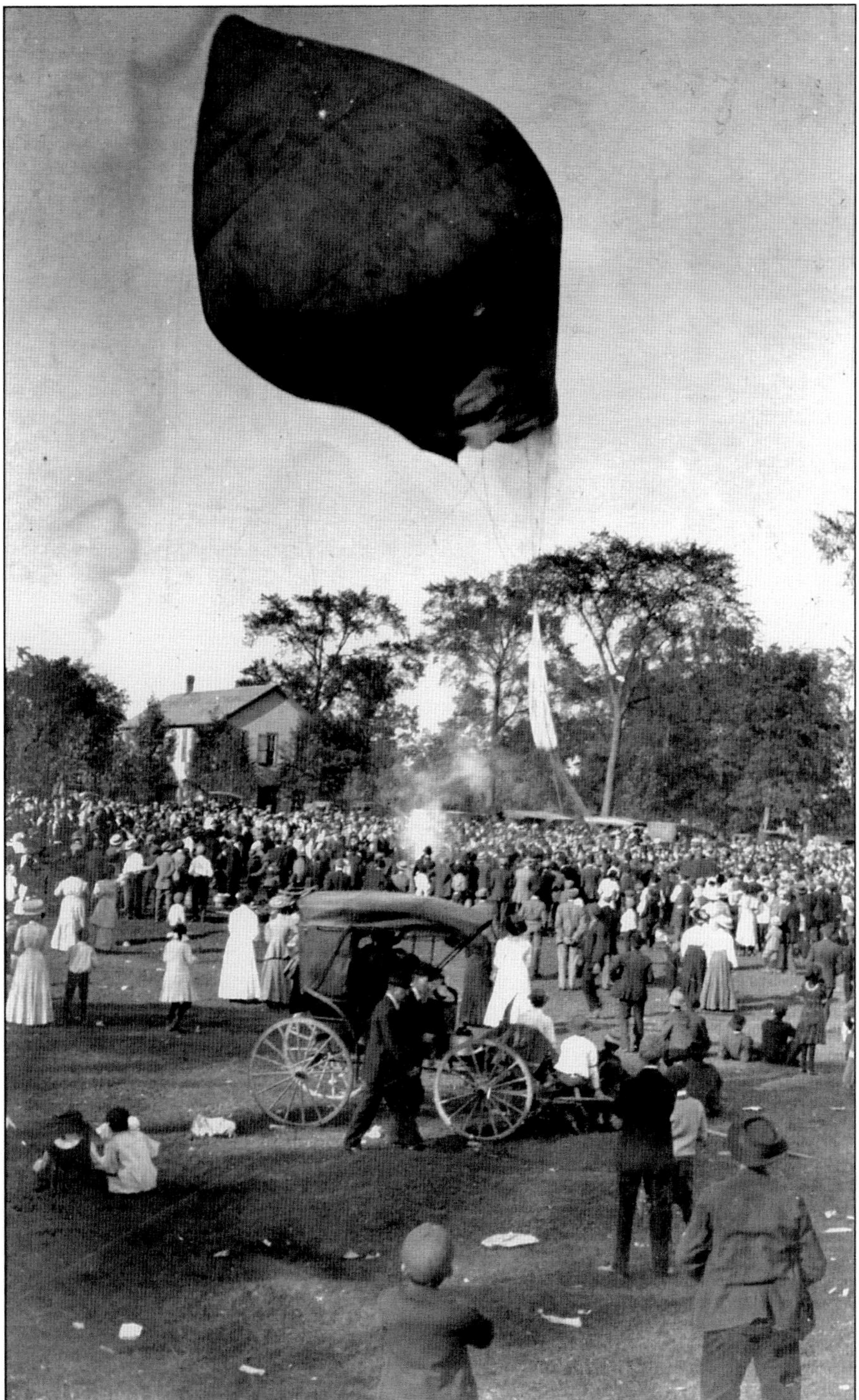

In this image the balloon ascends above the fairground. The fair was always the place to the see the latest things, from improved farm implements to the latest vehicles. The 1911 fair offered airship rides as well as four days of motorcycle races. (Ken Cripe collection.)

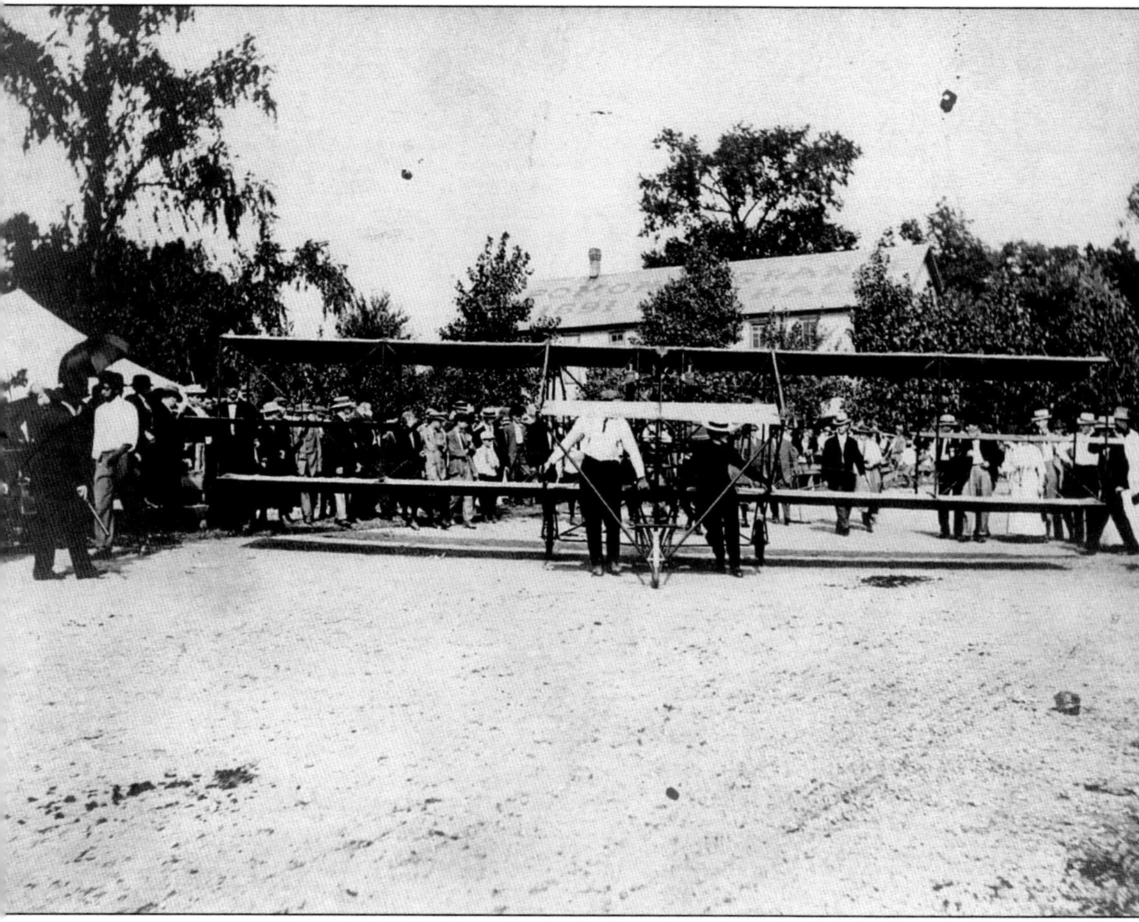

One of the most significant milestones at the fair occurred in 1912 when the first airplane to land in Van Wert County set down at the fairgrounds. In the background of the photograph was the Pomona Grange Hall, built in 1891. America's enthusiasm for air travel was reflected in the fair's attractions. Bob Bartley, "Dare Devil of the Air," performed his stunt-flying act in 1920. (Ken Cripe collection.)

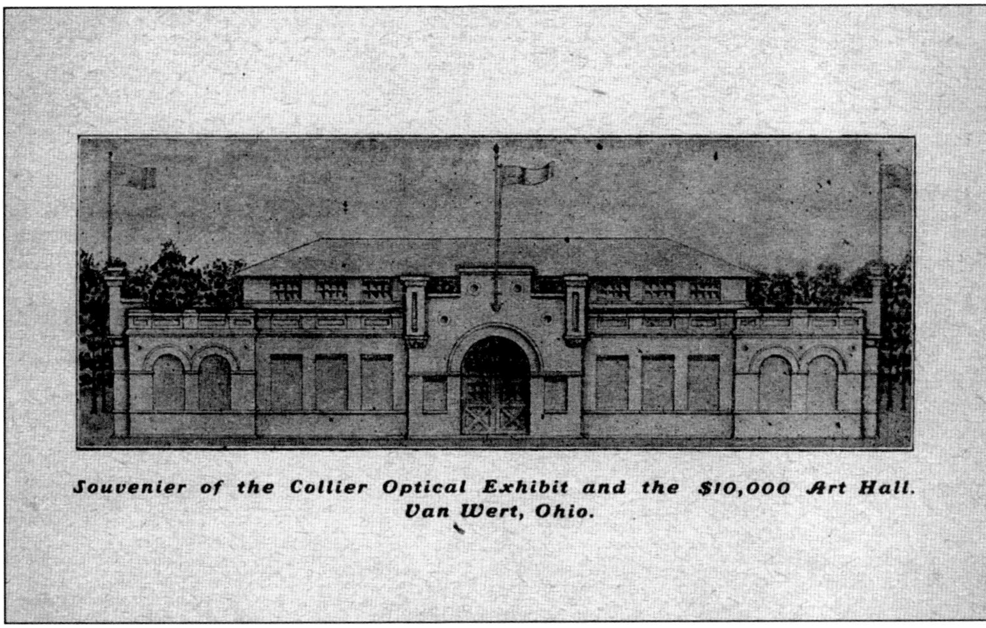

This drawing for the proposed new Art Hall indicated how big the fair had become by 1912. Completed for about $8,000, the Art Hall housed hundreds of exhibits until it was replaced by the Commercial Building in 1979. The new facility was built on top of the Art Hall's original cement floor. (Ken Cripe collection.)

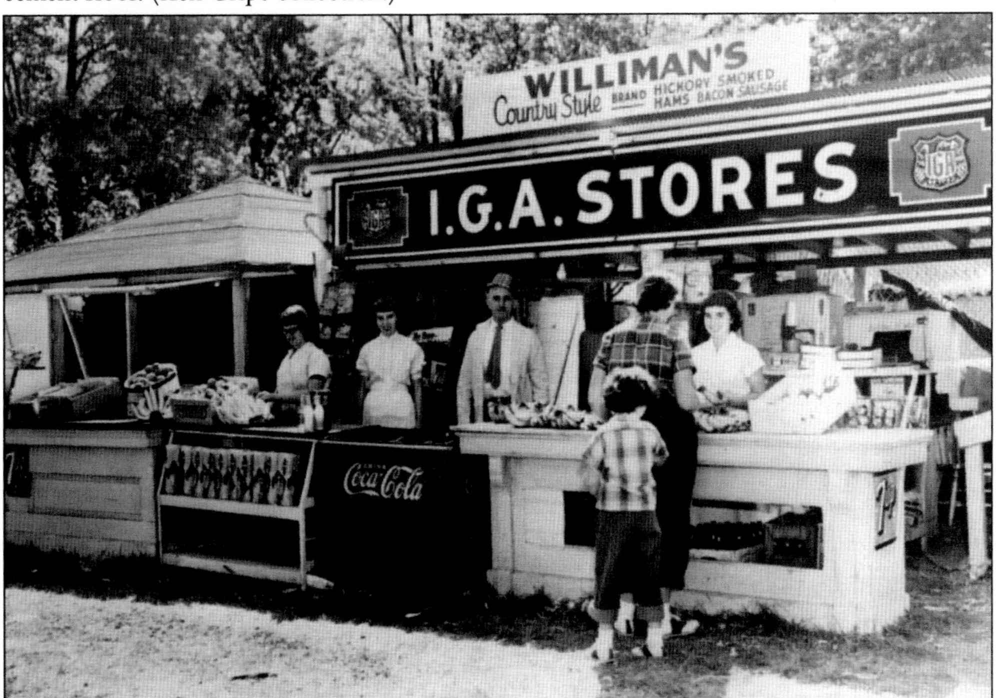

By the 1940s, local businesses were in full force at the fair. In this photograph, Charlie Williman (center) oversees Williman's I.G.A. (Independent Grocers Association) grocery store stand on the fairgrounds. The ladies are unidentified. (Ken Cripe collection.)

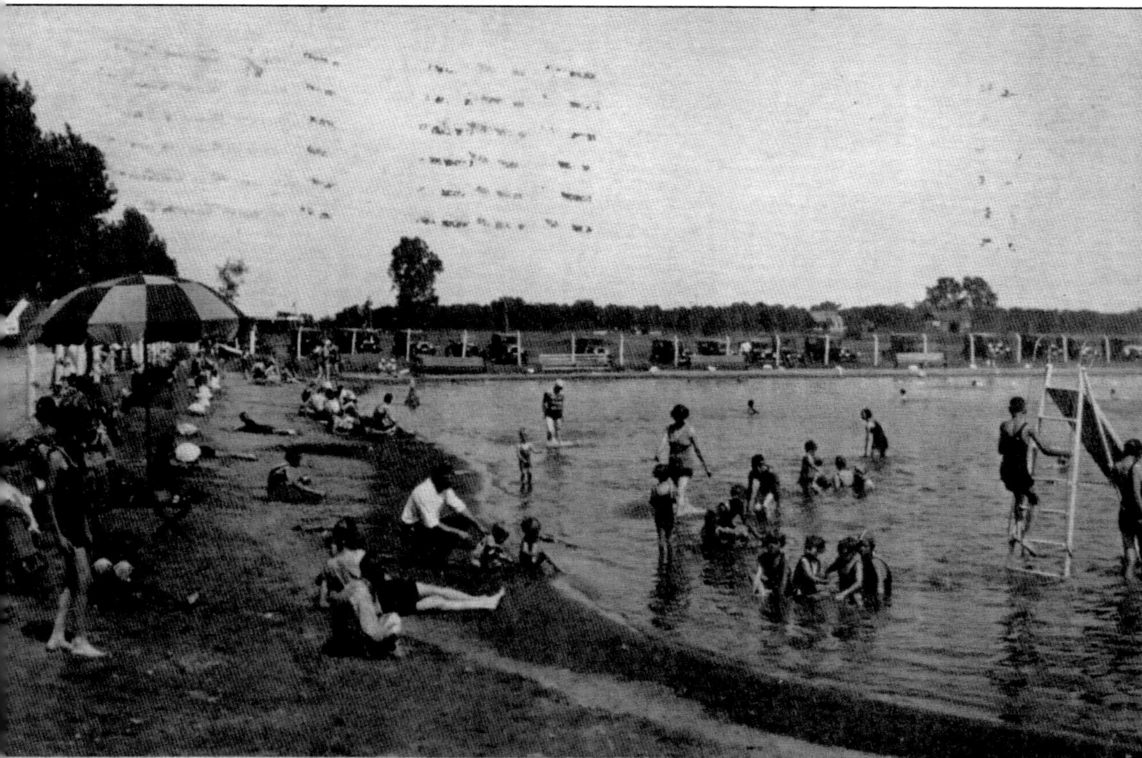

The Van Wert County Park Association Swimming Pool, Van Wert, Ohio

A special feature of the fairgrounds was the swimming pool built in 1930. The pool brought a bit of the beach to county residents during the summer, and was a popular site for family gatherings and church picnics. The pool eventually became part of the county park district and was used until it closed in 1964. (Ken Cripe collection.)

Three

PEONIES AND PARADES

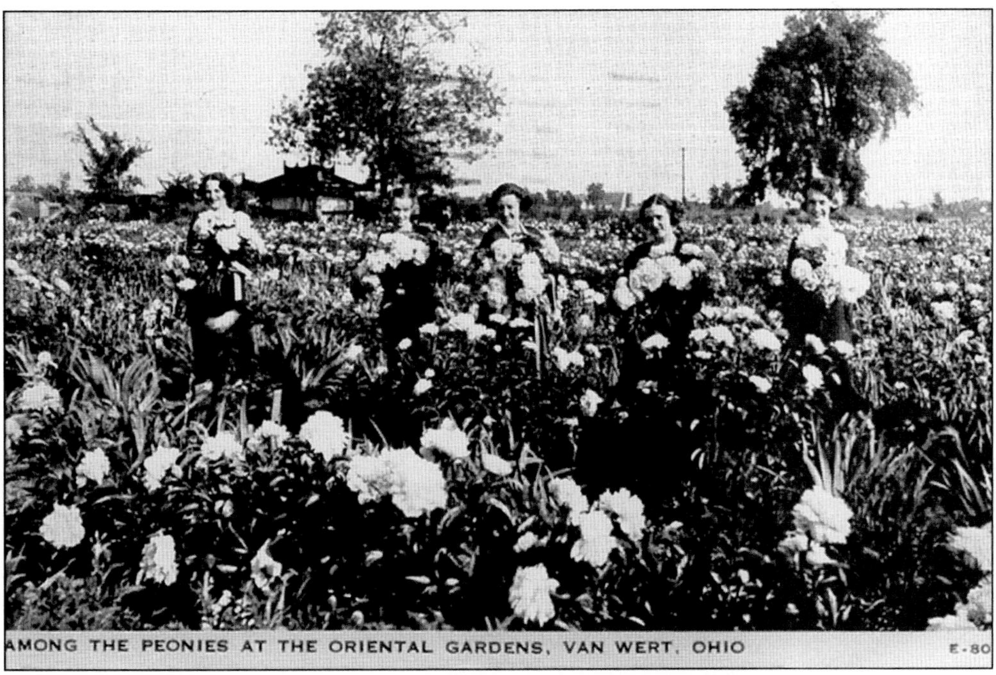

Five young, unidentified ladies just happened to be visiting the Oriental Gardens near Van Wert on the same day the postcard photographer visited. The card is postmarked 1944, but the photograph may have been taken much earlier. In the early 1900s, several flower farms specializing in peonies and other flowering perennials flourished around Van Wert. Clara Anderson, Louis J. Germann, Lee R. Bonnewitz, and Charles F. Wassenberg were among the county's top growers. (Author's collection.)

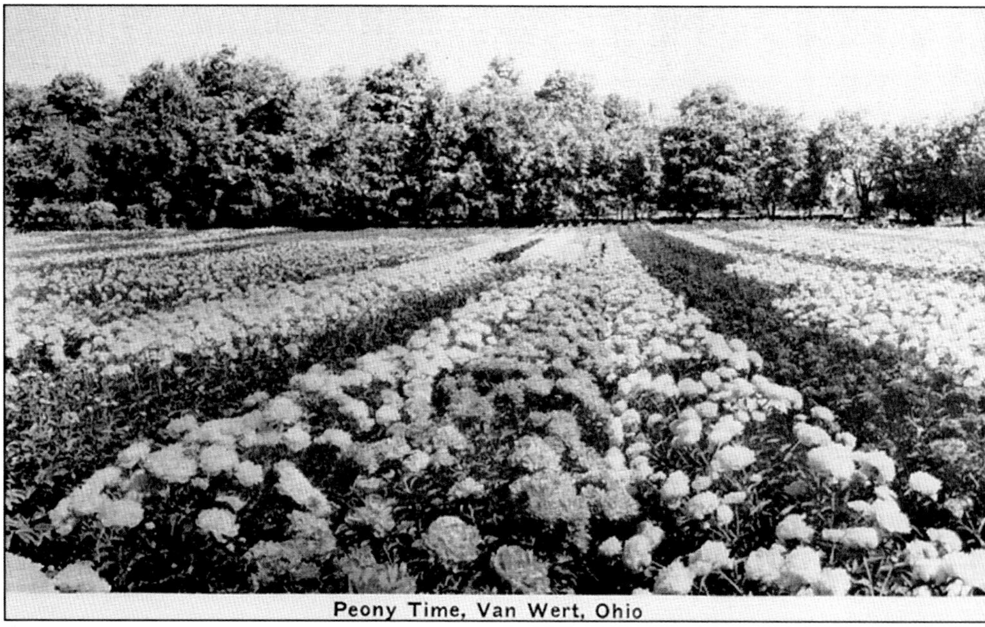

In 1902, peonies were so plentiful in the county that the first Sunday in June was designated Peony Sunday, and residents toured the beautiful peony fields in full bloom. They bought plants from local growers, who also mailed catalogues throughout the region. In 1917, Louis J. Germann entered a peony with a pointed bud, called the Jubilee, in the National Peony Show and was awarded the Finest Flower prize. (Author's collection.)

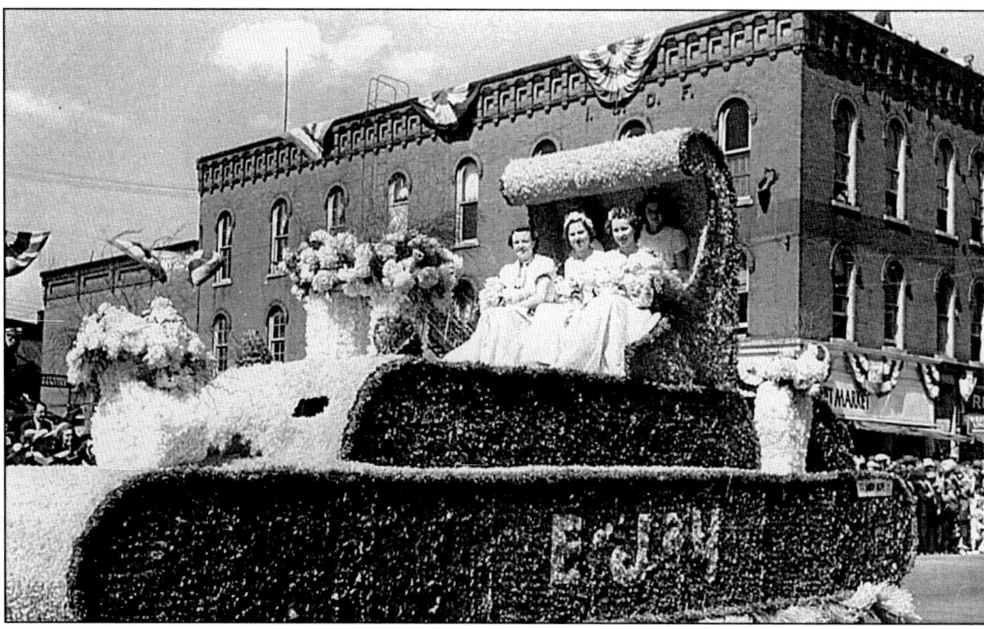

The Van Wert Men's Garden Club organized a peony festival and parade in 1932 to showcase local growers' achievements and entertain visitors who toured the peony farms each spring. Floats were totally covered with flowers and plant materials, and graced by lovely young women. The E-Jay float of 1939 was the entry of E. J. Evan Company, purveyors of coffees and spices. (Ken Cripe collection.)

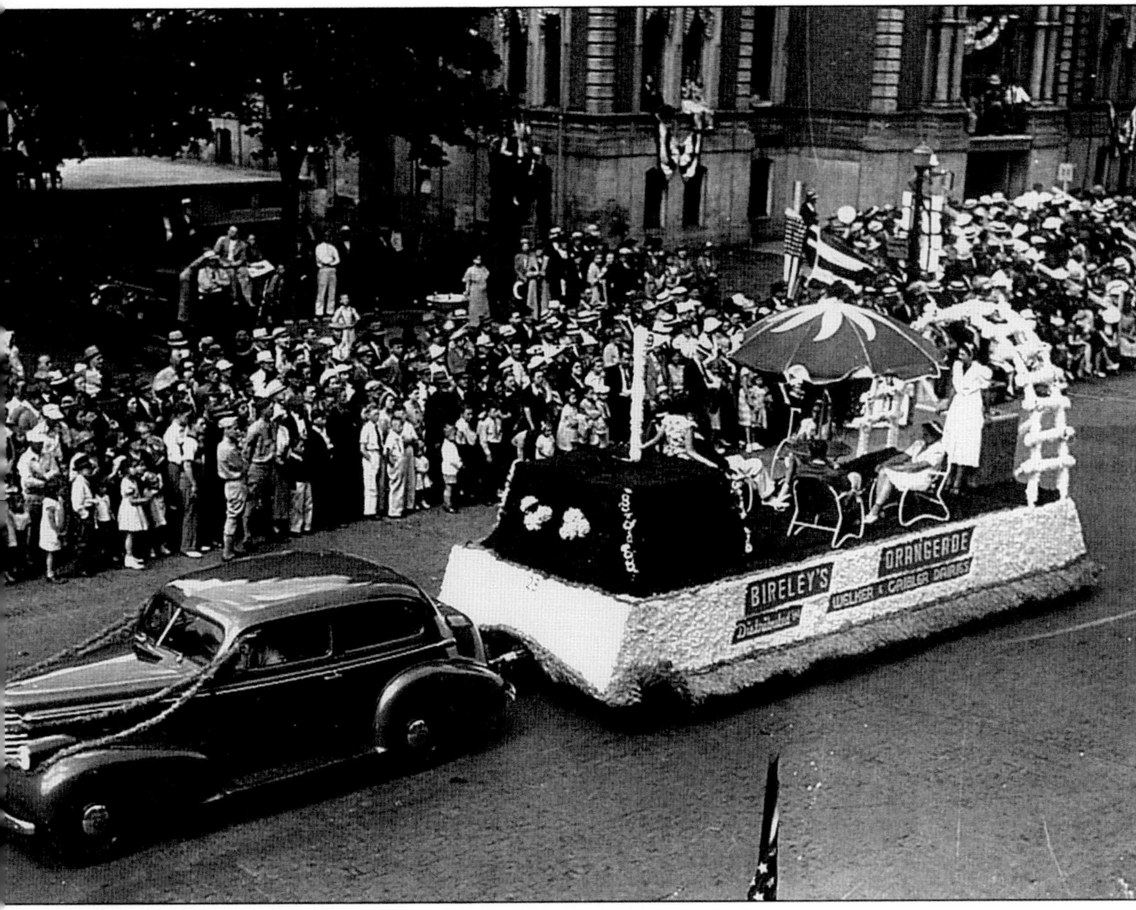

By the late 1930s, attendance at the annual festival topped 100,000. Dignitaries watched the parade from a reviewing stand built in front of the courthouse. The festival and parade rivaled Pasadena's Rose Parade. Corporations from across the country sponsored floats. In 1939, Bireley's Orangeade of Hollywood, California, was represented in the parade by its local distributor, Welker and Gribler Dairies. The Ocean Breeze Corporation of Camp Jester, Florida, was another national corporate participant. (Ken Cripe collection.)

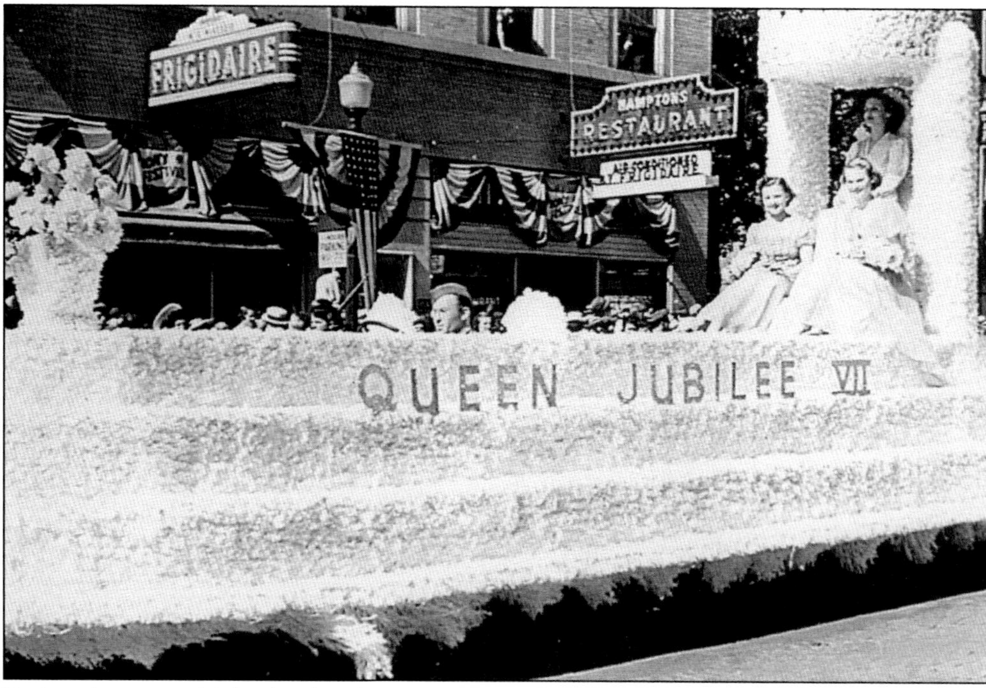

Each spring, every high school in the county selected a senior girl as their candidate for queen of the festival. Betty Joan Jones, the 1939 queen, sits beneath the arch on her float. The other two women are unidentified. Jubilee refers to the peony of that name. (Ken Cripe collection.)

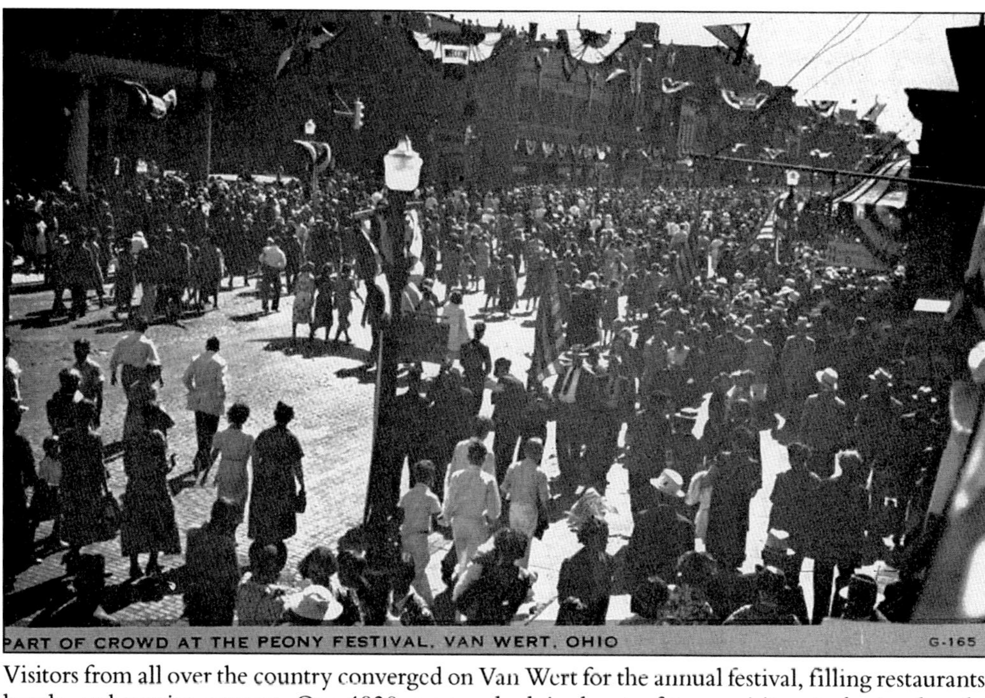

Visitors from all over the country converged on Van Wert for the annual festival, filling restaurants, hotels, and tourist cottages. One 1930s postcard advised out-of-town visitors to be in place by 8:00 a.m. on festival day to ensure a good viewing place. (Van Wert County Historical Society.)

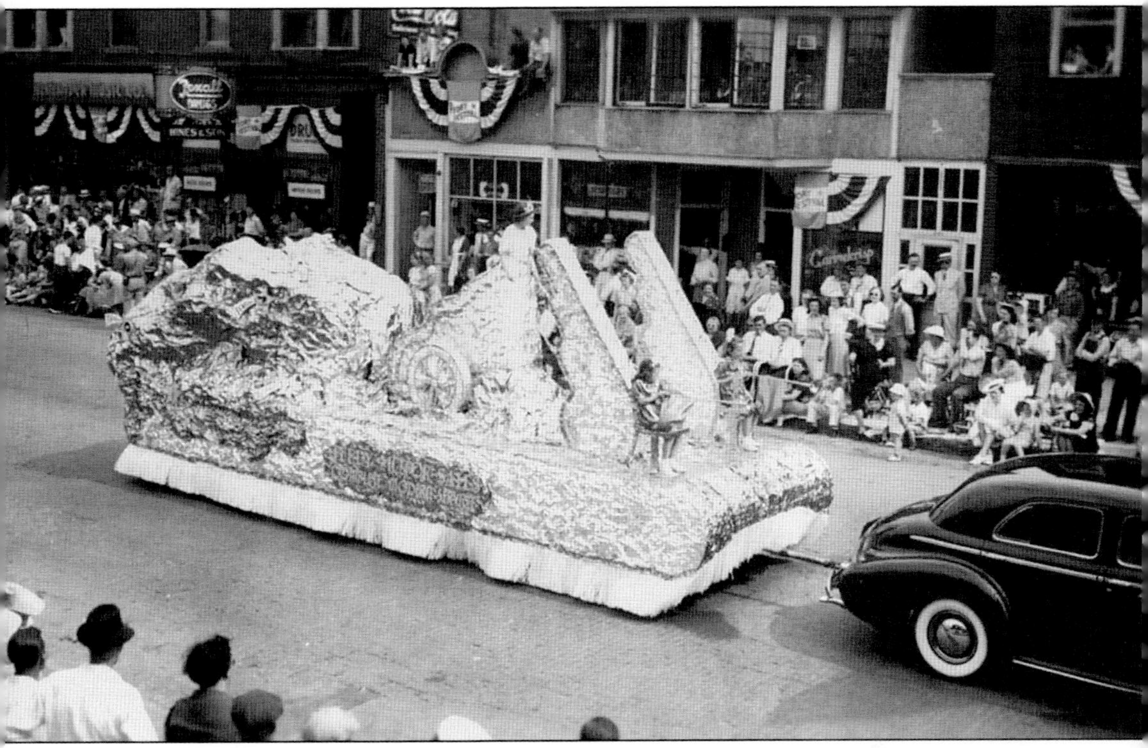

This 1939 float displays a lavish use of flowers and great artistry. Months of preparation went into each festival, and the public eagerly awaited the parade. People lined the streets, watched from upper story windows, and even perched on ledges to get the best view. By 1939, Van Wert was called the "Peony Capital of the World." The event had grown so large that two parades were held: a daytime event and an illuminated procession in the evening. As many as 45 floats and 40 marching bands entertained the crowds. A newspaper article boasted that the Peony Festival's floats were superior to those of the Mardi Gras parades. (Ken Cripe collection.)

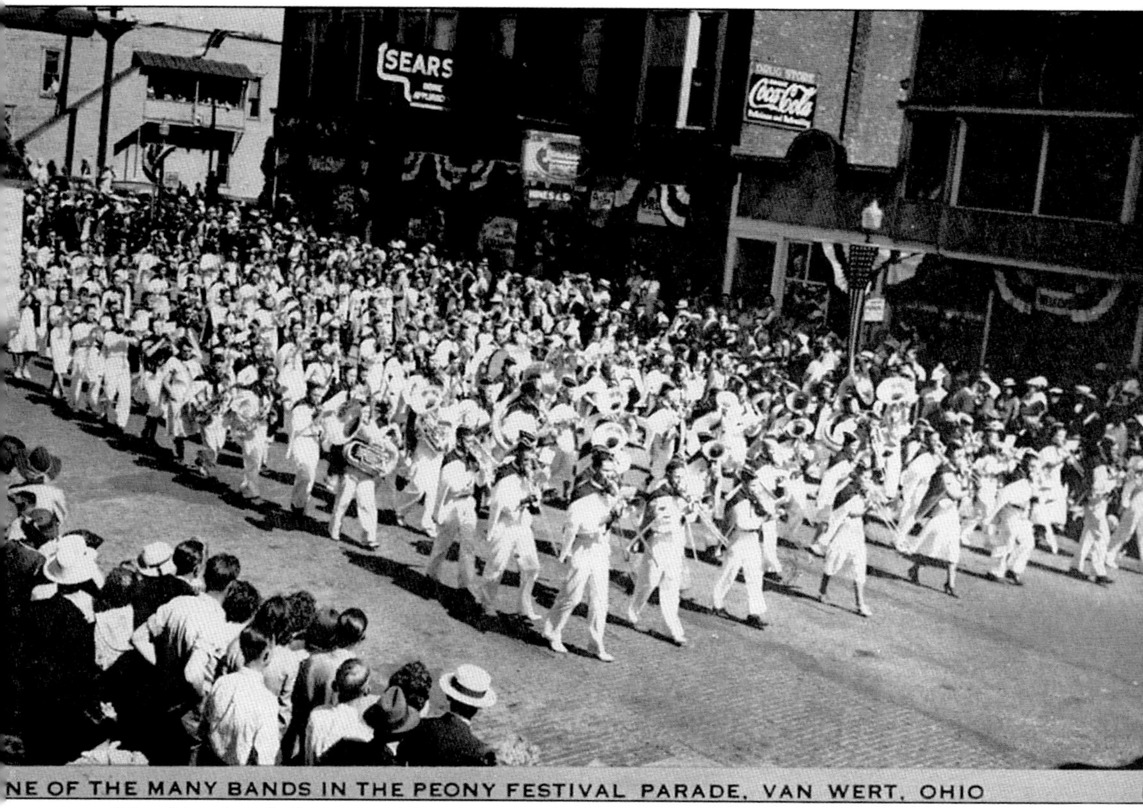

Marching bands from throughout the county and across the country performed in the daytime and evening parades. Between parades, the bands gathered on the Van Wert High School football field to perform mass concerts. One concert featured as many as 3,000 young musicians. The festival thrived throughout the Depression but was interrupted by World War II. The 1941 parade was the last for 14 years, as Americans turned to other pursuits and forms of postwar entertainment. (Ken Cripe collection.)

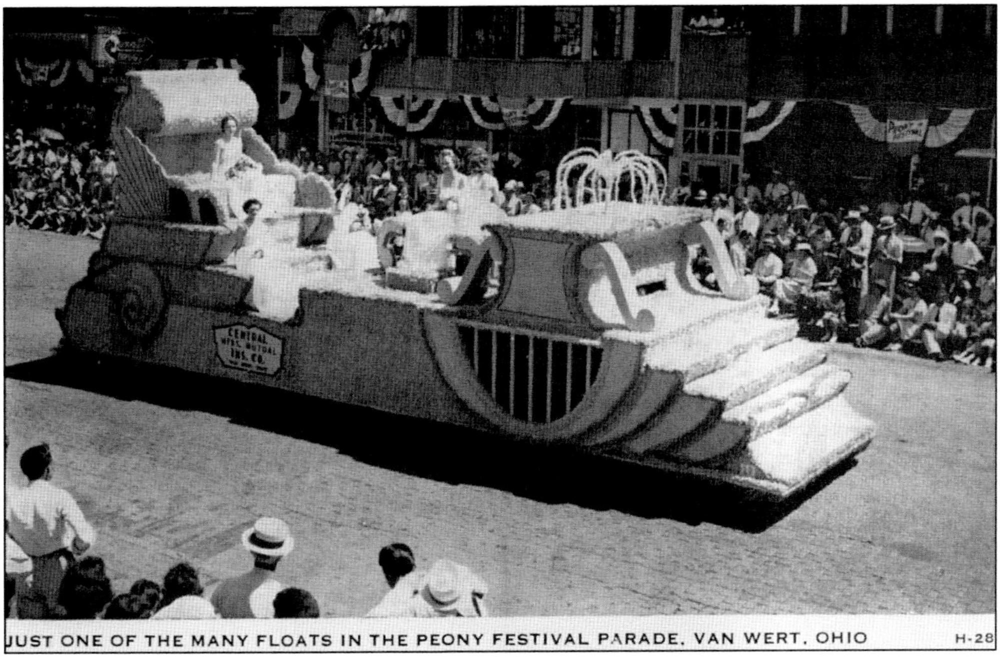

Central Mutual Insurance was one of the oldest businesses involved in the festival. Central Mutual was incorporated in 1876 in Van Wert as a fire insurance company and has remained active in the community since then. (Ken Cripe collection.)

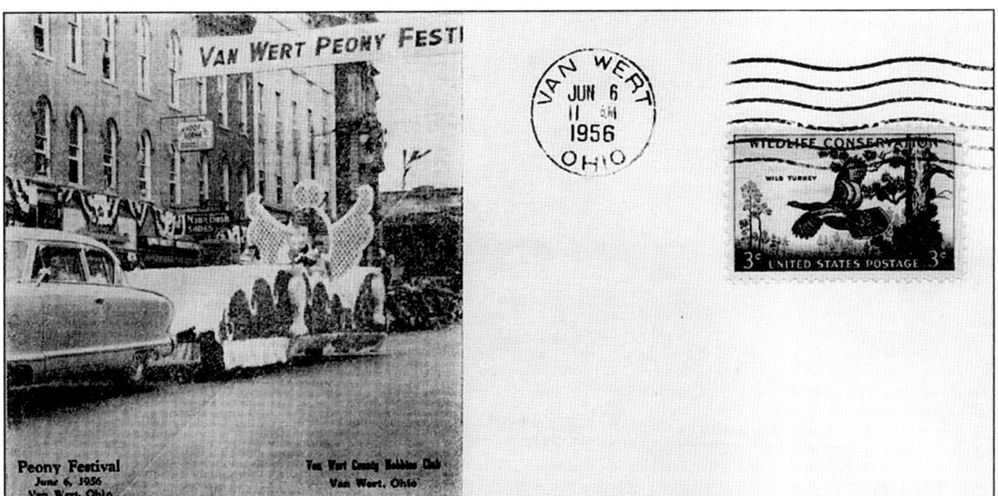

The Peony Festival was revived by Van Wert business people in 1955. The Van Wert County Hobbies Club issued a commemorative envelope in 1956 to help promote the festival. Queen Janis Beatty is shown riding on the float with her court. (Author's collection.)

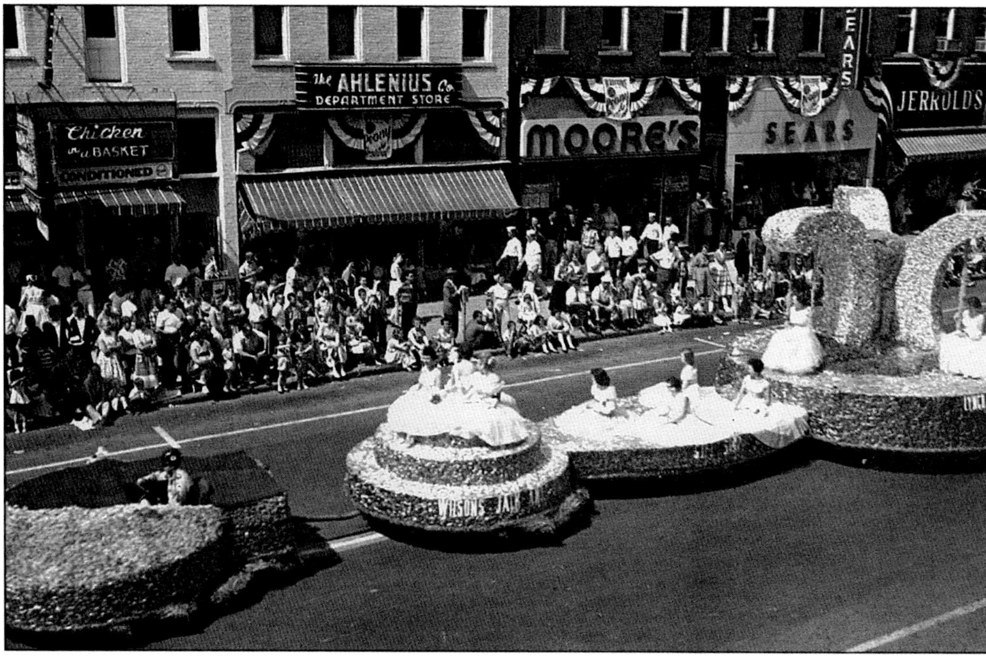

Creativity never faltered as floats became more elaborate and varied over the years. This beautiful 1958 entry, with its circular style, was a departure from the usual rectangular floats. (Ken Cripe collection.)

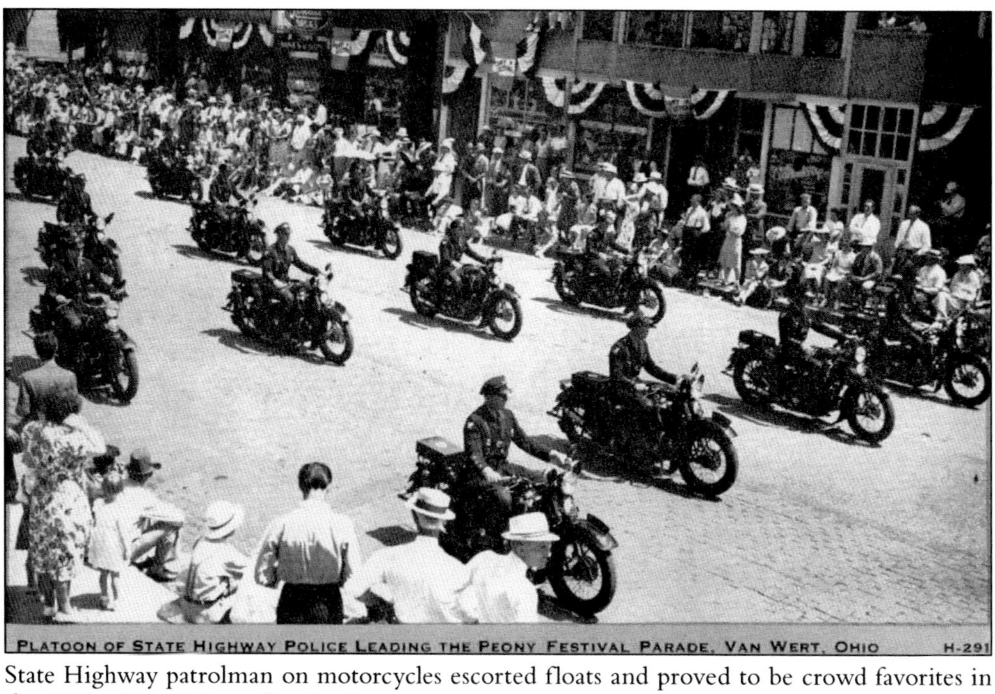

State Highway patrolman on motorcycles escorted floats and proved to be crowd favorites in the 1950s. (Ken Cripe collection.)

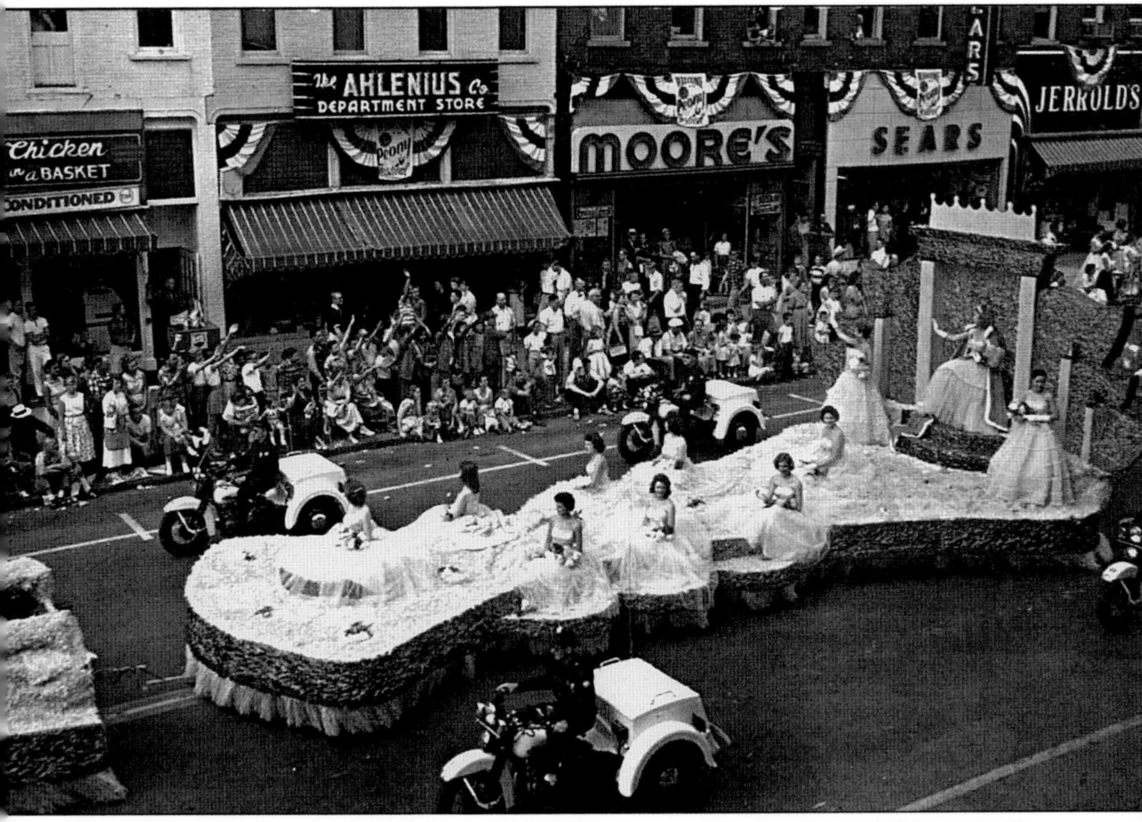

Queen Pat Taylor's float is seen here accompanied by motorcycle escorts in the 1958 parade. By the end of the decade, the Peony Festival attracted around 200,000 people. But the demise of the last commercial peony farms in the county led to another long hiatus for the festival. The festival was started again in 1992 and has been held the first weekend in June since then. (Ken Cripe collection.)

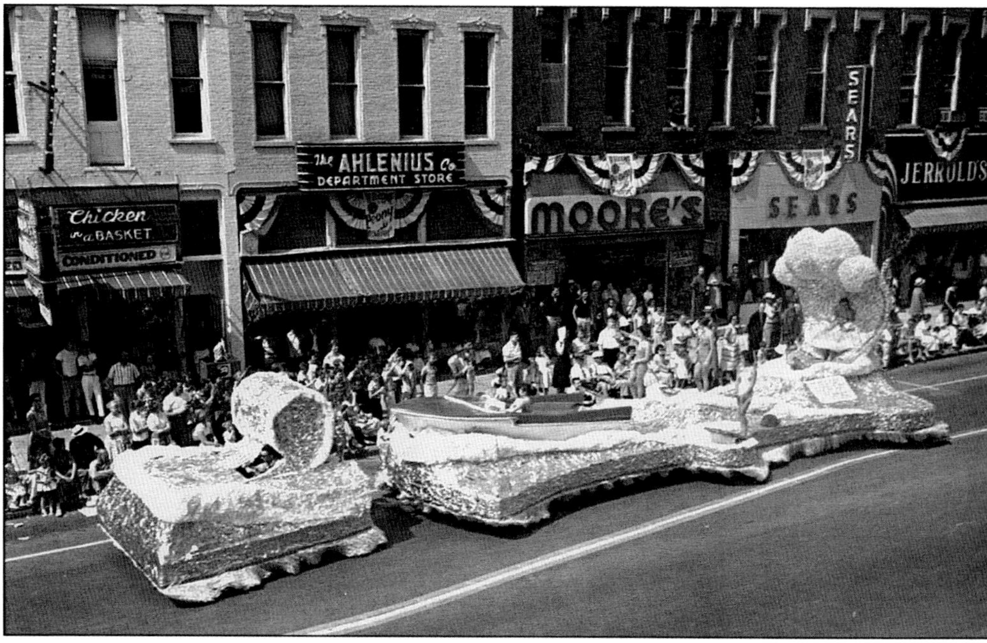

This 1958 float reflects the interest in recreational boating that was building at the time. The county's proximity to Grand Lake St. Marys provided residents with the opportunity to vacation on the water close to home. (Ken Cripe collection.)

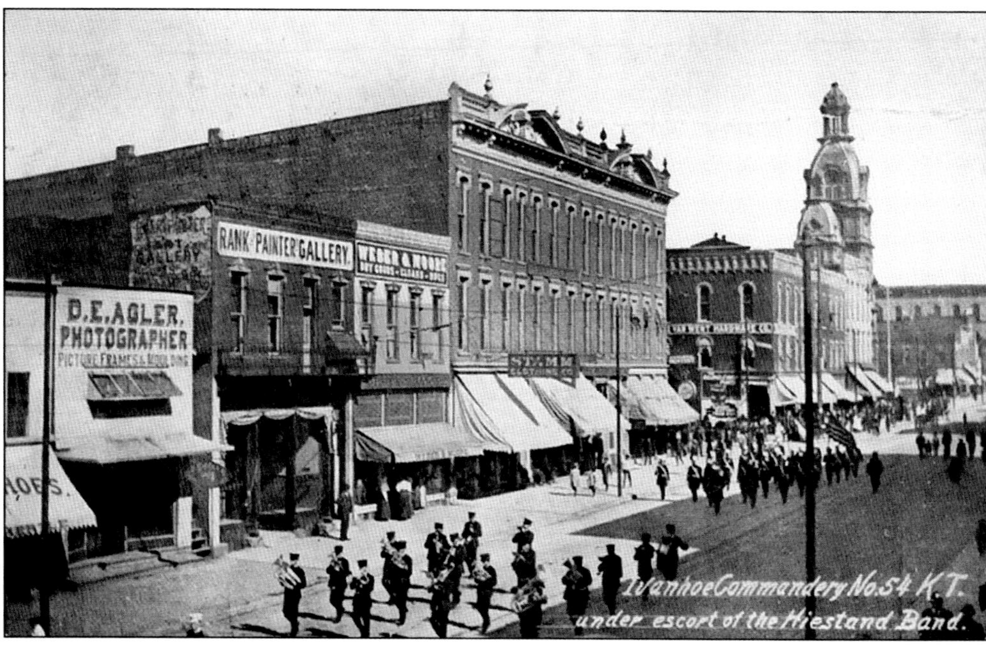

Van Wert County citizens have always loved a parade, as this card, dated June 1, 1909, shows. The W. H. Hiestand Band, which performed for over 50 years at area events, escorted the Ivanhoe Commandry No. 54 of the Knights Templar at this parade. Hiestand Band performed regular summer concerts in Fountain Park and played the Strand Auditorium at various times. (Author's collection.)

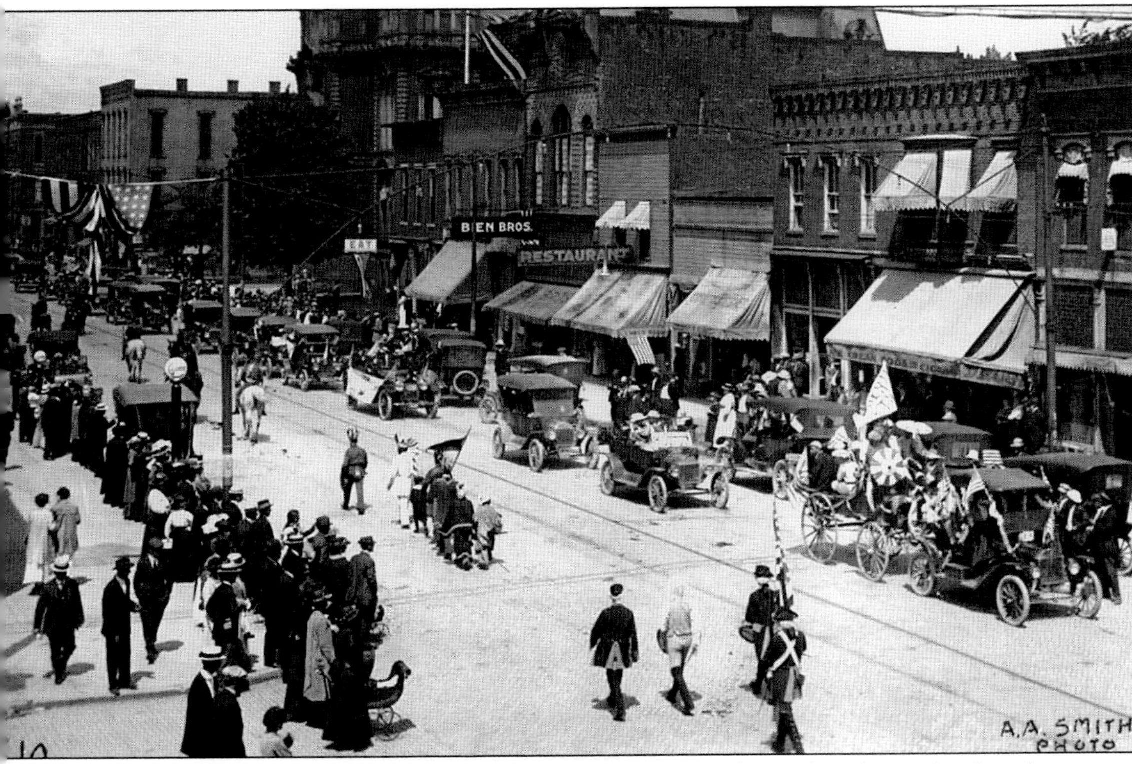

The men dressed in colonial-era uniforms in the foreground indicate that this undated card may commemorate Van Wert's founding. The county was formed in 1820, and named for Revolutionary War hero Isaac Van Wart, a Dutch immigrant who helped to thwart Maj. John Andre's plot to smuggle the plans for West Point to his British superiors. The change in spelling from Van Wart to Van Wert is attributed to a clerical error. David Williams and John Paulding, who with Van Wart captured Andre, also had Ohio counties named for them. In 1835, James Watson Riley, George Marsh, and Peter Augenbaugh purchased and surveyed 240 acres, which they divided into 78 lots and called Van Wert. The county seat was moved from Willshire to Van Wert in 1839. Van Wert was incorporated as a village in 1848. (Ken Cripe collection.)

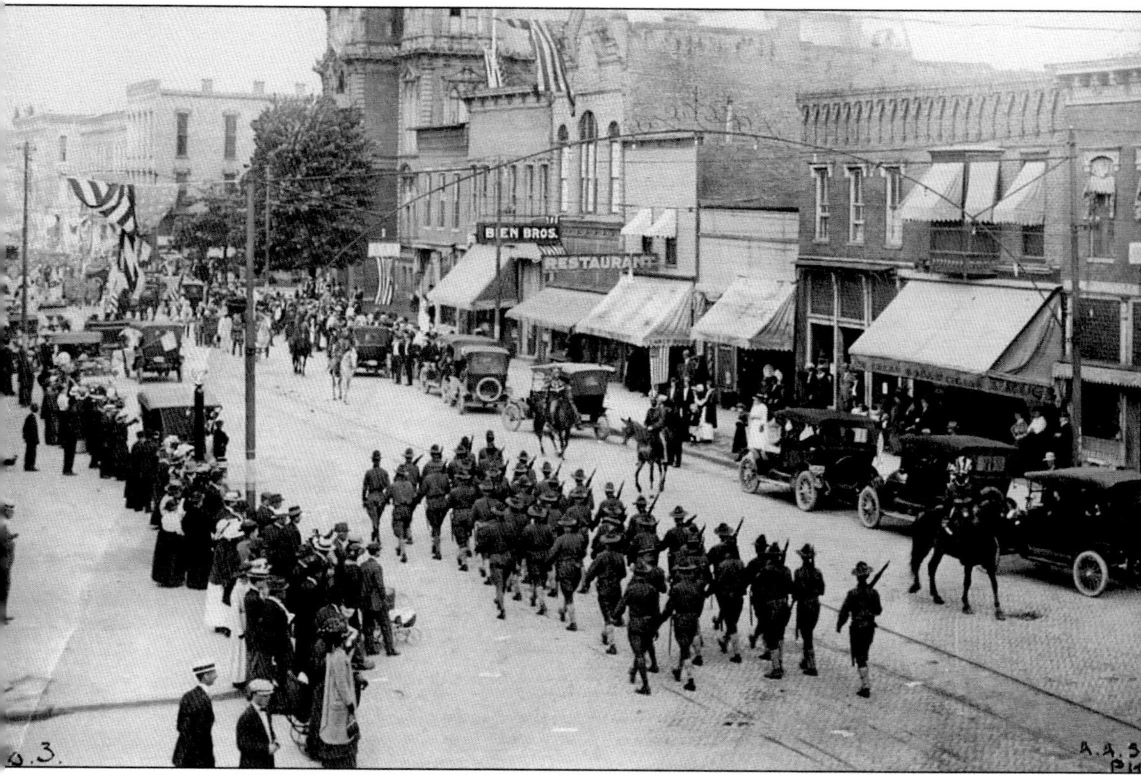

Americans gathered together, first in shock, then in resolve, to meet the challenges of World War I. Parades, like the Van Wert one featured in this undated postcard, honored servicemen and bolstered citizens' spirits. As the war intensified and claimed more young men, some citizens transferred their anti-German feelings to the county's German immigrants, who were a large percentage of the population. Several churches that had held services in German switched to English to avoid harassment and show solidarity with their fellow Americans. Three hundred and eleven county residents served in the war; 41 gave their lives. (Van Wert County Historical Society.)

Four

Transportation and Travel

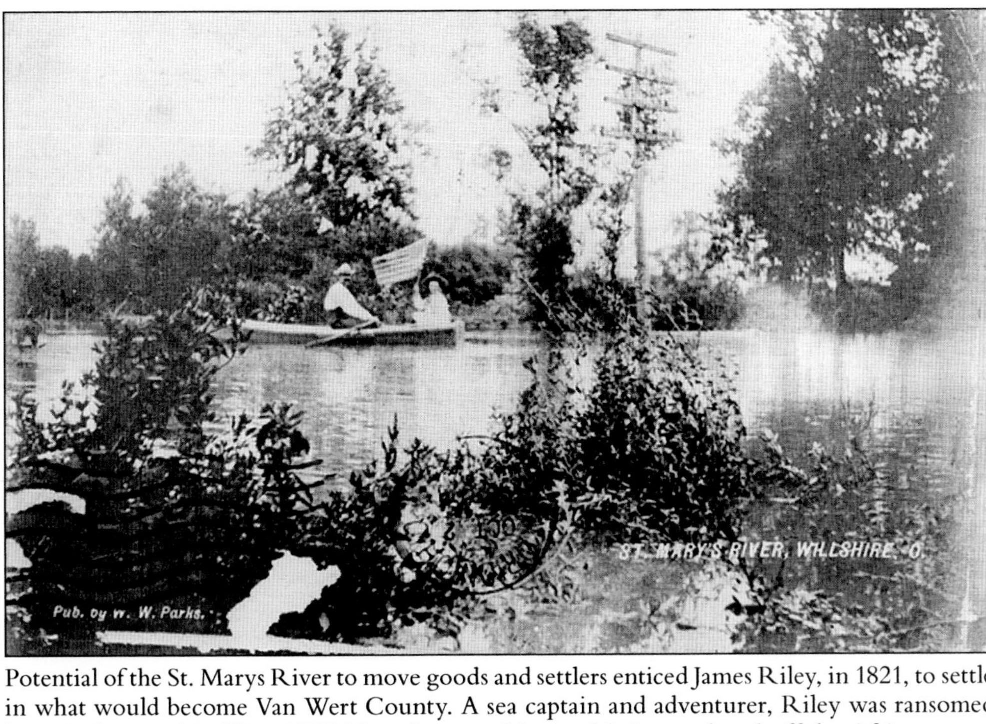

Potential of the St. Marys River to move goods and settlers enticed James Riley, in 1821, to settle in what would become Van Wert County. A sea captain and adventurer, Riley was ransomed by British consul William Willshire after wrecking and being enslaved off the African coast. Riley became the county's first white settler and named his village for Willshire. By the time this postcard was mailed in September 1912, this section of the river was used more for pleasure than commerce. "These are fine days if one has time to enjoy them," the sender wrote in inviting a relative to visit Willshire. (Author's collection.)

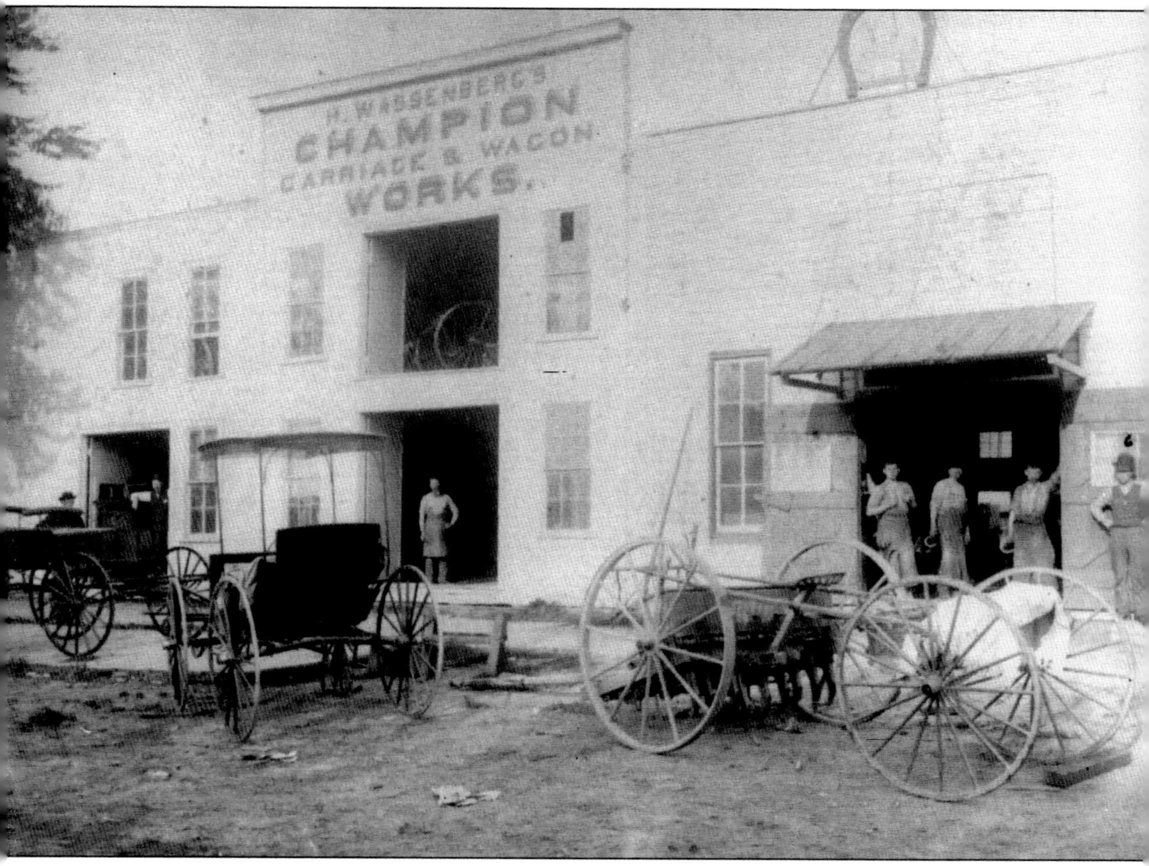

From the mid-1800s through the early 1900s, horses and wagons provided most of the daily transportation throughout the county. Many businesses developed to meet this basic transportation need. One of the most successful was Henry Wassenberg's Champion Carriage and Wagon Works in Van Wert. Wassenberg moved from Tuscarawas County to Van Wert in 1871, and worked as a journeyman for W. H. Himmelreich before opening his own business on North Jefferson Street in 1874. Champion Works manufactured carriages and wagons, and also sold farm implements and bicycles. Wassenberg was elected to the Van Wert city council in 1893. His son Charles (shown in the center of the photograph) also became a successful businessman and patron of the arts. (Ken Cripe collection.)

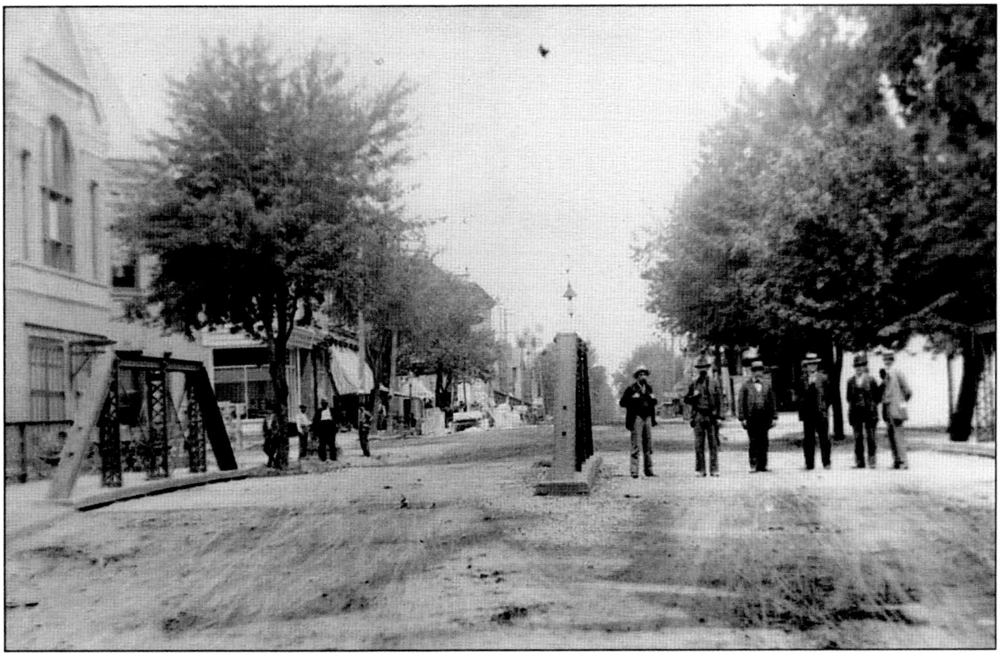

Street and bridge improvements in Van Wert were frequent from the 1890s to the 1920s as the county seat grew. These men pose with supports for a new bridge that was being planned for South Washington Street. The bridge was constructed in two sections of oak planks, each 15 feet long. (Ken Cripe collection.)

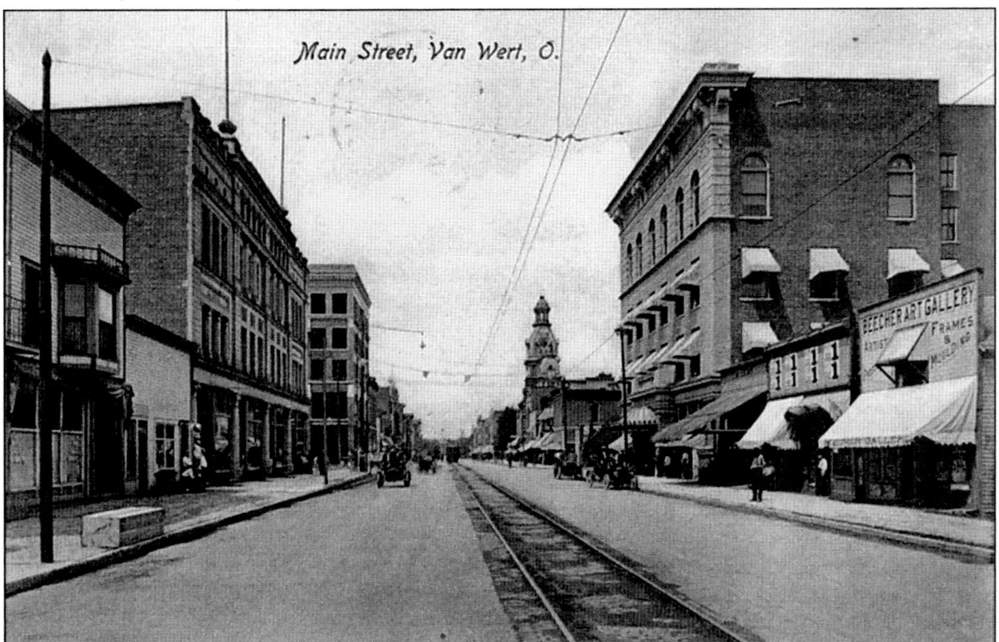

This card, postmarked 1908, shows a thriving downtown Van Wert. Handsome building facades, the stately courthouse, and the interurban railroad track running down Main Street attested to the city's vitality. Among the storefronts and offices, the Beecher Art Gallery (right) spoke of the residents' love for art and culture. (Author's collection.)

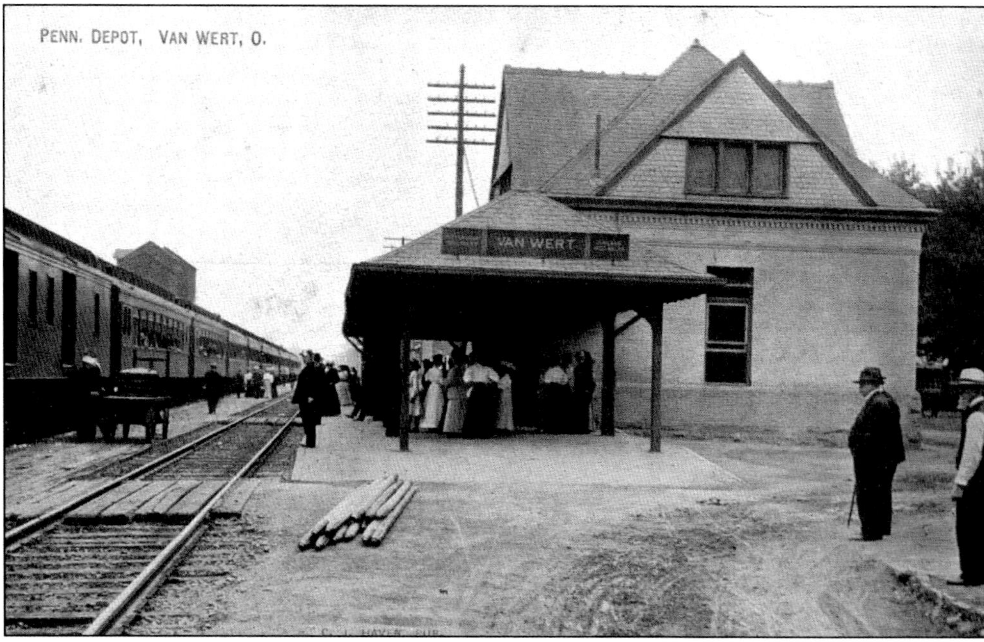

The Pennsylvania Railroad connected Van Wert County to the country. First called the Ohio and Indiana Railroad, the line ran through the county seat to Fort Wayne, Indiana, by the mid-1850s. The line passed through Middle Point, Convoy, and Dixon, with smaller depots in the first two villages. (Ken Cripe collection.)

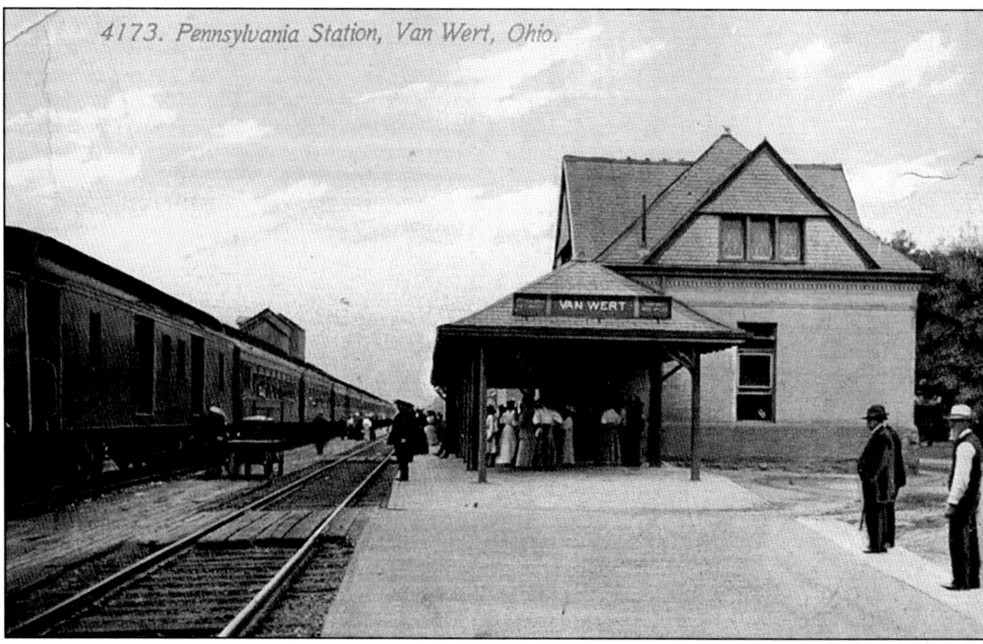

Collectors enjoy examining this type of retouched postcard. An artist took the black and white, *c.* 1914 photograph card above and retouched it. In addition to coloring the card in pastels, the artist removed the telegraph lines to the left rear of the depot and the pile of boards in the foreground near the tracks. The artist added a narrow sidewalk for the gentlemen in the right foreground to stand upon. (Author's collection.)

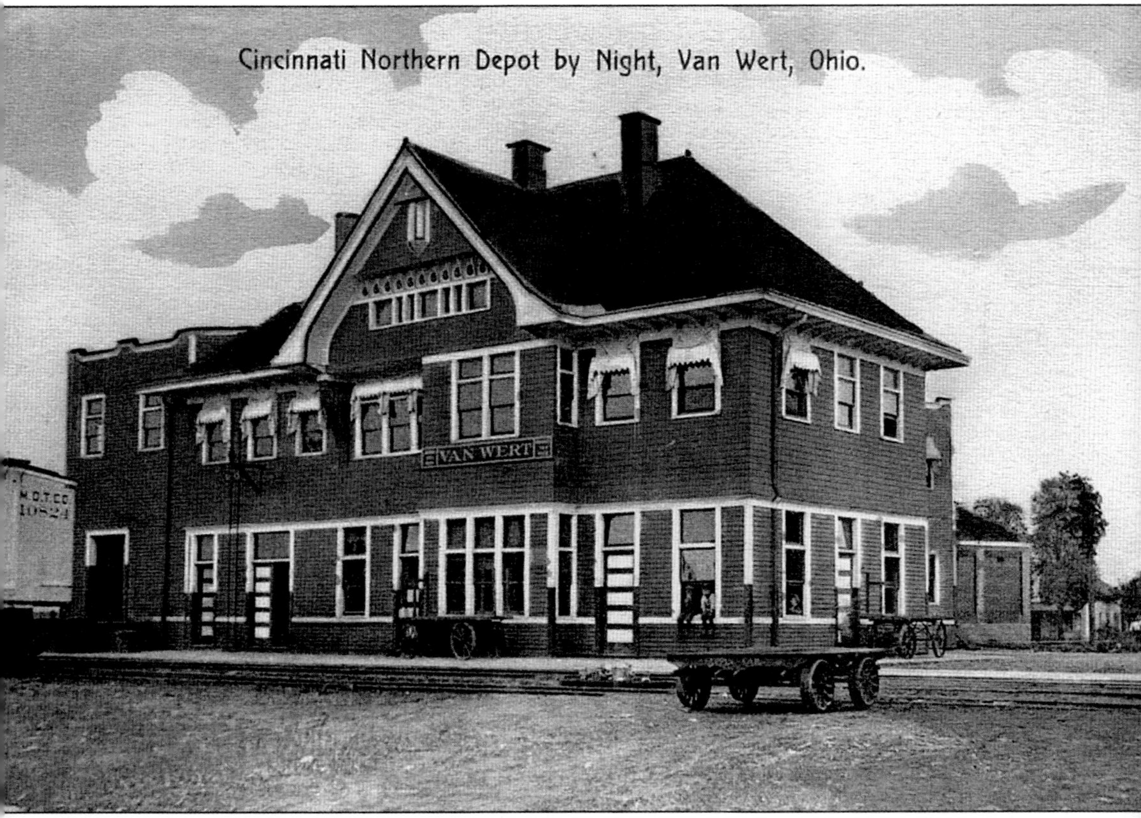

The Cincinnati Northern Railroad had a passenger station, including a restaurant at Fulton and Elliott Streets in Van Wert. Cincinnati Northern dated back to 1880 and evolved out of the Cincinnati, Jackson and Mackinaw Railroad, which was laid out by Henry E. Butler and J. S. Brumback. Butler owned a stave plant in what later became Ohio City and made sure that the tracks would run through that community. Cincinnati Northern and Pennsylvania Railroads became major employers in the city with more than 100 workers. On April 7, 1903, a boiler in an old Cincinnati Northern engine being worked on in the Anderson Avenue roundhouse exploded, leveling the brick structure. Four men who were working in and around the cab at the time miraculously escaped with minor injuries. Most of the Cincinnati Northern workers had already cleared the area for lunch. A ride on the Cincinnati Northern line from Van Wert to Ohio City cost 25¢ in 1910. Passenger service continued until September 1938. (Ken Cripe collection.)

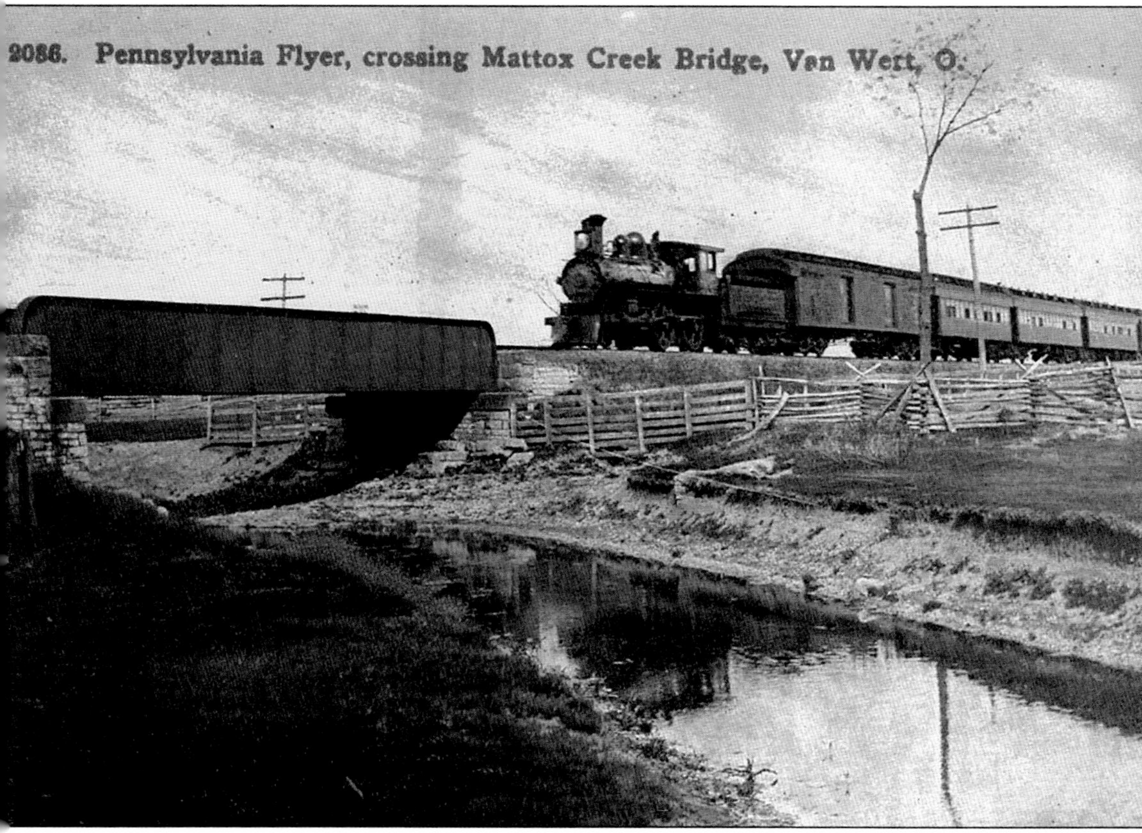

The powerful Pennsylvania Flyer engine symbolized the push of American capitalism at the beginning of the 20th century as it rushed people and freight across the country. The Flyer came to a tragic halt one October day in 1906 in Van Wert. The train was coming into town from the west when it hit an open switch west of the Burt Street crossing. The engineer and the baggage man were killed in the wreck. This *c.* 1910 postcard shows that the line recovered to run another day. The caption should read Maddox Creek Bridge. (Ken Cripe collection.)

A horse and delivery truck were not nearly as exciting as a locomotive, but they got the job done. This unidentified deliveryman took good care of one of his biggest investments—his horse—by protecting the animal from the winter weather with a blanket as he made his rounds around 1916. (Van Wert County Historical Society.)

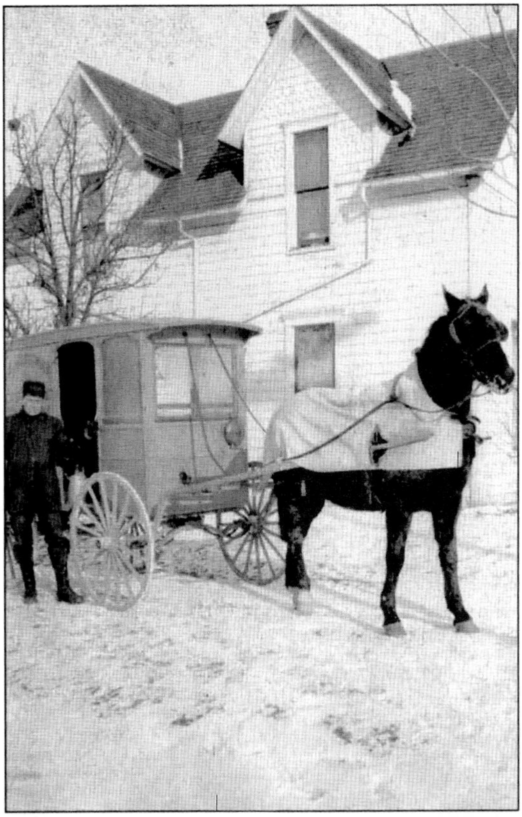

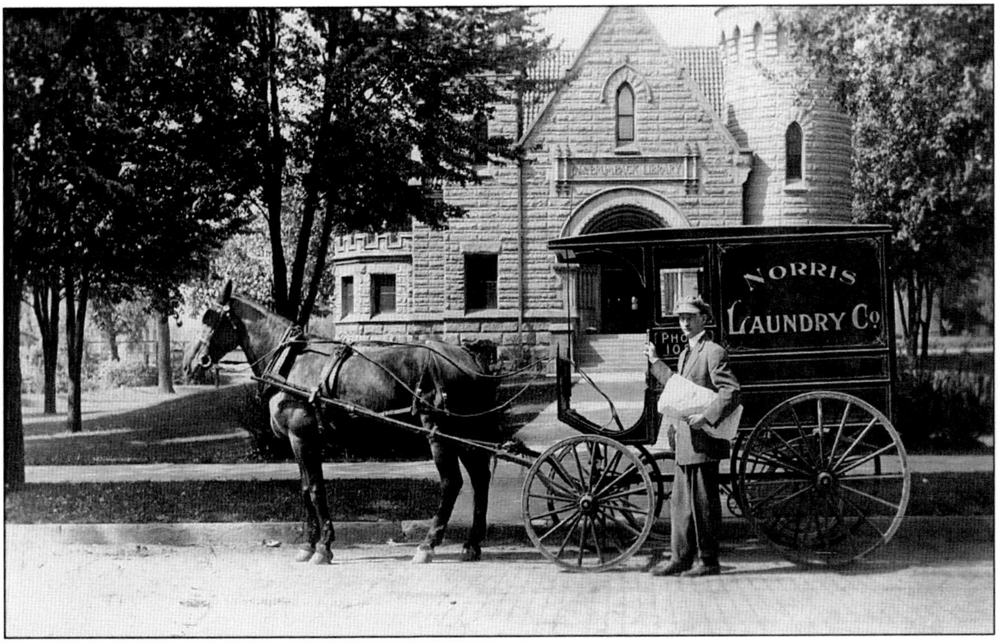

Ray Arnold poses outside the Brumback Library with his delivery truck for Norris Laundry in this *c.* 1920 postcard. The laundry is listed at 219 North Market Street, Van Wert, in the 1910 county directory. (Van Wert County Historical Society.)

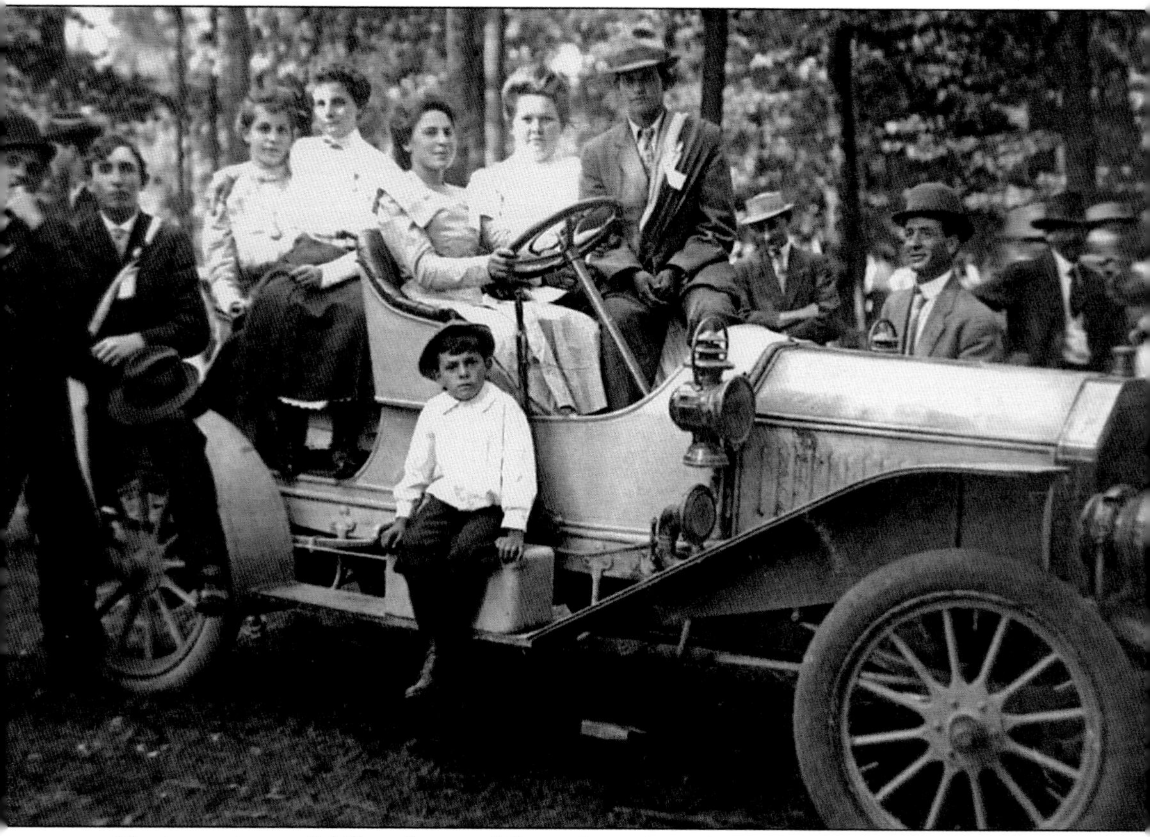

The increasing availability of automobiles in the early 20th century turned drivers into explorers and passengers into admirers. Van Wert County residents had a special love for the automobile because one of their own, Ohio City's John W. Lambert, was credited with producing the first gasoline engine vehicle built in the United States in 1891. The original three-wheeler was powered by a two-cylinder engine. A four-wheel buggy soon followed, and Lambert built a factory in Indiana where the Lambert was produced until 1917. Lambert's success influenced a whole generation of independent Indiana automakers and several generations of car lovers. This group posed with a favorite car at the Van Wert County Fairgrounds. The only people identified are Clarence Williman (second from left) and Emily Snyder (fourth from left). The couple married in 1910. (Ken Cripe collection.)

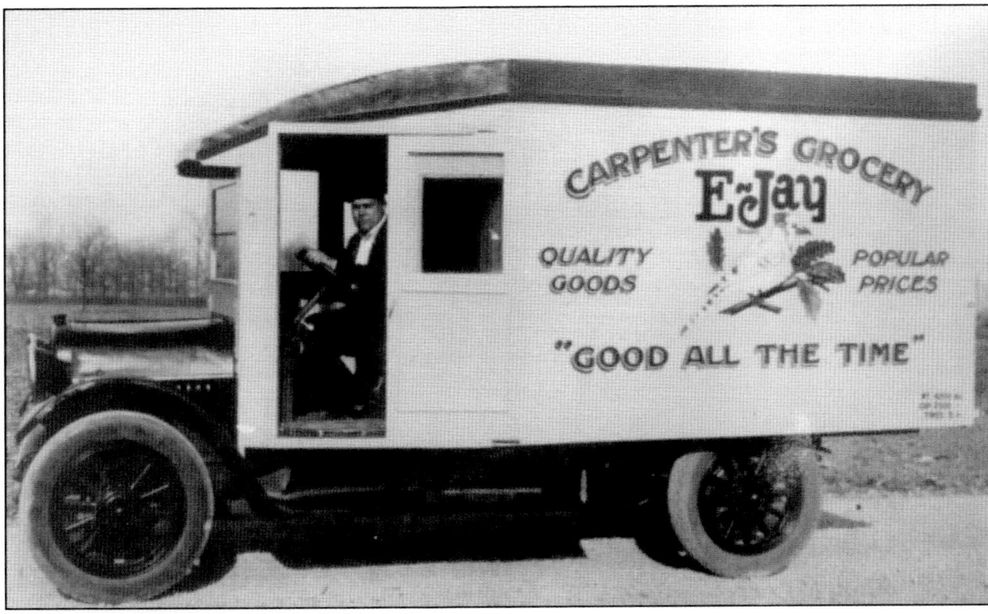

Carpenter's Grocery delivered products to customers around Van Wert in the 1920s. The store carried the popular E-Jay brand of goods and boasted that their products were "good all the time." (Ken Cripe collection.)

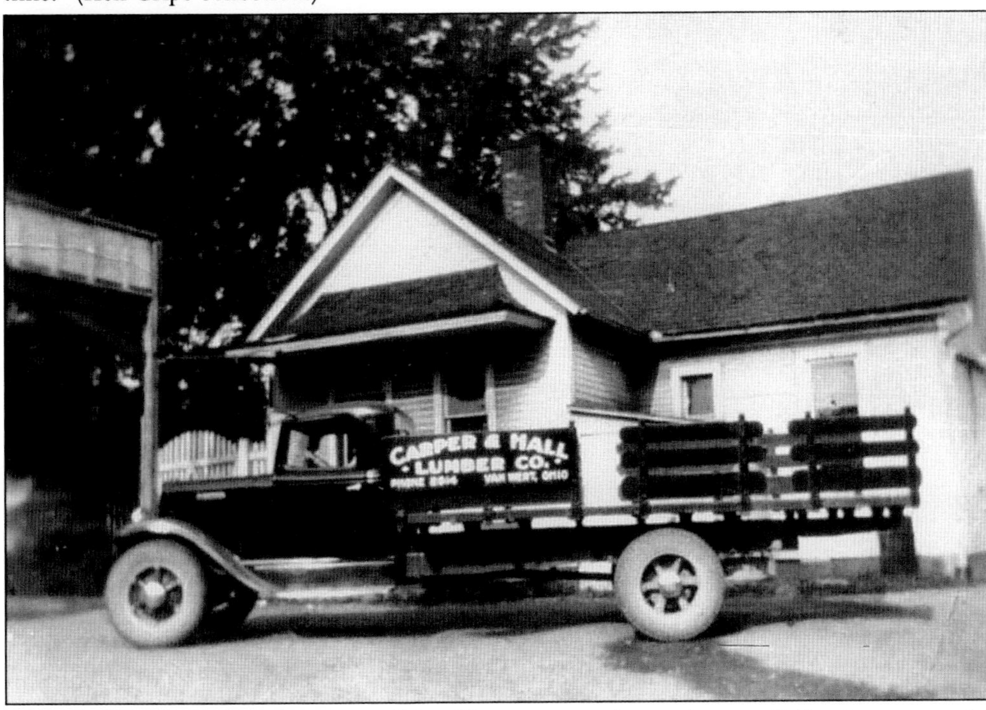

Carper and Hall Lumber Company of Van Wert was one of several successful lumber companies operating in the county by the 1920s. The region's lumber business dated back to the 19th century when thousands of trees harvested during the clearing of the Black Swamp resulted in numerous sawmills and stave factories. Timber from Tully Township was reportedly used in building the U.S.S. *Monitor* warship during the Civil War. (Ken Cripe collection.)

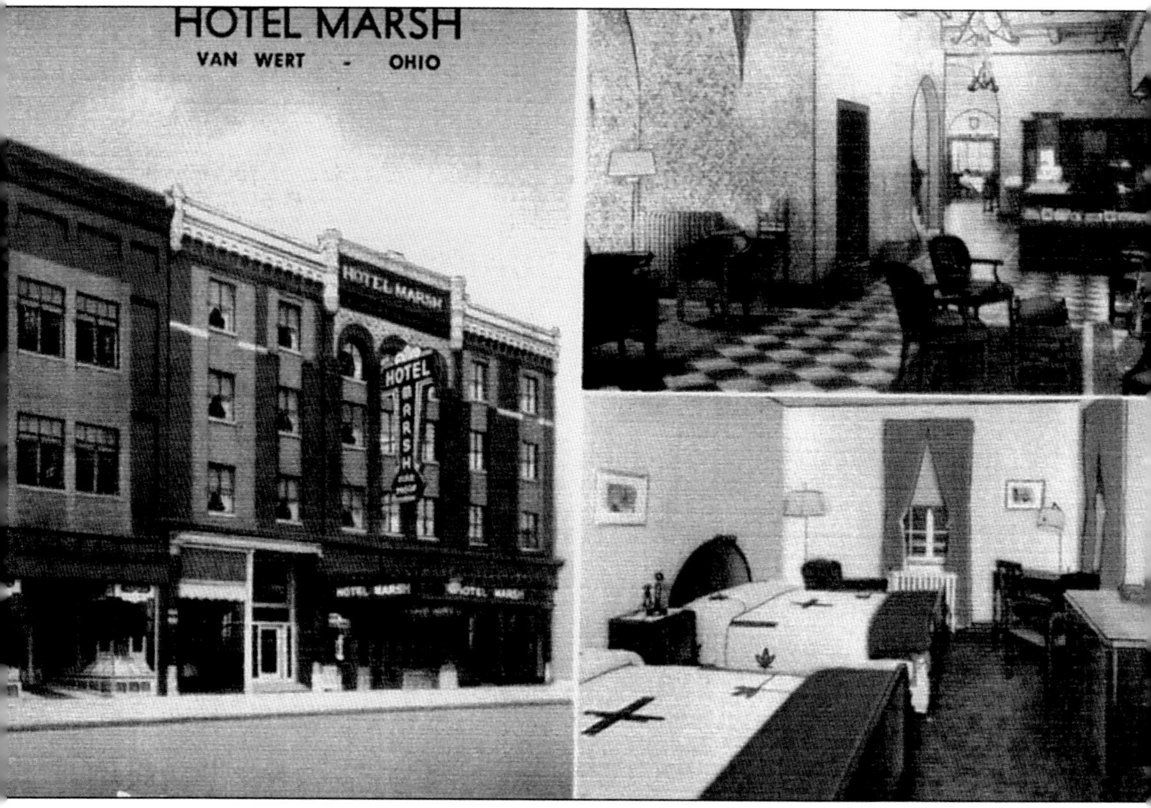

By the 20th century, three national highways ran through the county: U.S. 127, U.S. 224, and U.S. 30. Visitors, who once arrived by train, were greeted by porters of Van Wert's four major hotels and were then checked into a growing number of hotels, tourist cabins, and motels. George H. Marsh built the Hotel Marsh in 1884 in Van Wert. Marsh, who became a household name in the county due to his philanthropy, had business dealings and land holdings throughout the state. The hotel survived long after his death. This card, postmarked 1942, shows Main Street's "new" Hotel Marsh, which boasted 90 fireproof rooms and proclaimed itself the "Best in Middle West." (Author's collection.)

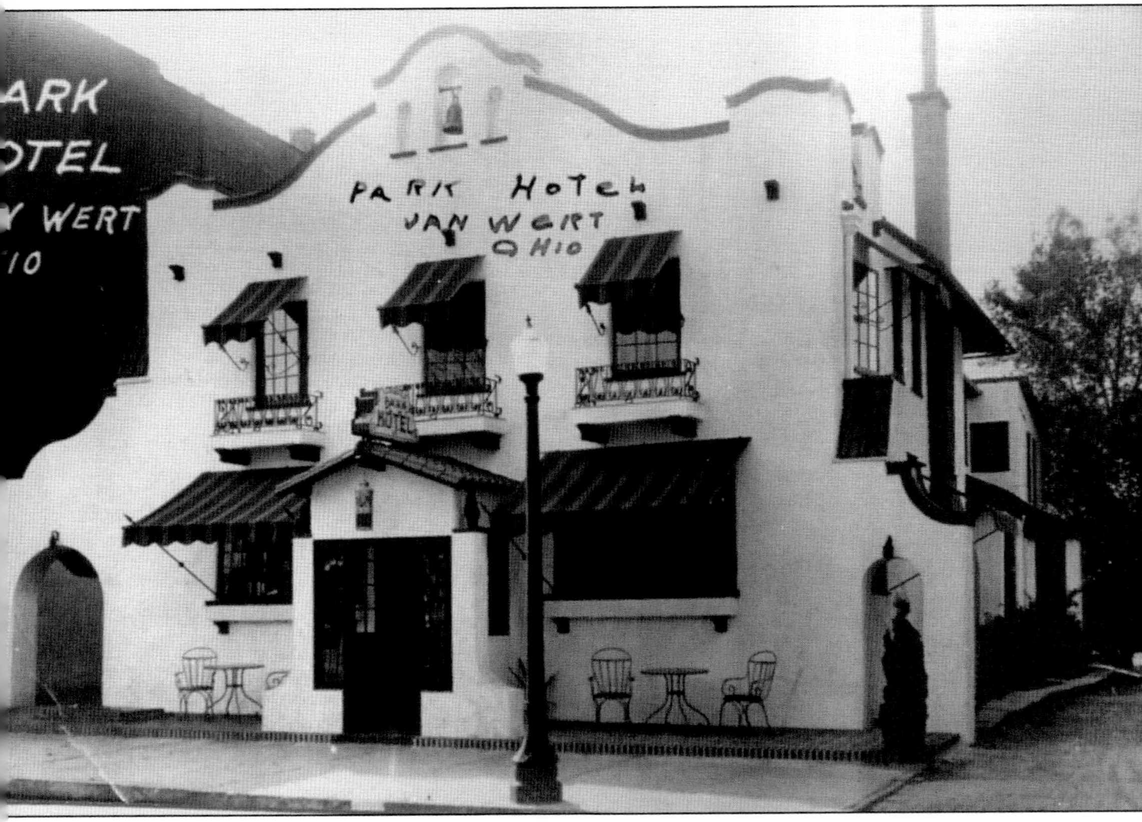

With its tile roof, stucco exterior, and bell, the Park Hotel brought a touch of the Southwest to Van Wert. The Park Hotel, seen in this *c.* 1936 postcard, operated for decades on Washington Street. It became a local landmark while 19th-century establishments, including the DePuy, American, Davis, and Van Wert House, faded. When most long-distance travel was by train in the 1800s, even larger villages, including Convoy, Scott, Willshire, and Wren, had hotels. (Ken Cripe collection.)

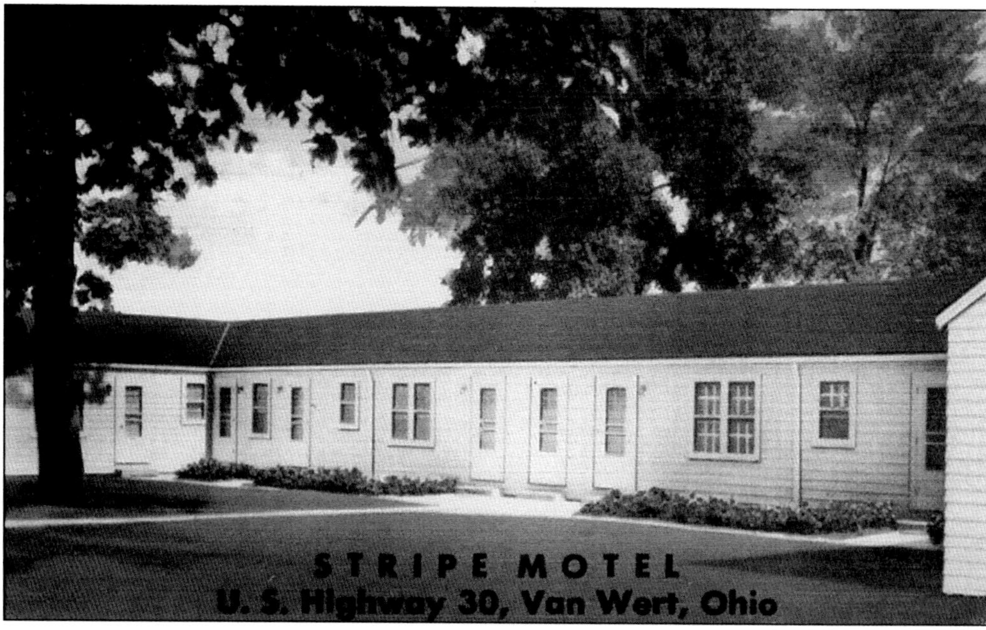

Motels, where travelers could pull up right to their doors, were popular by mid-20th century. The Stripe Motel, west of downtown Van Wert on U.S. 30, boasted 12 completely modern units. Emmett Stripe and his sons Robert and Richard built the motel in 1950. "We are staying at this motel and it is real nice," wrote the sender of this card in 1957. "Large trees in front which makes it shady. This is a nice town and grand farms." (Author's collection.)

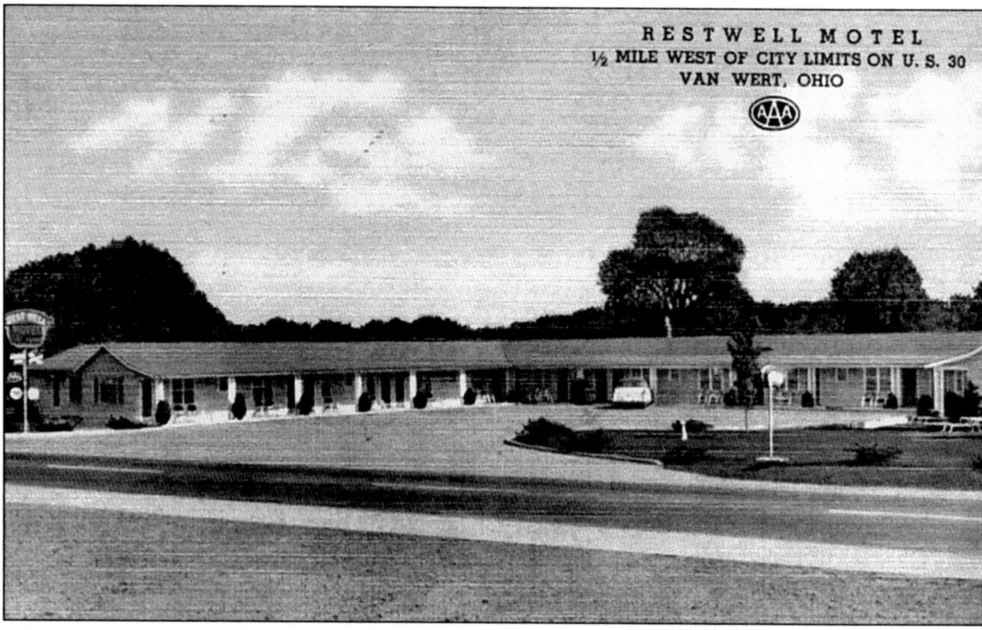

The Restwell Motel, just west of Van Wert on U.S. 30, earned the coveted AAA seal of approval. The 15-room unit advertised private baths, hot water heat, and cross ventilation, an important consideration in the days before air conditioning became prevalent. The Restwell prided itself as family friendly and noted the proximity of the Brookside Restaurant and Drive-In Theater. (Author's collection.)

Five

Heart and Soul

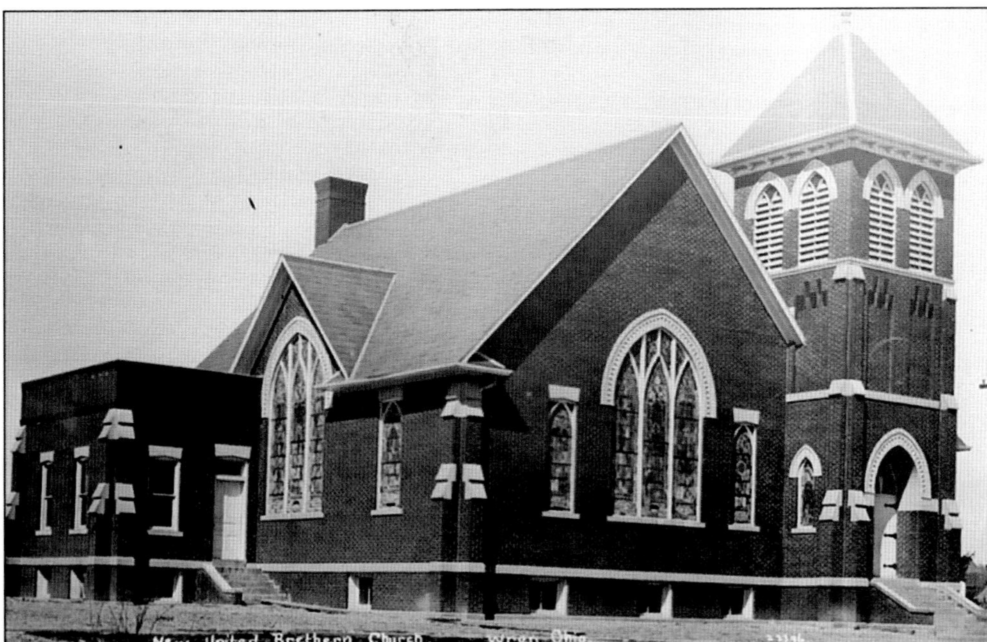

The United Brethren Church of Wren, shown in this 1913 postcard, traces its heritage to a handful of people who began worshipping together in the village school building in 1853. They raised funds to build a frame church in 1858. An internal dispute over doctrine led to the church being called the Liberal United Brethren church for years. The cornerstone for this building was laid on June 12, 1910. The church, built for $12,500, was dedicated in February 1911. (Author's collection.)

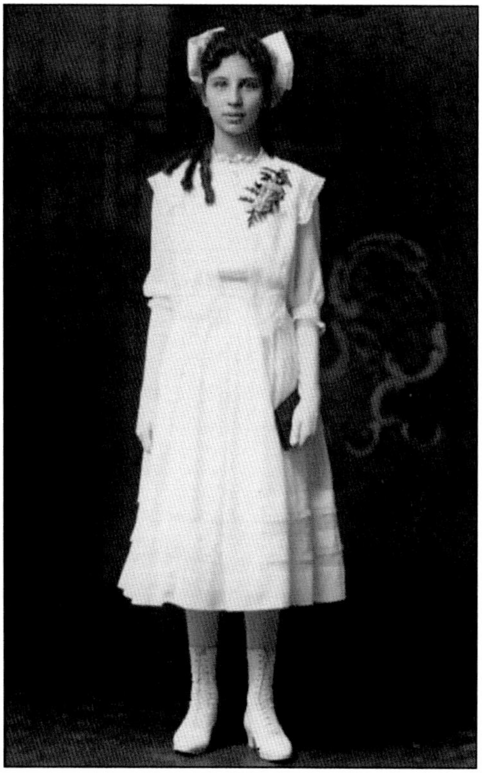

Elsie Elvera Bauer was confirmed into the Lutheran faith at St. John Church in Harrison Township around 1915. Her catechism classes as well as worship services were conducted in German. Elsie was the daughter of Frederick J. Bauer and Elizabeth Bauer (née Steinbauer) of Tully Township, and the author's aunt. As was common in those days, Elsie walked several miles to church for instruction. (Author's collection.)

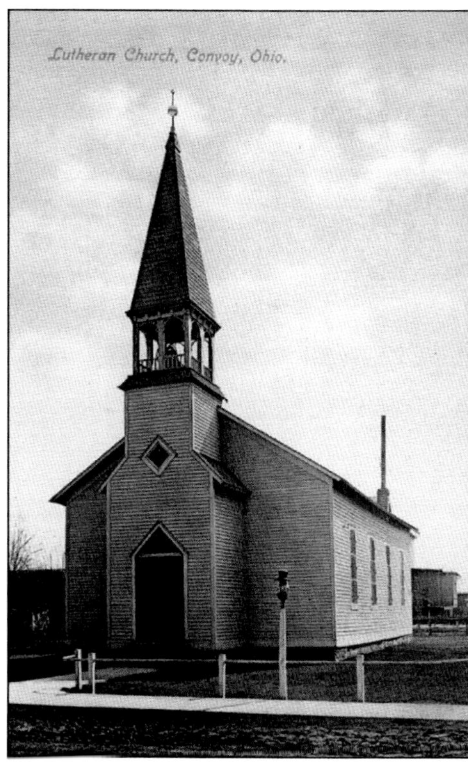

This church was home to two Lutheran congregations in Convoy's early days. The Evangelical Lutheran Church first called it home in the 1870s. The building was moved from Tully Street to North Liberty Street in 1911 where it became home to St. Paul Lutheran Church. This card is postmarked 1909. (Author's collection.)

After selling their old sanctuary, the Evangelical Lutheran Church built this brick structure on their original Tully Street site in 1912 for $16,000. The congregation received a matching grant from the Carnegie Foundation for a pipe organ. The congregation adopted the name Trinity Lutheran in the late 1920s. (Author's collection.)

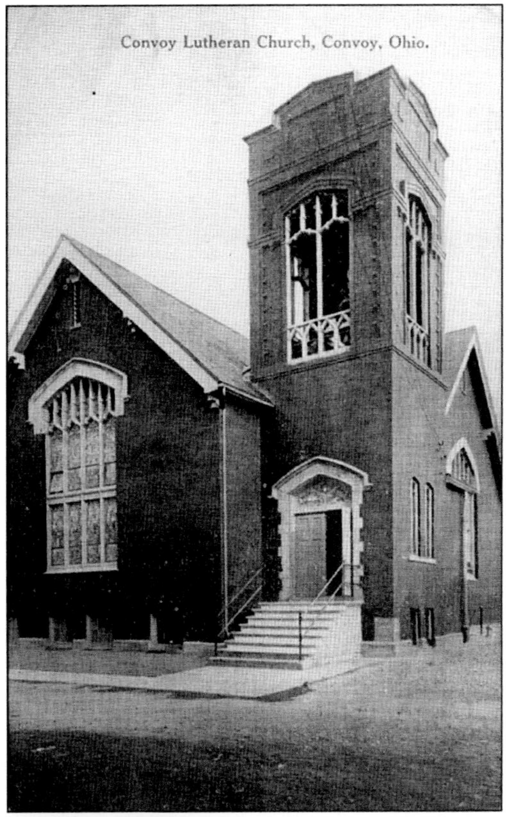

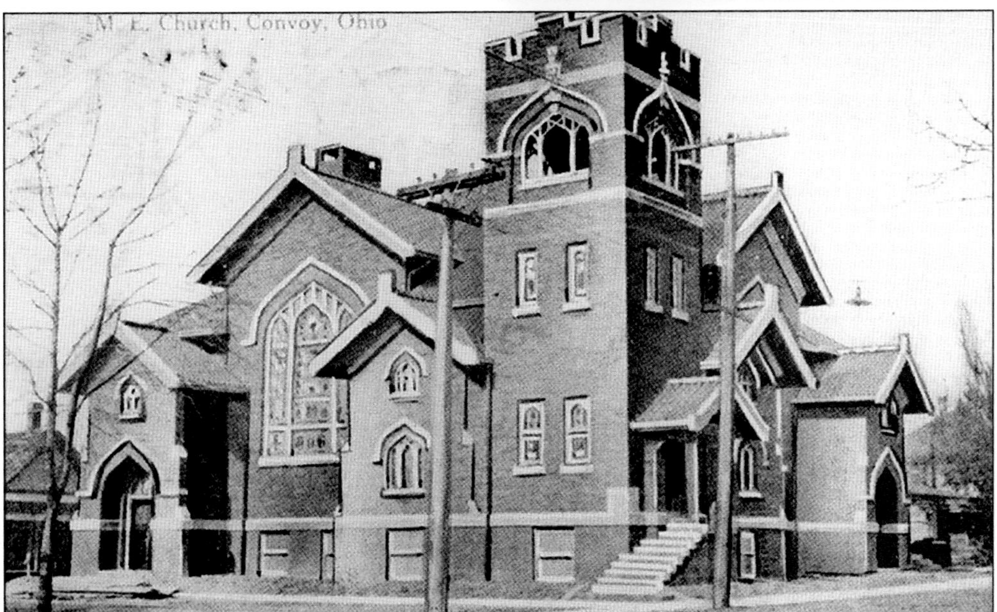

The Methodist Episcopal Church began in Convoy with a Sunday school class in 1867. A brick church was built at Sycamore and North Main Streets in 1878. This card, postmarked 1940, shows additions and renovations made in 1915. (Author's collection.)

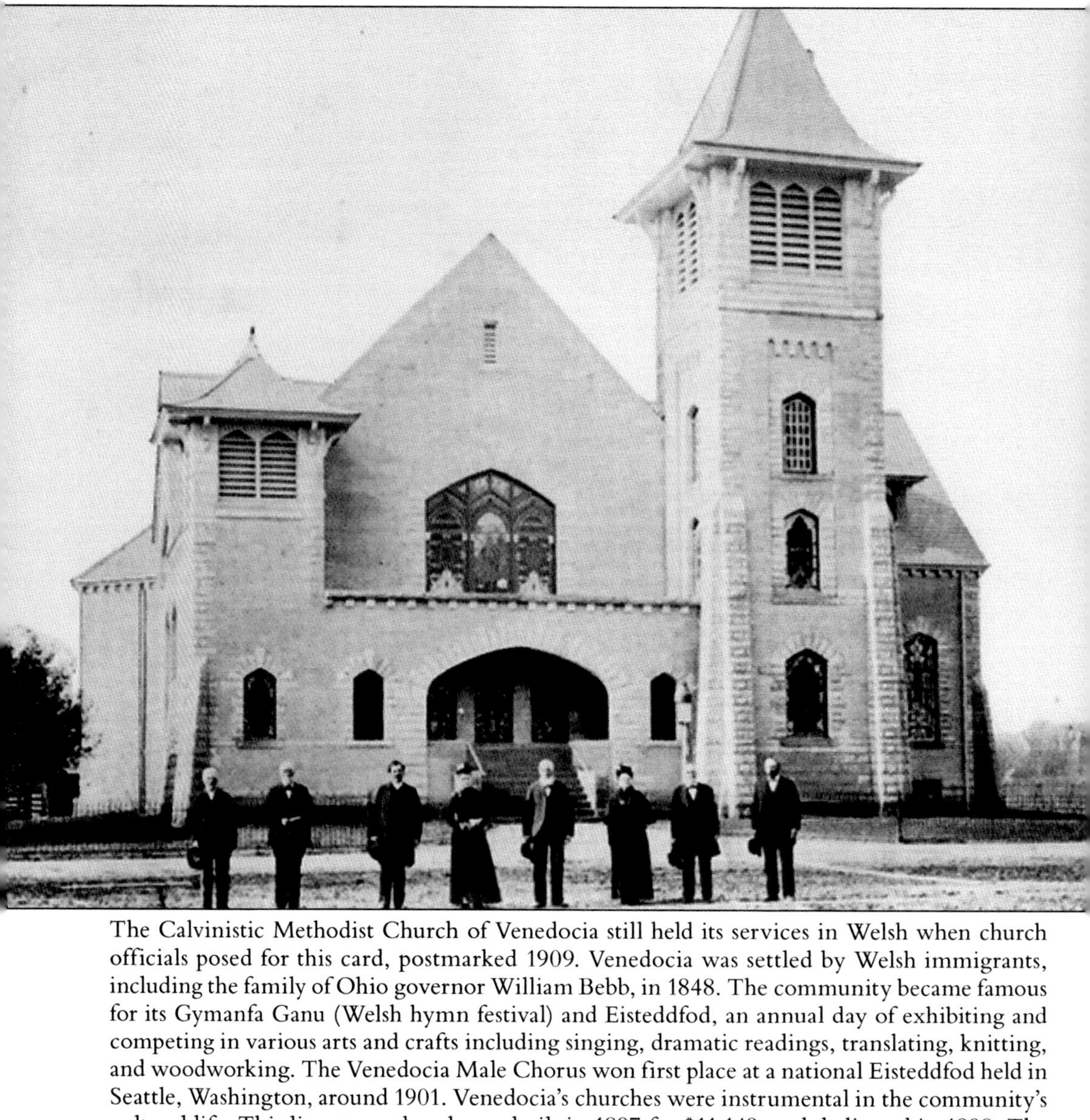

The Calvinistic Methodist Church of Venedocia still held its services in Welsh when church officials posed for this card, postmarked 1909. Venedocia was settled by Welsh immigrants, including the family of Ohio governor William Bebb, in 1848. The community became famous for its Gymanfa Ganu (Welsh hymn festival) and Eisteddfod, an annual day of exhibiting and competing in various arts and crafts including singing, dramatic readings, translating, knitting, and woodworking. The Venedocia Male Chorus won first place at a national Eisteddfod held in Seattle, Washington, around 1901. Venedocia's churches were instrumental in the community's cultural life. This limestone church was built in 1897 for $11,149, and dedicated in 1898. The congregation later joined with the Presbyterian denomination and was known as Salem Church. (Author's collection.)

St. John the Evangelist, a Roman Catholic congregation, began holding services in Delphos in 1853. S. W. Lane of Cleveland designed a sanctuary, which was built and dedicated in 1879. A thriving membership resulted in numerous expansions over the years, resulting in the building shown in this 1950s-era card. (Author's collection.)

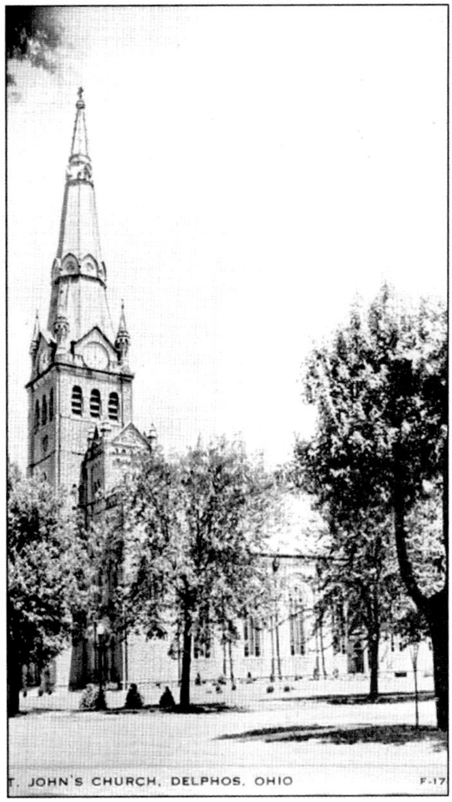

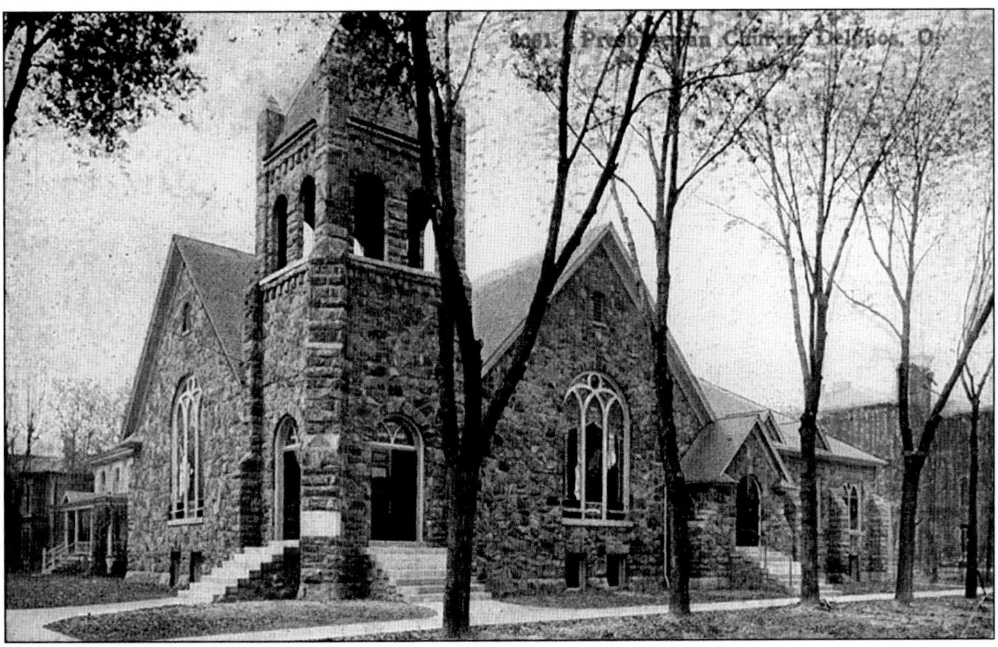

The congregation of the Delphos Presbyterian Church organized in 1849. This church dates to 1869 when the Ladies Sewing Circle raised almost one-third of the $6,000 construction cost. (Author's collection.)

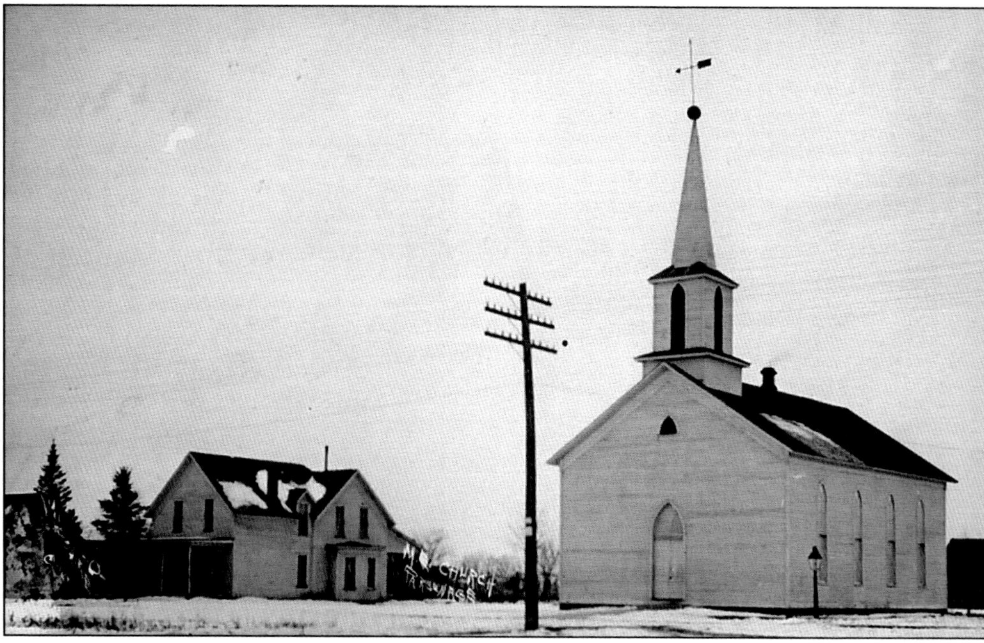

Willshire's Methodist Episcopal Church and parsonage are shown in this *c.* 1908 postcard. The Methodists first organized in Willshire in 1829 in a one-story log building that had housed an early courthouse, tavern, and shoe shop. This frame church was built in 1860 under the leadership of Rev. John C. Miller. (Author's collection.)

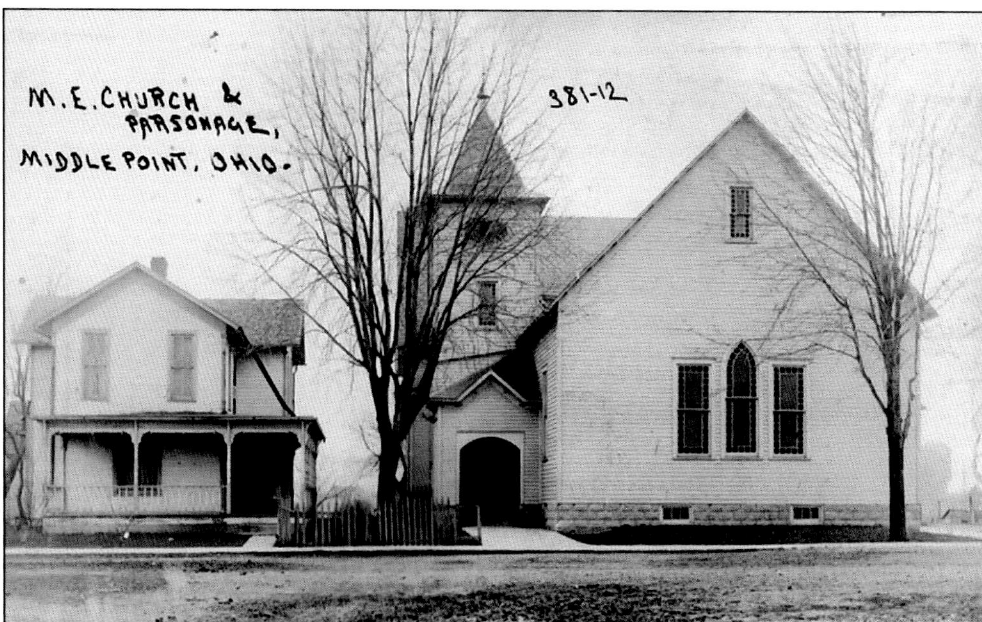

The Middle Point Methodist Circuit began around 1872. The congregation's first church was completed in 1874 for $2,000. The building was enlarged and remodeled in 1908. The parsonage shown in this card, postmarked 1917, was replaced in 1926. (Author's collection.)

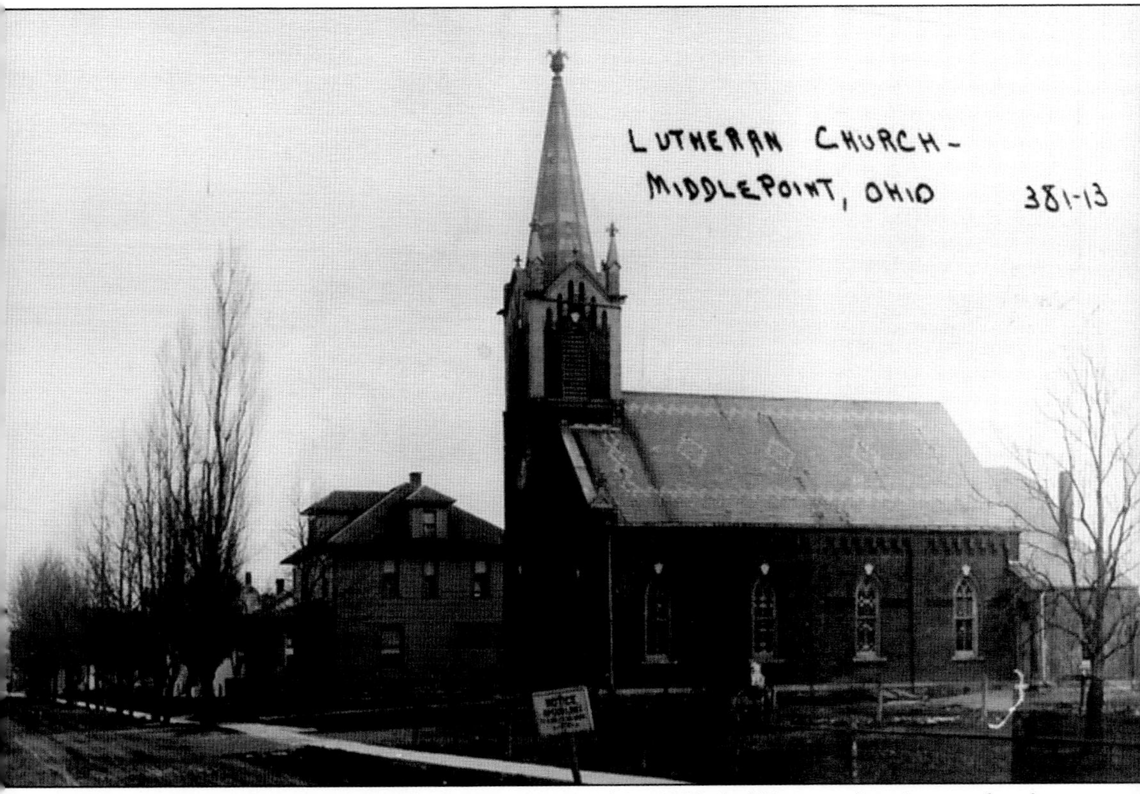

Trinity Lutheran Church of Middle Point organized in 1853, holding services in members' homes until a frame church was built on Main Street in 1858. The church was so respected in the community that in 1892, its pastor, Dr. Luther McCreery, was asked to lead the Middle Point Normal School, a training school for teachers. As the congregation grew over the years, so did the building. An addition was made and a pipe organ installed in 1911. At first, the bellows of the pipe organ were filled with air pumped by hand by two young men; later a gasoline engine was used. This card, postmarked 1916, shows the convergence of two centuries: the buggy in the church lot and the street sign limiting speed to eight miles per hour, and the horse-drawn wagon almost parallel to the automobile in the distance. Middle Point was a thriving, growing community in 1916. (Author's collection.)

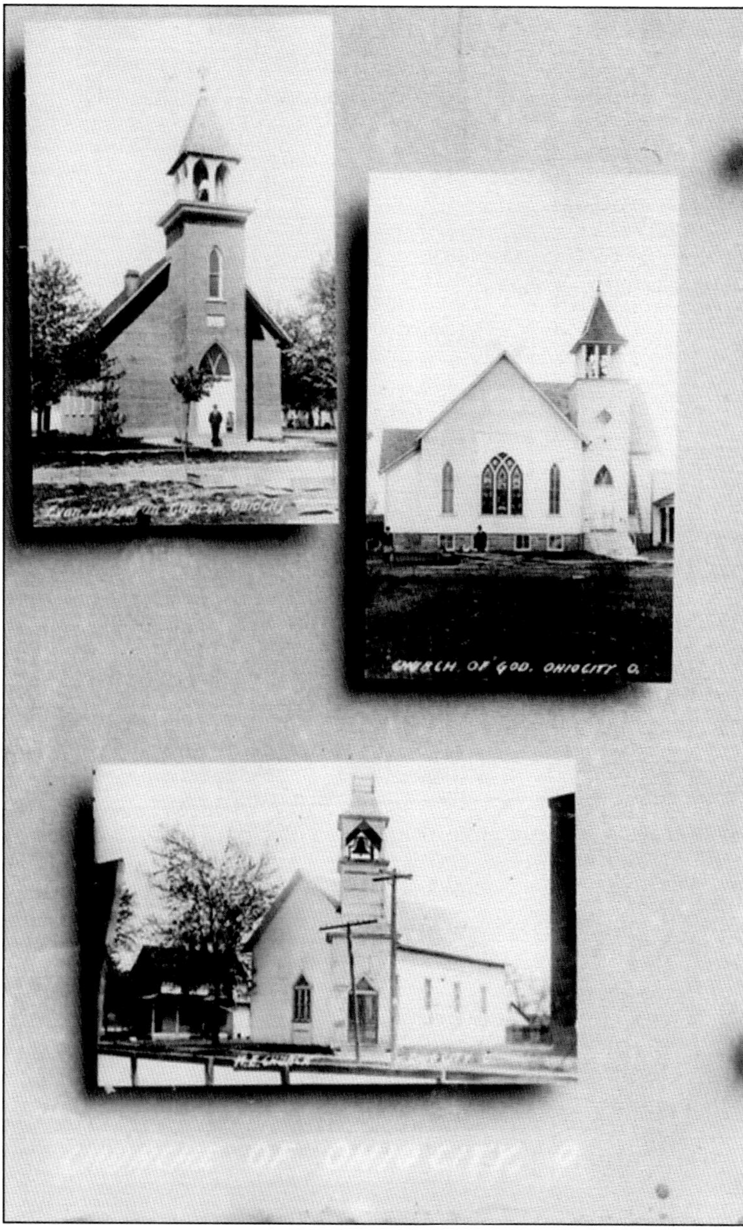

Ohio City's Evangelical Lutheran Church (top), Methodist Episcopal Church (bottom), and Church of God (center) are shown in this early-20th-century card. All three churches formed in the 1800s when Ohio City was still called Enterprise. R. B. Bolton formed the Church of God congregation in 1861. Church meetings were held in various places throughout Liberty Township until a church was constructed in 1885 in the village for $2,000. The church was remodeled in 1909. Rev. David Thomas led the first Methodist congregation in the community. A small church (shown in this card) was built in 1882 on Carmean Street; a larger brick church was constructed on North Main Street in 1910. Rev. C. Caskey organized Lutherans in Liberty Township around 1858. Preparations for a new church in the village started in 1894 when the congregation exchanged their old church property for 80,000 bricks and some money to construct the new sanctuary shown in the card. (Author's collection.)

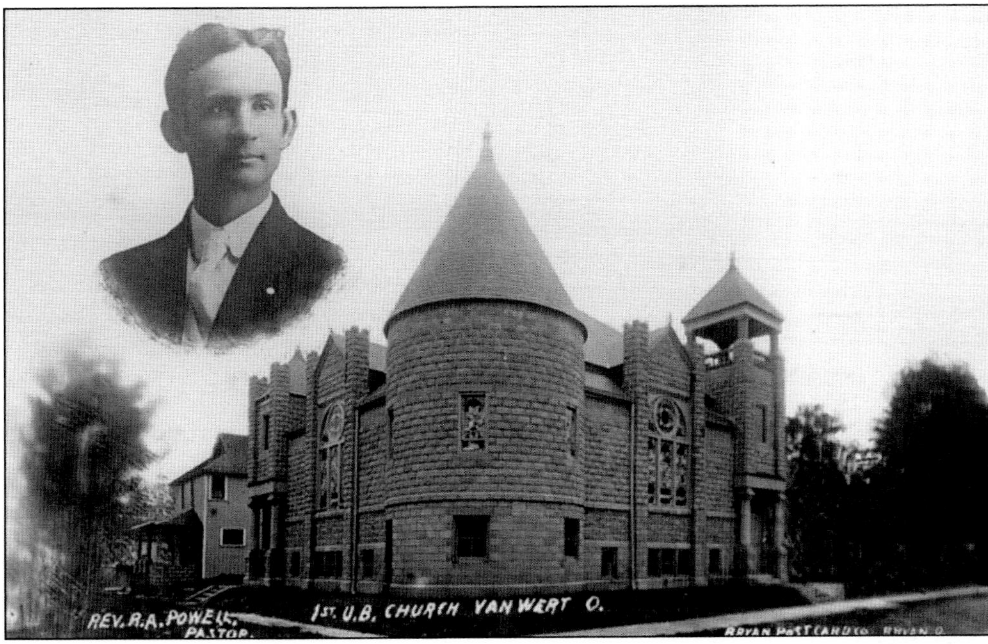

Rev. R. A. Powell's photograph is seen in the insert of this card of the First United Brethren Church in Van Wert. The sender mailed this card to a lady in Venedocia on April 3, 1909, to let her know he had arrived safely in Van Wert. (Author's collection.)

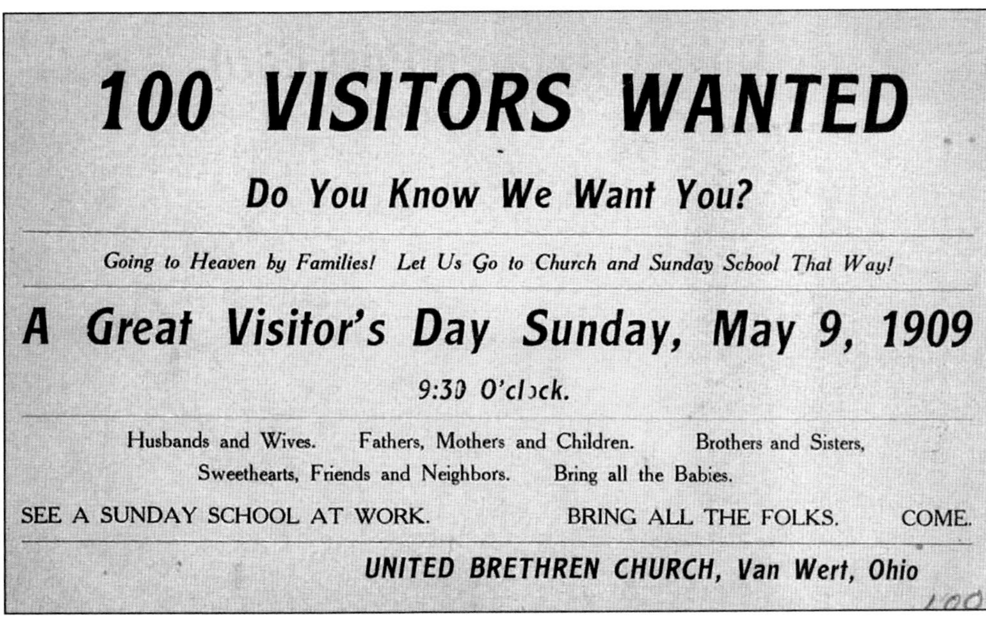

100 VISITORS WANTED

Do You Know We Want You?

Going to Heaven by Families! Let Us Go to Church and Sunday School That Way!

A Great Visitor's Day Sunday, May 9, 1909

9:30 O'clock.

Husbands and Wives. Fathers, Mothers and Children. Brothers and Sisters, Sweethearts, Friends and Neighbors. Bring all the Babies.

SEE A SUNDAY SCHOOL AT WORK. BRING ALL THE FOLKS. COME.

UNITED BRETHREN CHURCH, Van Wert, Ohio

The United Brethren Church sought out visitors and new members through a mailing campaign in the spring of 1909. "Going to Heaven by Families!" the card declared. "Let Us Go to Church and Sunday School That Way!" (Ken Cripe collection.)

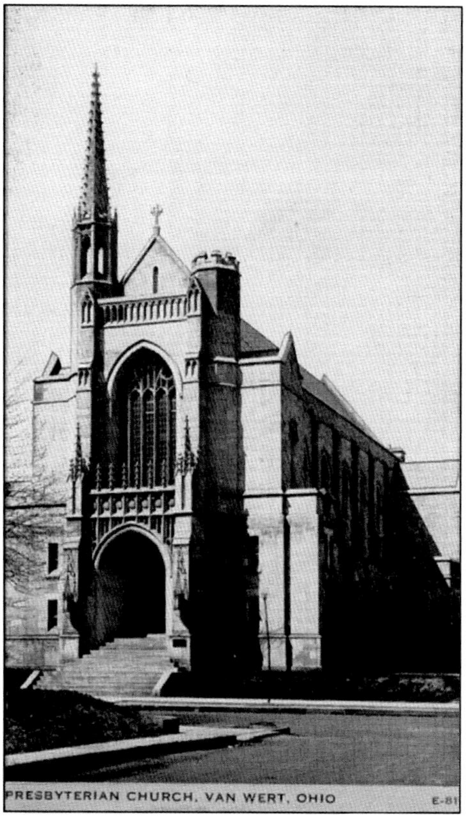

The Presbyterian Church in Van Wert formed on June 10, 1843. The 1924 church, shown in this 1930s card, is one of the purest examples of Gothic architecture in the region. The church is one vast, self-supporting unit of aspiring arches, buttresses, and piers, graced with a series of stained-glass windows in the sanctuary that depict *The Revelation of God in the Old and New Testaments.* (Author's collection.)

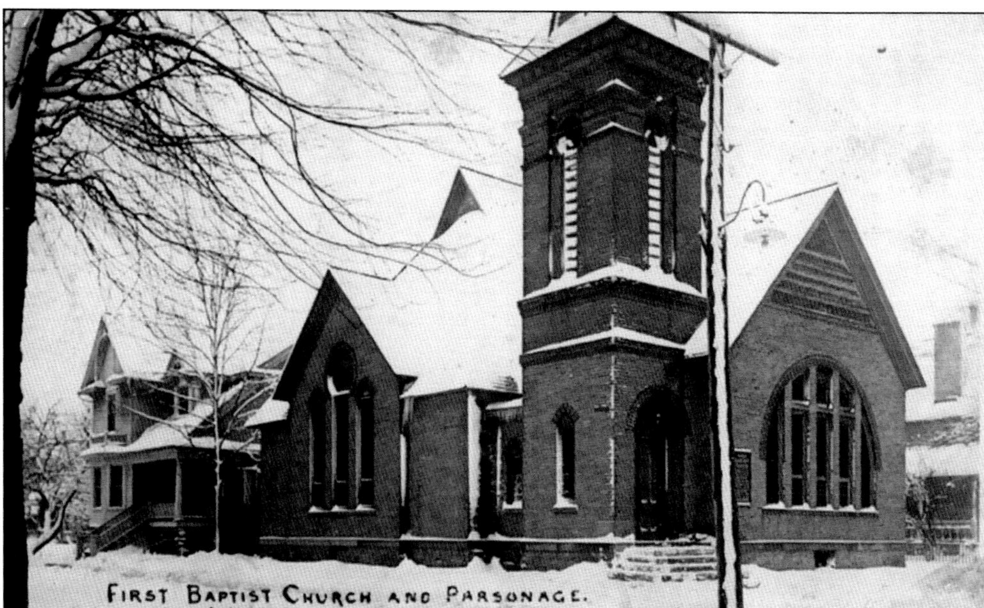

A snow-capped First Baptist Church and parsonage at Crawford and Taylor Streets in Van Wert is featured in this 1920s card. The congregation first organized in 1847 and met in various locations before this church was built. (Author's collection.)

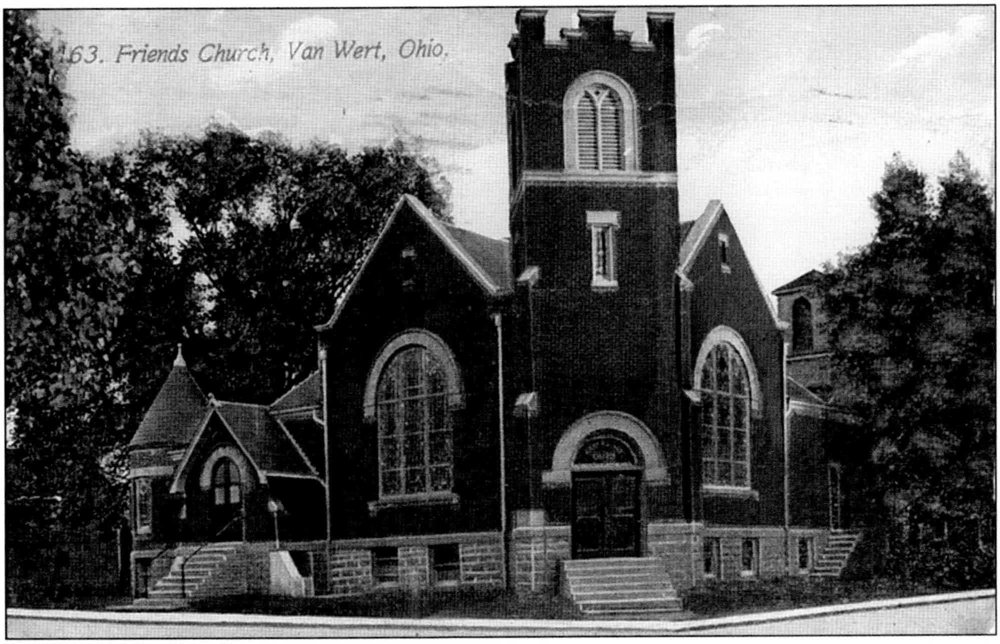

The First Friends Church, East Central and Franklin Streets, Van Wert, is shown in this card postmarked October 17, 1919. The brick and stone church was dedicated in 1910 with Tennyson Lewis as the first pastor. The church's distinctive round room was once used for prayer services. Joseph Wakefield first gathered a Friends congregation in Van Wert in 1873. (Author's collection.)

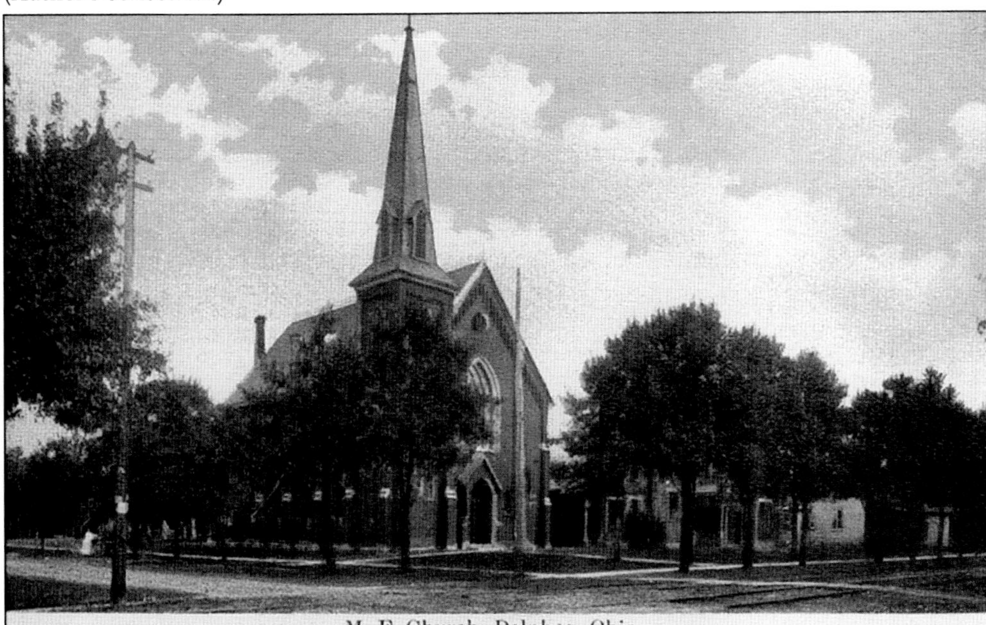

The Methodist Episcopal Church in Delphos is shown in this 1920s postcard. The church dates to 1846 when members worshipped in one another's homes. Rev. John Graham was the first pastor. The building shown was completed in 1880 for about $6,000, half of that was raised by ladies of the church. (Author's collection.)

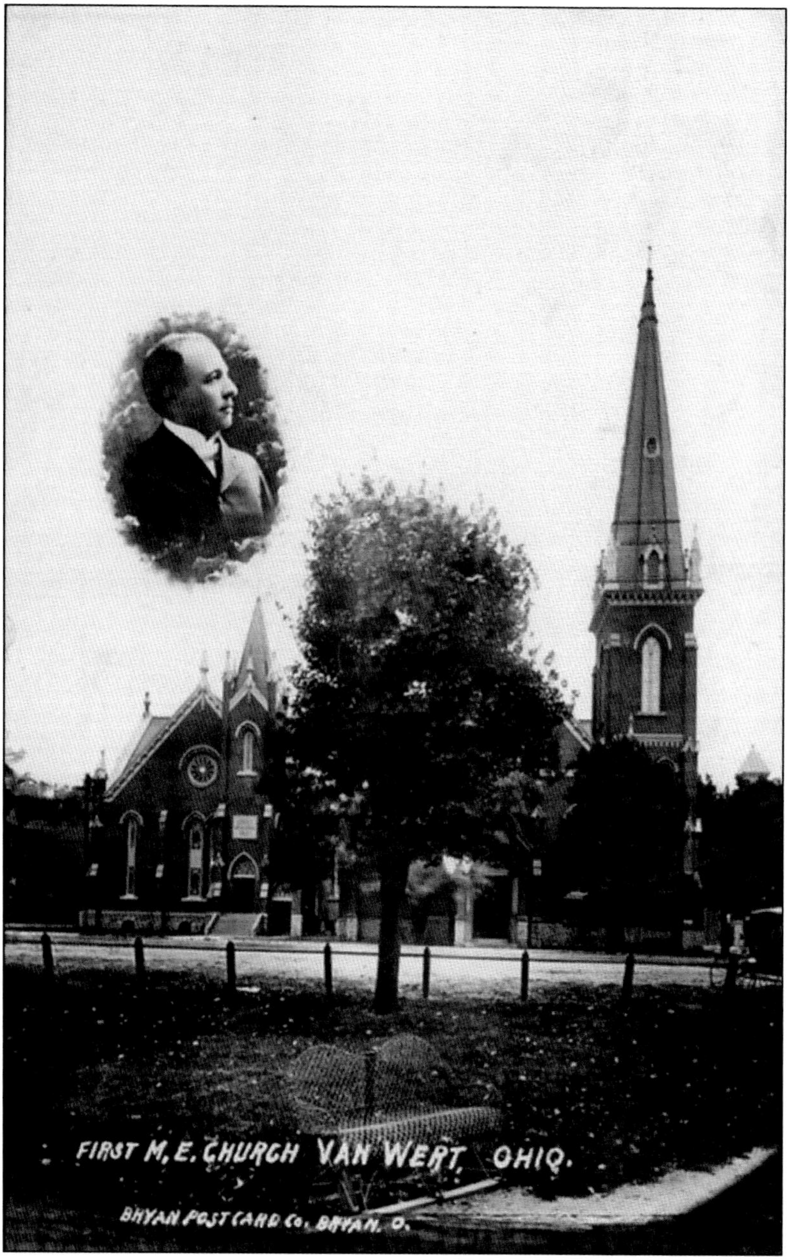

A participant at a Methodist conference held in Van Wert in September 1908 sent this postcard to a loved one in Roswell to report that his work was going well. First Methodist pastor Rev. Jesse Swank is shown in the inset photograph. The Methodist Church had a respected place in the community since 1838 when the Van Wert Circuit began meeting. Early members met in each other's homes or in the old log courthouse in town. Sunday school was held by 1864. A church was completed in 1889 for approximately $35,000 at the corner of Jefferson and Water Streets (now Central Avenue). When the cornerstone was laid, a copper box was enclosed containing a Bible and Methodist hymnal and theology book; items donated by the Masons, Odd Fellows, and Order of Red Men (a fraternal group), and copies of medical ethics and fees donated by the Van Wert Medical Society, along with other contemporary papers. (Author collection.)

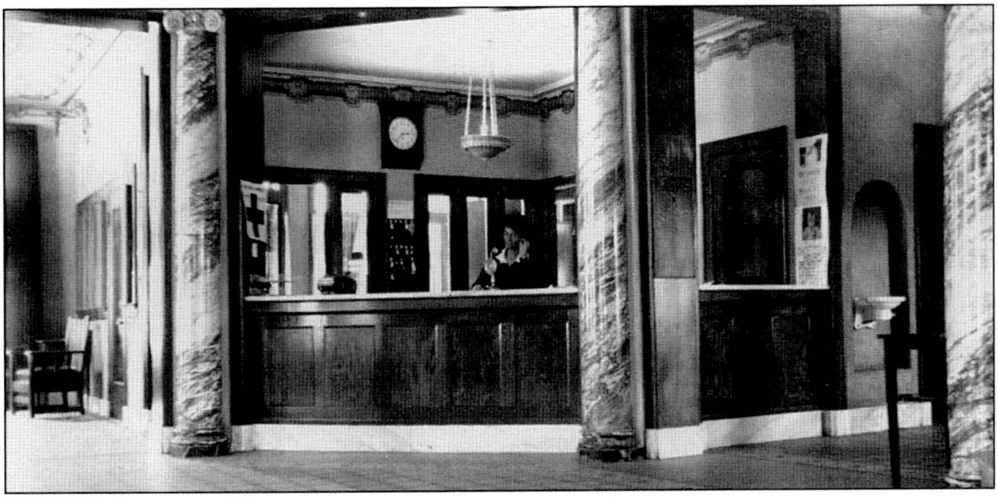

The Young Women's Christian Association opened a new facility for county women in 1916 in Van Wert, largely through the generosity of businessman George H. Marsh. Marble, tile, and gleaming woodwork greeted those entering the lobby of the Van Wert YWCA. (Ken Cripe collection.)

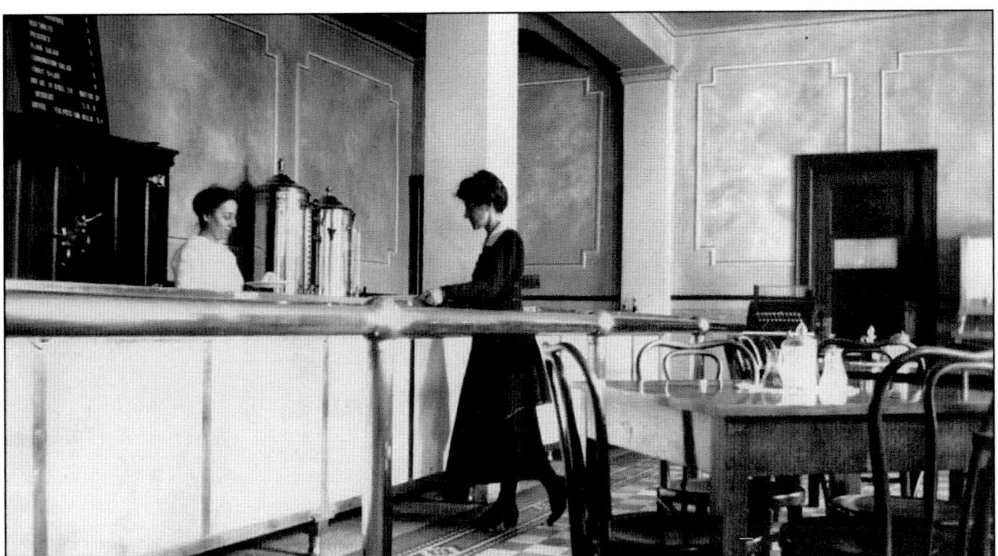

The YWCA offered recreation, education programs, and housing for women in a Christian environment. Meals were offered at nominal prices in the attractive cafeteria. (Ken Cripe collection.)

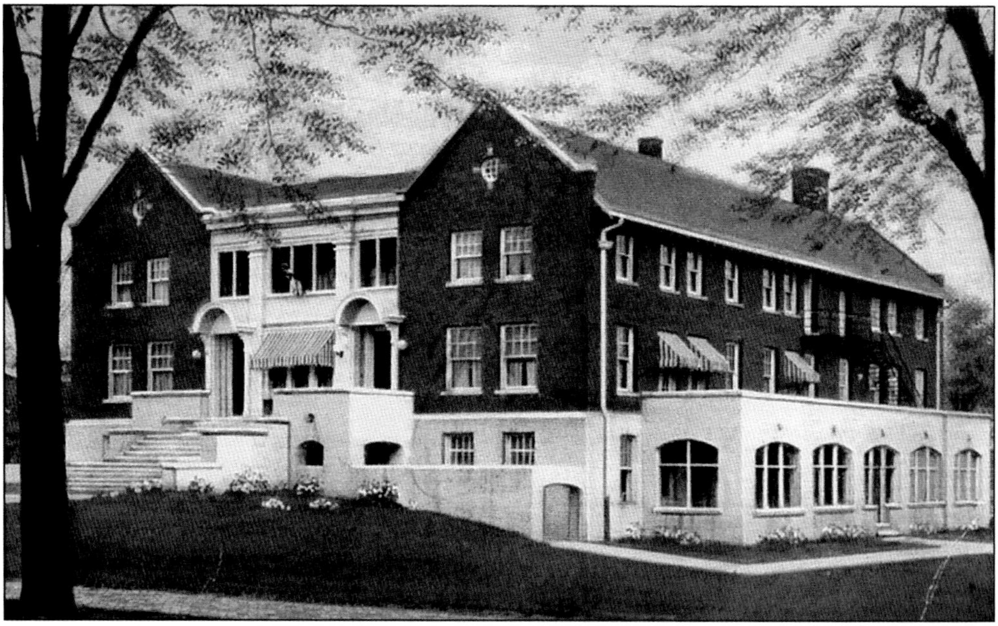

The Young Men's Christian Association also opened its new facility in Van Wert on West Main Street in 1916. The building and program were funded primarily from the estate of John Strandler, a successful Van Wert harness maker and businessman. The YMCA shared the objectives of the YWCA in similarly stately surroundings. This card is postmarked 1921. (Author's collection.)

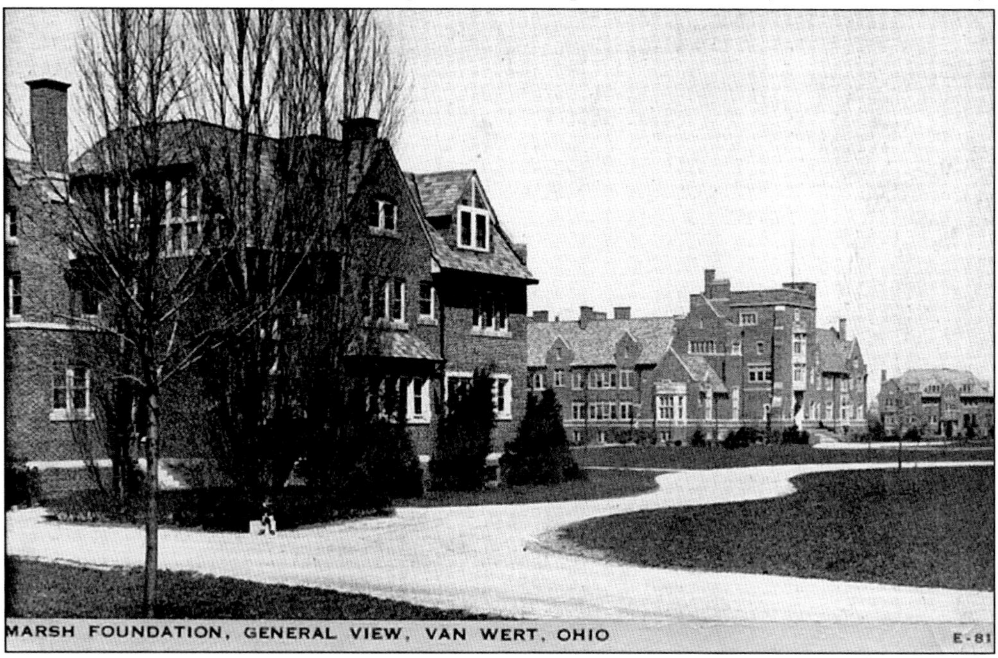

The Marsh Foundation provided guidance, education, and a home for boys in need. The foundation was created in 1921 through the estate of businessman and community leader George H. Marsh. The foundation covered 1,400 acres off of East Ridge Road. Facilities included an administration building, a director's residence, dorms, a power plant, barns, shops, a greenhouse, and pastures. (Author's collection.)

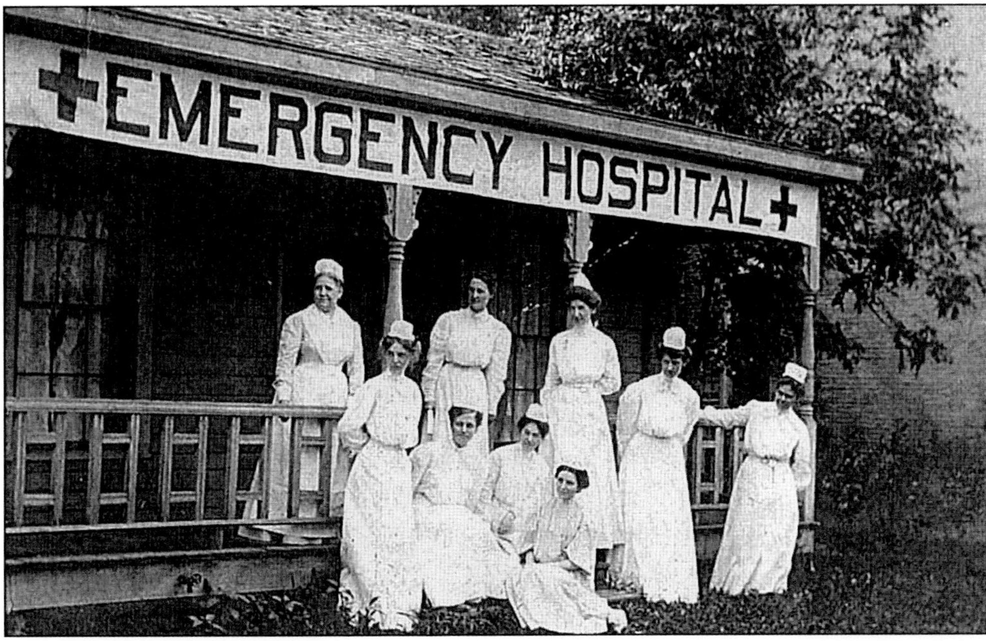

Dr. C. A. Files opened Files Emergency Hospital at 311 East Main Street, in Van Wert, in 1905. His daughters, Rilla Mooney and Mabel Whittington, were his first nurses. The Van Wert Hospital Association leased the property from Files in 1912 and began a training school for nurses there. The nurses on this card are unidentified. (Ken Cripe collection.)

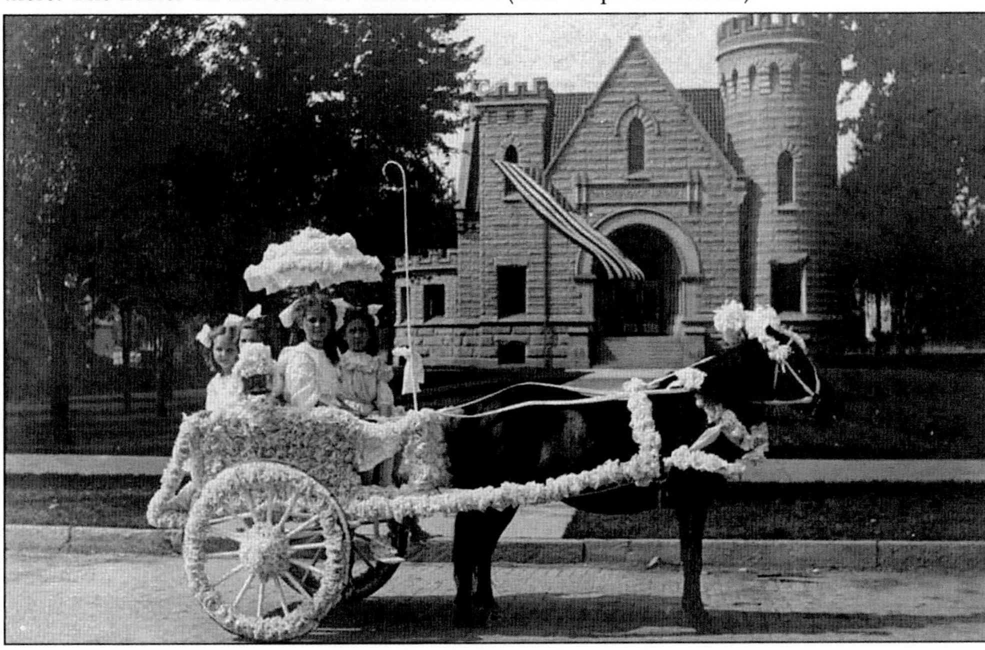

The Van Wert Hospital Association held a carnival and parade on September 21, 1905, to raise money for hospital expansion and nurses' training. Driver Lucile Woodruff decorated her pony and cart in white chrysanthemums and posed in front of the Brumback Library. The little girls in the back are identified only as Will Young's children. The girl next to Lucile is unidentified. (Ken Cripe collection.)

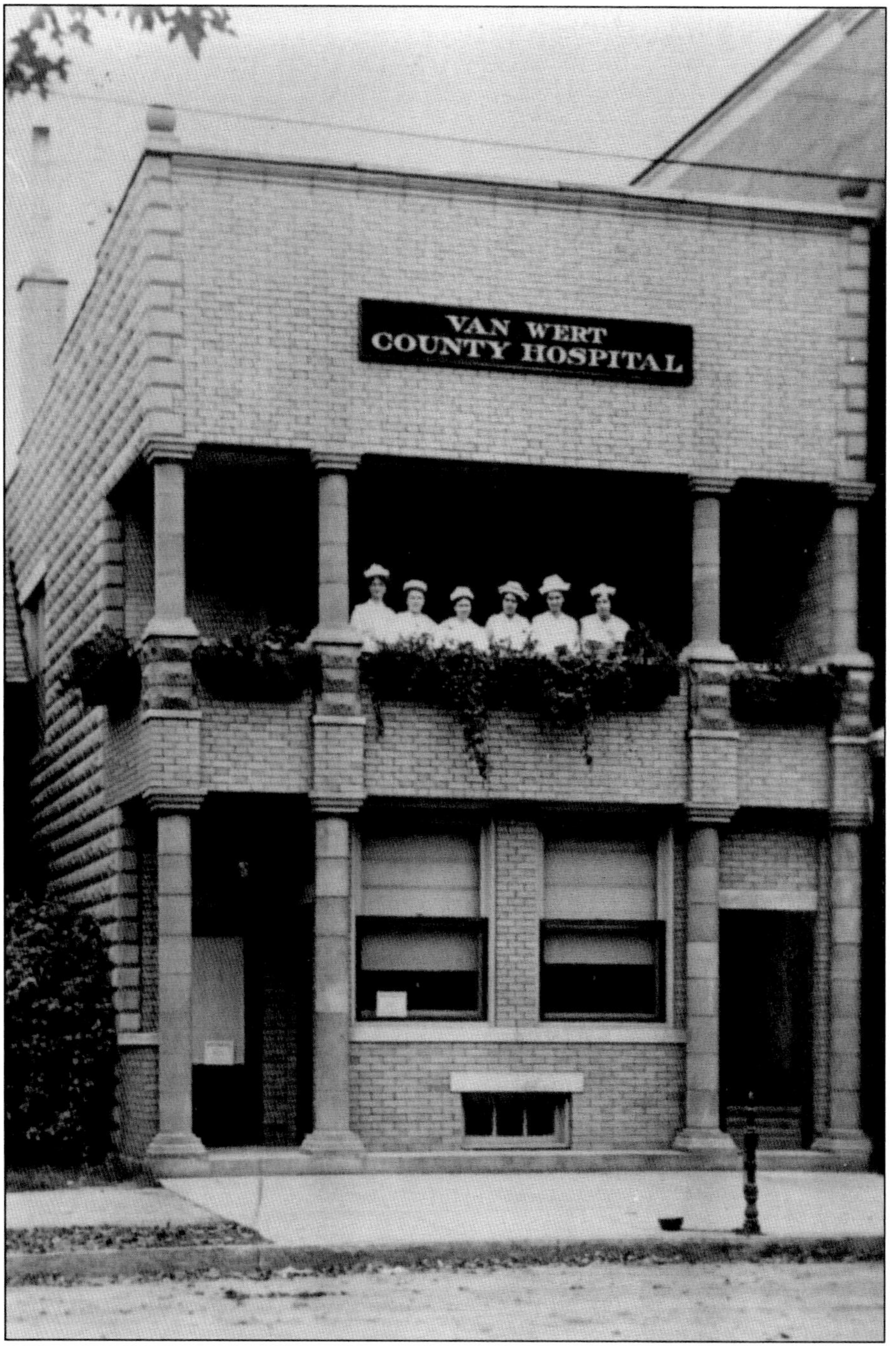

Funds from George H. Marsh helped transform the former Fourth Ward School on East Central Avenue in Van Wert into the first county hospital and built a nurses' home on South Race Street. Student nurses lived at the new YWCA while the home was being constructed. The Van Wert County Hospital officially opened on November 29, 1916. Bernice Wells of Middle Point was the first patient. A nursing school affiliated with the hospital and Cincinnati General Hospital operated in the city until 1933. The county hospital operated on Central Avenue until 1960. The nurses on the balcony are unidentified. (Ken Cripe collection.)

Six

Education and Entertainment

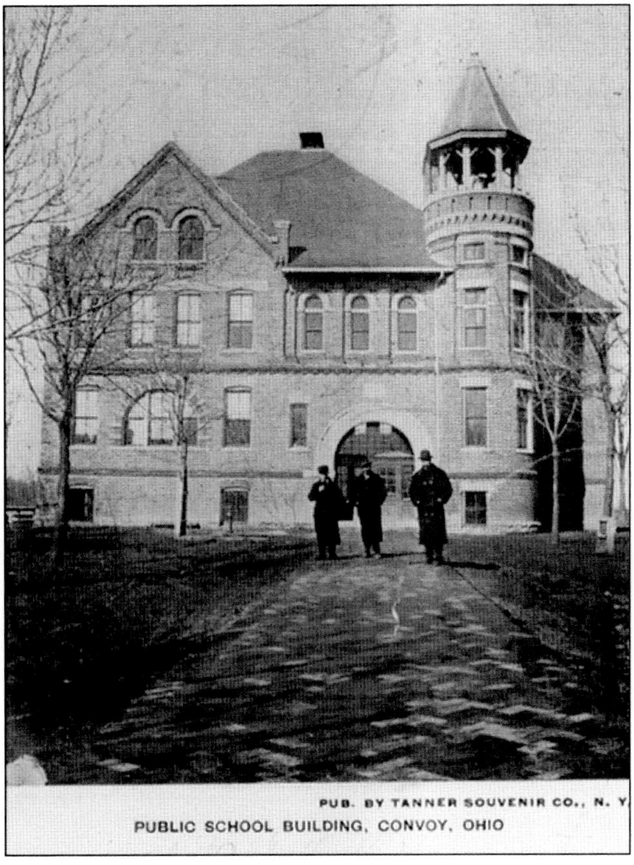

Leaders in Van Wert County communities were eager to provide a quality education in attractive settings to local children. The first public school near Convoy was the District No. 1 School, started in the northeast corner of Tully Township in 1852. Convoy's first public school was a brick, two-story building constructed on Sycamore Street in 1874. Additions and improvements were made to this building in 1892. Although the people in this early-1900s card are unidentified, records show that around that time, John Greulach was superintendent and teachers included William F. Henry, Frieda Giessler, and Georgia Leslie. (Author's collection.)

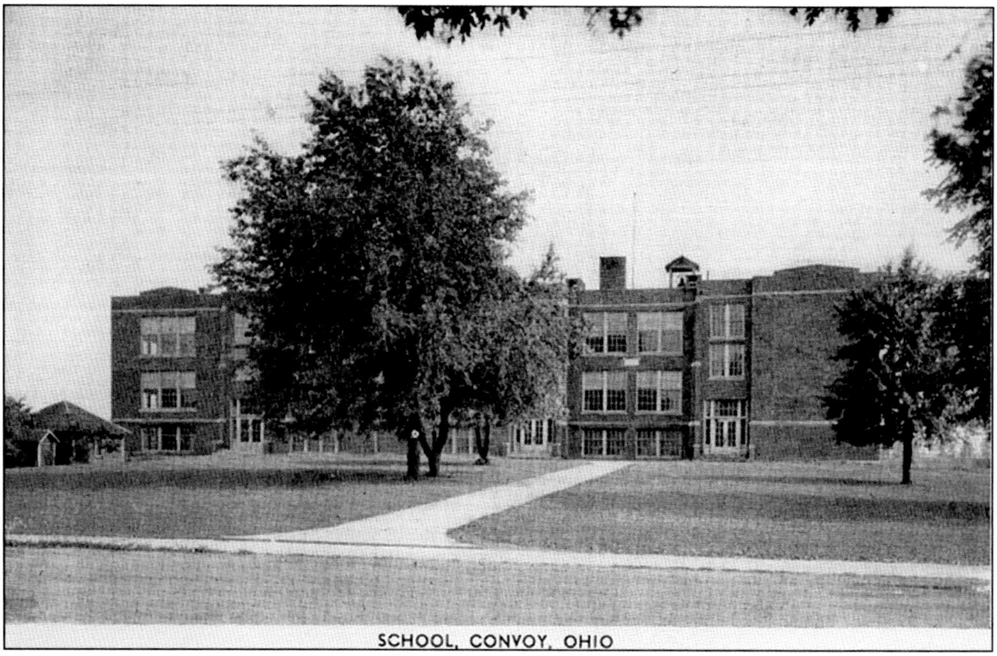

The Convoy School Board purchased seven acres on East Tully Street in 1918 to build a larger, more modern school. That building was enlarged in 1923 as township schools began to consolidate with the village school. Union Township School joined with Convoy in 1952, and Wren School joined in 1960 to form Crestview Schools. (Author's collection.)

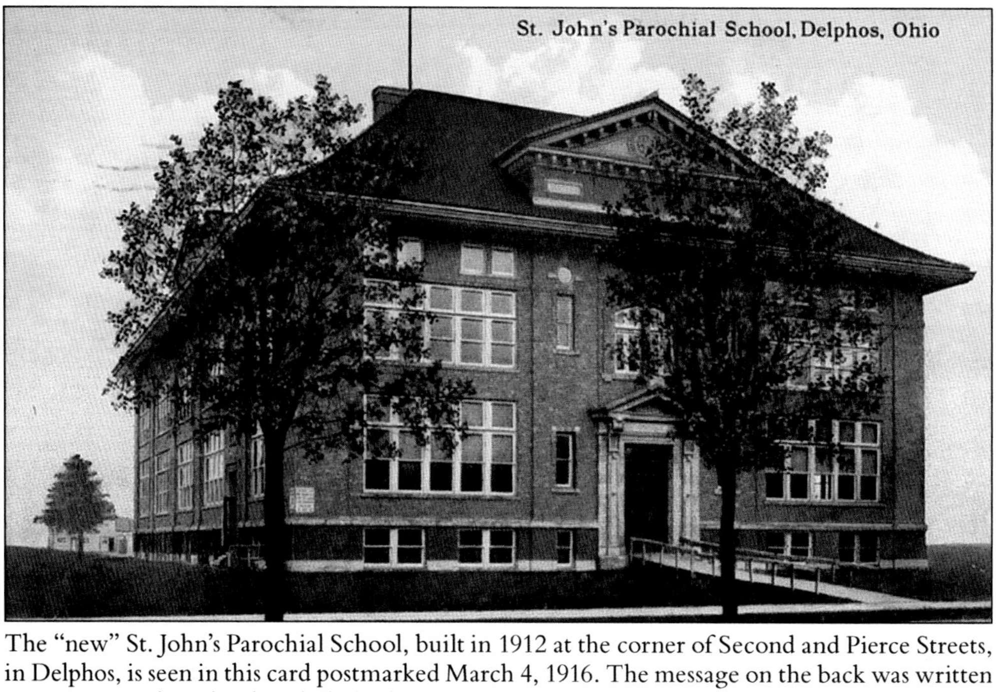

The "new" St. John's Parochial School, built in 1912 at the corner of Second and Pierce Streets, in Delphos, is seen in this card postmarked March 4, 1916. The message on the back was written in German. The school included a large auditorium and 12 spacious classrooms. Parochial education started in St. John the Evangelist's parish in 1859 and continued to thrive into a new century. (Author's collection.)

Union School in Middle Point is featured on this card postmarked November 25, 1909. Western Ohio Normal School, an institute to train teachers, operated for many years in Middle Point. When the institute closed, the building was used by the public schools. Note the cross at the tip of the tower. (Author's collection.)

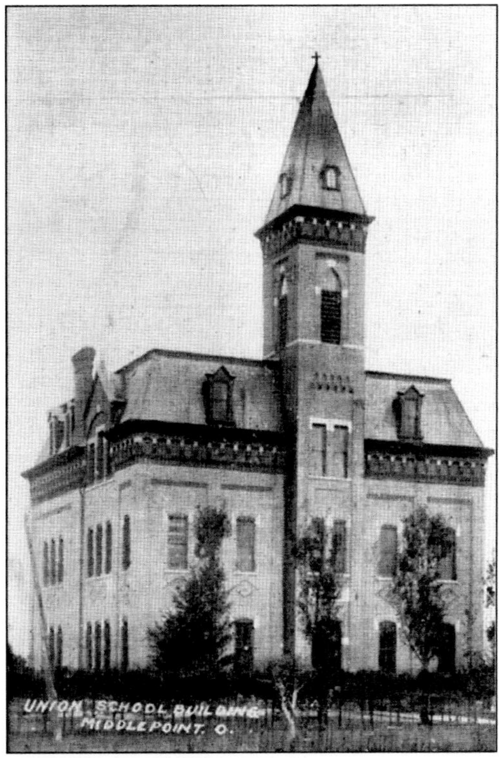

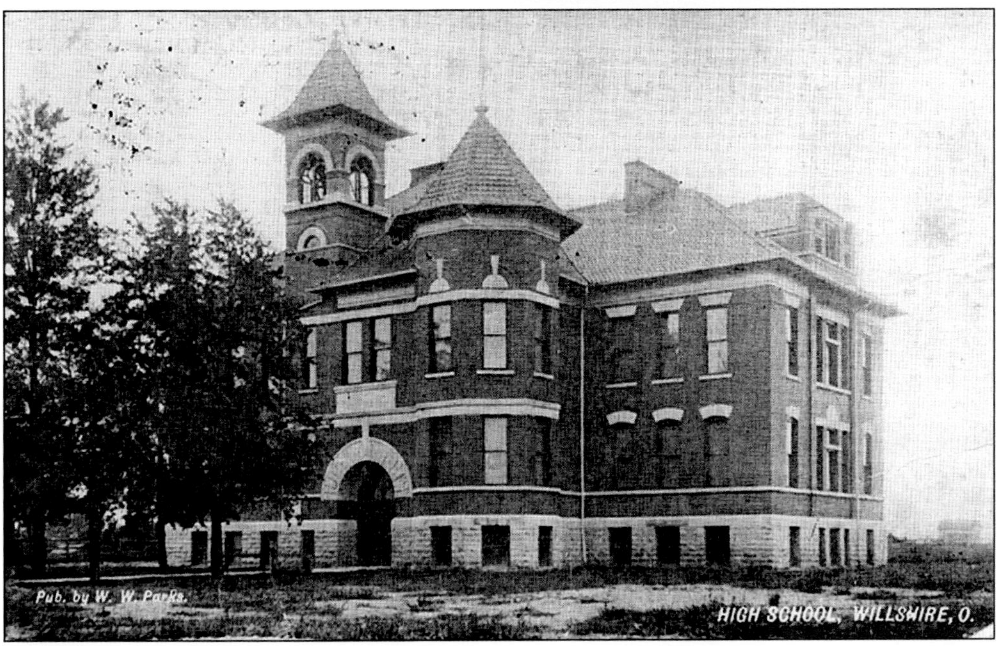

Willshire's second public school building, shown here, was completed in 1900. James Riley's daughter Amelia held the county's first classes in 1827 in what may have been a subscription school where neighbors paid an individual to teach their children. Public schooling was available by 1848, and the first brick school constructed in the 1860s. This card is postmarked February 2, 1911. (Author's collection.)

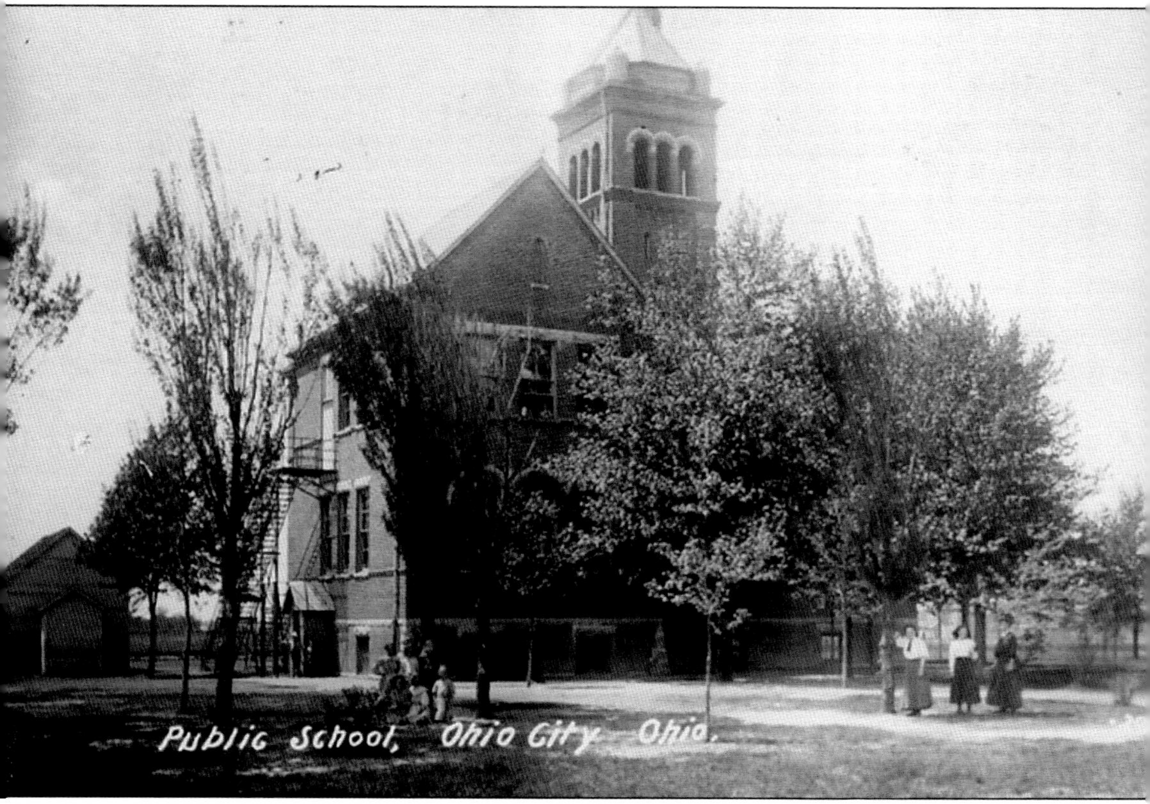

Staff and students of the Ohio City School in this early 1900s card seem to be having fun with the photographer. The photograph has to be examined carefully to find all 14 individuals who are shown. Schools such as this provided not only an education for children, but entertainment, culture, and social events for all members of the community. Ohio City residents passed a bond issue in 1889 to build this brick school. The building housed grades one through twelve. Township families had to provide their children's transportation to school. Increased growth in the community resulted in another school being built in the village in the 1920s. (Author's collection.)

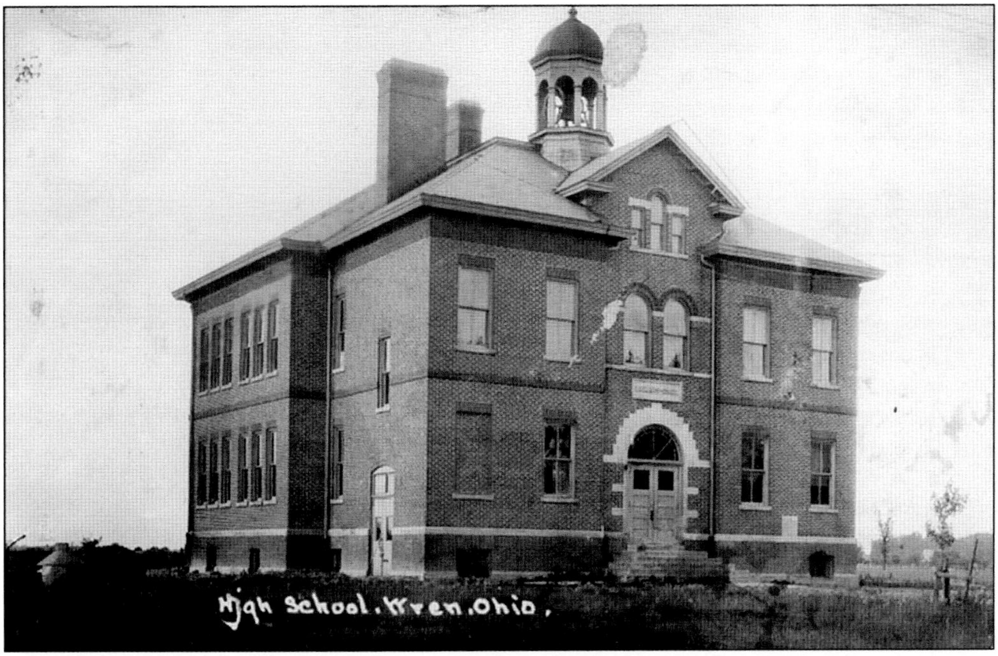

"This school house is being built 2 new additions, so will look better in no time," the sender wrote to a friend in Toledo on July 30, 1928, of Wren School. "Mary graduated from here. Great, eh!" The school had been built in 1908 to house all grades. It was the fourth school built for Wren, with the first being a one-room school in 1856. (Author's collection.)

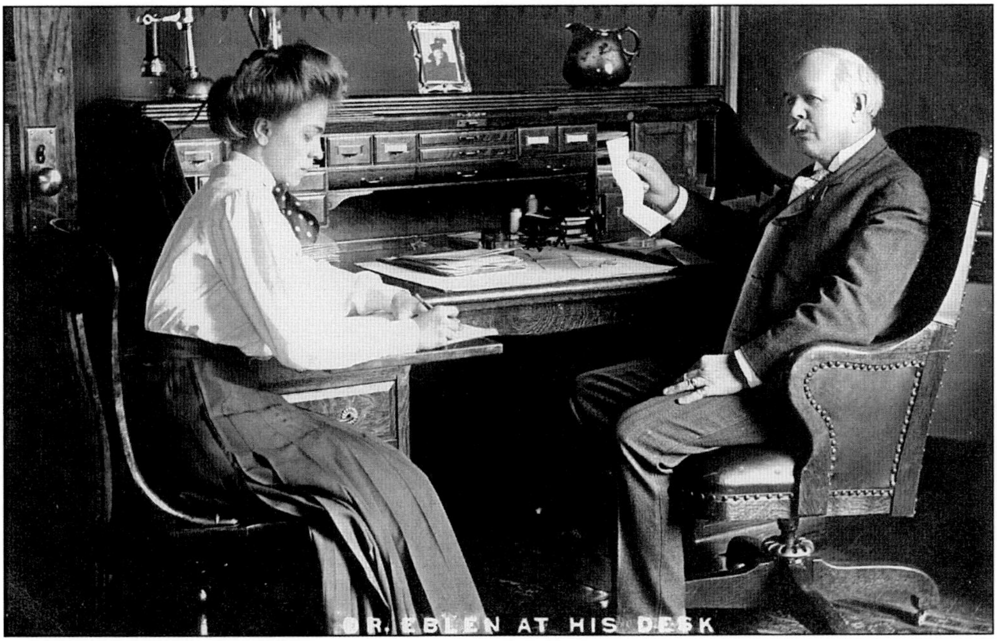

Dr. George J. Eblen, shown in a 1909 postcard with his unidentified assistant, was a true Renaissance man. He grew up in Switzerland County, Indiana, where he became a schoolteacher. After teaching for several years, he trained in medicine and around 1880, moved to Van Wert County where he worked as a doctor for many years. (Van Wert County Historical Society.)

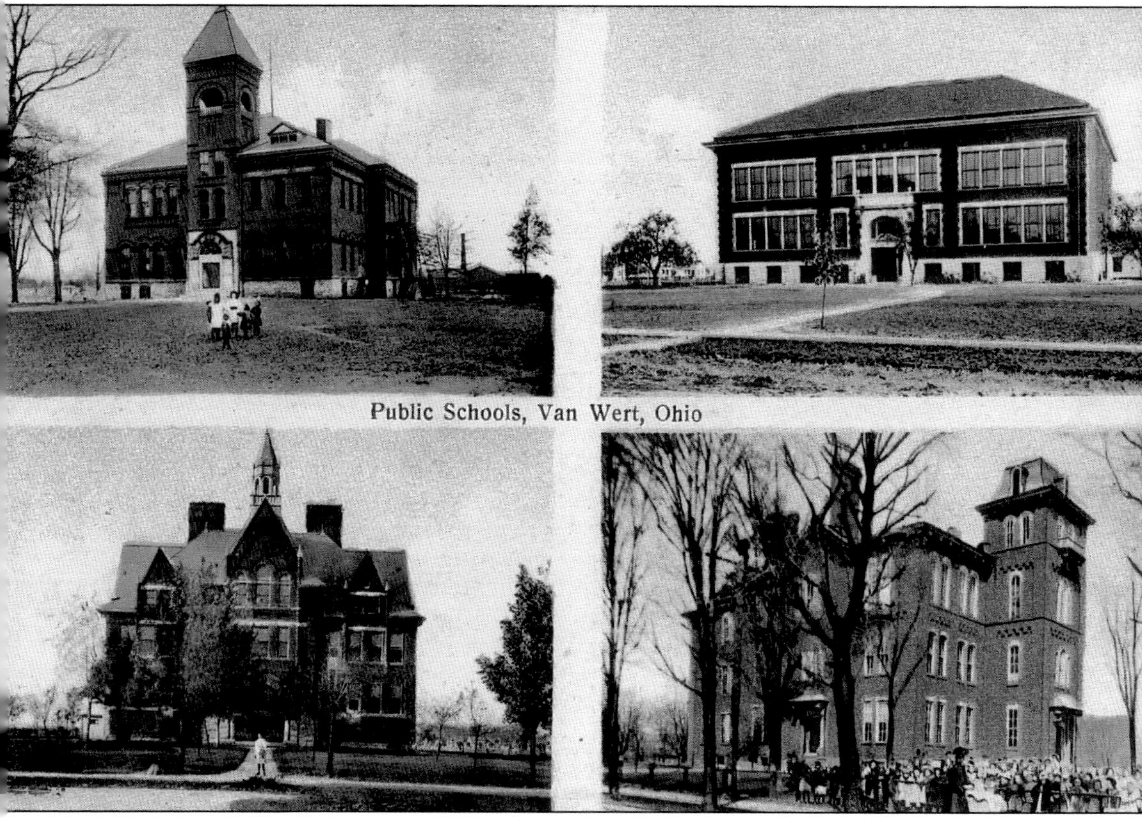

This postcard was printed around 1909 after the "new" Fourth Ward School had been built in 1904 at the corner of South Walnut Street and Frothingham Street in Van Wert. The change from Gothic-inspired towers and spires to a more simple modernity signaled the Van Wert schools' readiness for a new century. The new school replaced the Fourth Ward School, which had been built on East Central Avenue around 1883 for about $9,000. Other schools shown in the card are the Second Ward School on North Jefferson Street, built in the 1880s for around $12,000; the First Ward School on East Third Street, built in the 1890s; and the Third Ward School, which dates back to 1867 and later became Central High School. Although not every student graduated from high school in the 1800s and early 1900s, community leaders realized that education was vital to a successful future. In the 1880s, the Van Wert board appointed a number of women to visit destitute and orphan children in each ward to encourage school attendance. (Ken Cripe collection.)

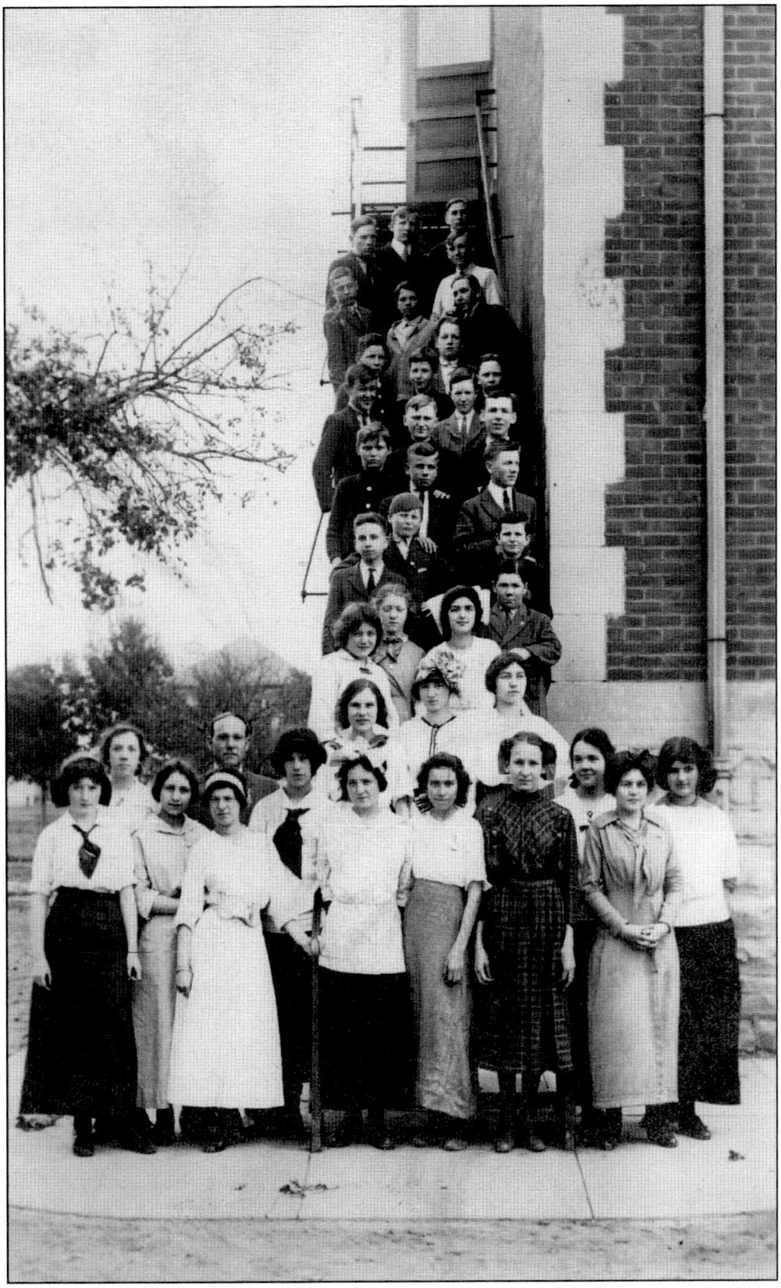

Eighth graders in S. E. McConahy's classroom at Van Wert's Fourth Ward School pose in this early-1900s postcard. Students are not listed in any particular order but the class included Raymond Hertel, Orville Shurtleff, Jessie Baker, Ruth Creech, Bradford Smith, Deann Cogat, Ruth Hennerman, Margaret Hennerman, Frank Munday, Donald Jacobs, Mervin Neely, Richard Webster, Russel Yoh, Doyt Walters, Russel Jacobs, Mabel McCollum, Marjorie Wagner, Pauline Harris, Belva Johnson, Elmer Collins, Gladwin Fauble, Marjorie Stutsman, Florence Stupp, Kenneth Everett, Leona Parker, Evelyn North, Don Dasher, George Sells, Robert Conn, Paul Blank, Albert Fortner, Bruce Reed, Dean Mauk, Lewis Graham, Vivian Bair, Gertrude Ball, Lavella Hernstead, and Raymond Blume. (Ken Cripe collection.)

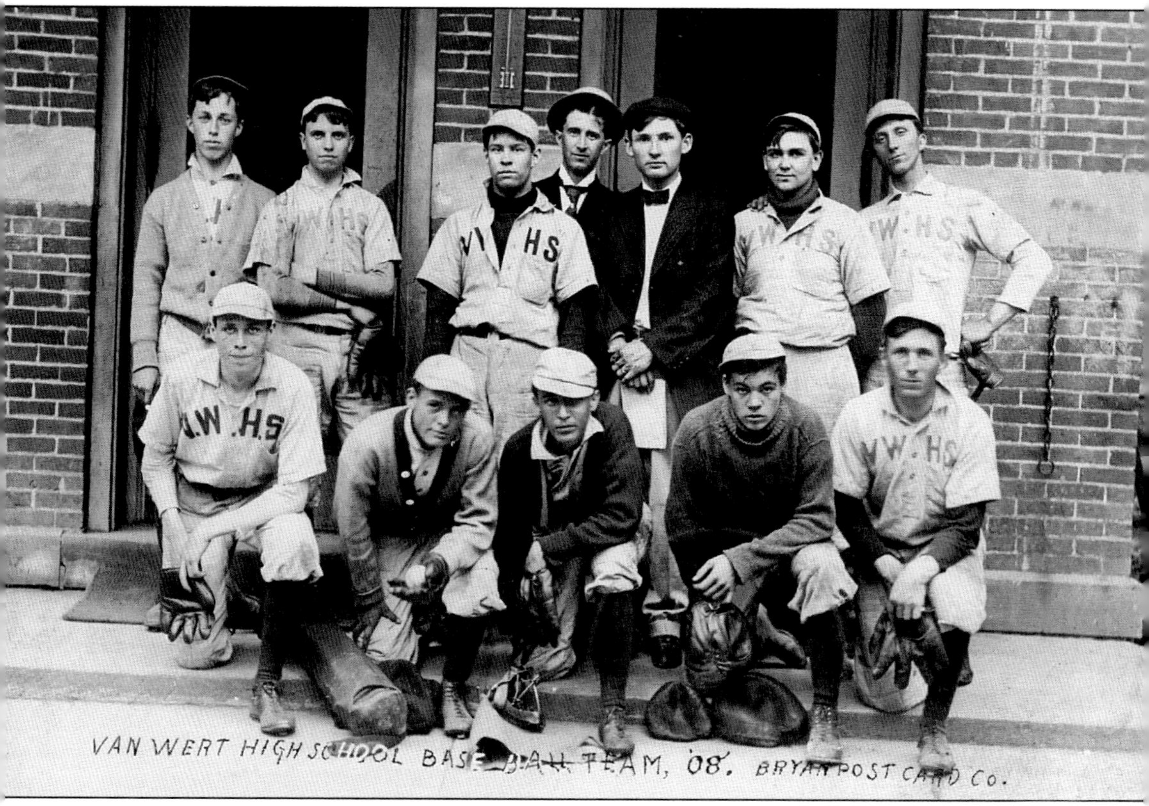

The Van Wert High School baseball team of 1908 pose for this card that was probably sent to friends, family, and school supporters. Picture postcards of the era were accumulated and traded by collectors and often ended up in interesting places. This card was directed to Rome, Italy, with a personal message from William Baldasseroni to a lady named Ethel. Unfortunately, neither the players' names nor team's statistics were given. (Ken Cripe collection.)

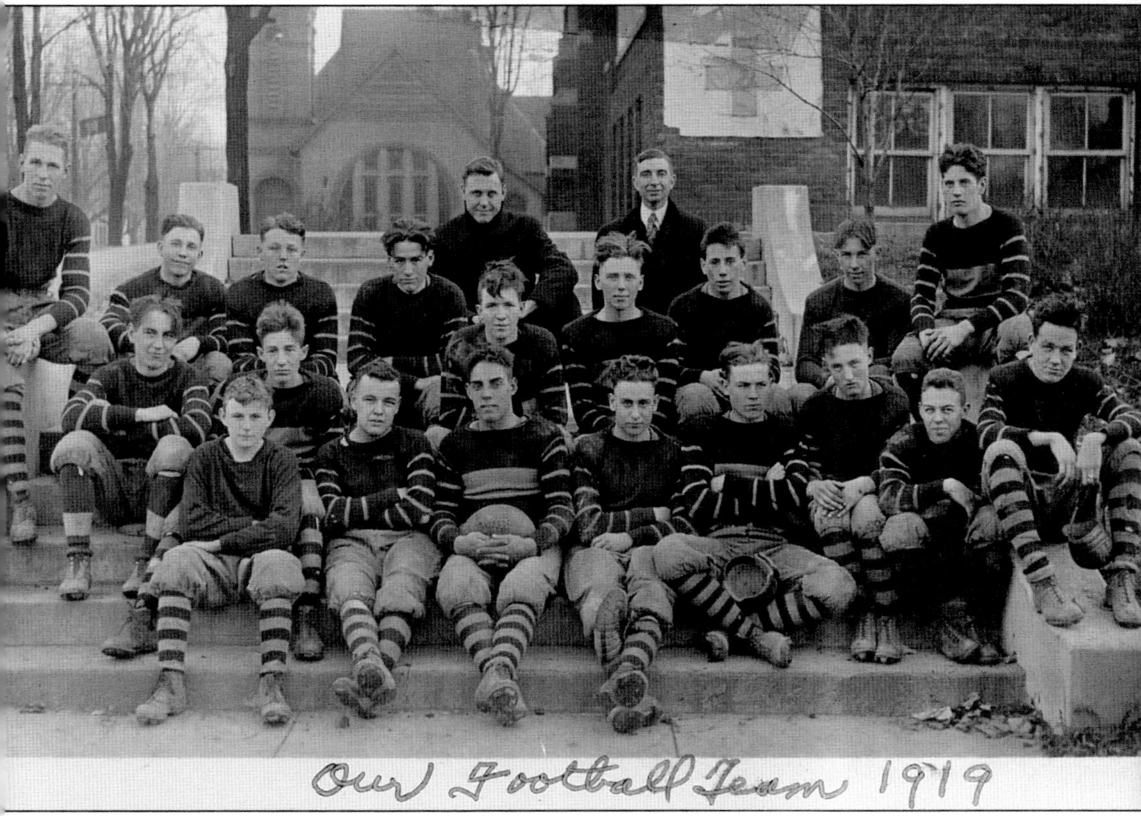

The Van Wert High School football team of 1919 appears confident and relaxed in this postcard portrait. From left to right are (first row) Leonard Sidle, Vaughan Davies, Lawrence Connolly, Howard Hines, Walter Burrell, Harvey Miller, Joyce Gottschall, and Ray Finkhouse; (second row) Alfred Kessel, Richard Grunewald, Paul Barfell, Wyler Swick, Mark Kemper, ? Lintermoot, and Robert Kahn; (third row) Albert Johnson, Burdette Todd, David Bonnewitz, unidentified, principal Chester Johnson, and manager Augustus Karns. (Ken Cripe collection.)

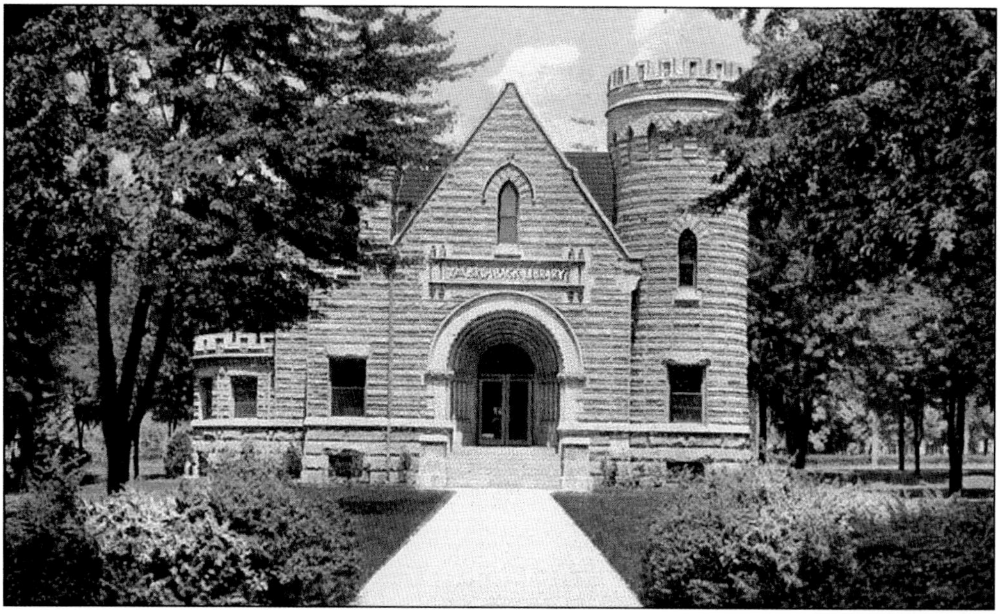

The Brumback Library became the first county library in the United States when it was dedicated on January 1, 1901, in Van Wert. John Sanford Brumback bequeathed the funds to create the library. The castle-like structure, which combined Gothic and Romanesque architecture, quickly became the county's most recognizable landmark and a favorite backdrop for photographers. This card is postmarked 1923. (Author's collection.)

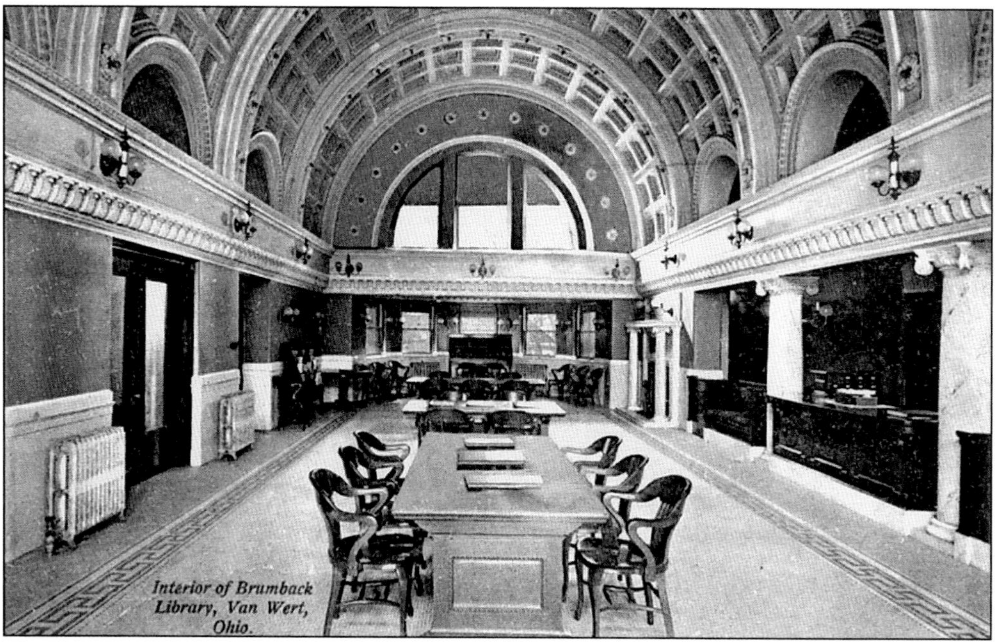

The reading room of the Brumback Library reflected the lofty ideal of its founders—bring literacy and books to the entire county. Back in 1891, a dozen Van Wert women started the Reading Room Association. Within five years, they formed the Library Association and created a small circulating library. In 1896, voters passed a tax levy to create a free library. This card is dated 1917. (Author's collection.)

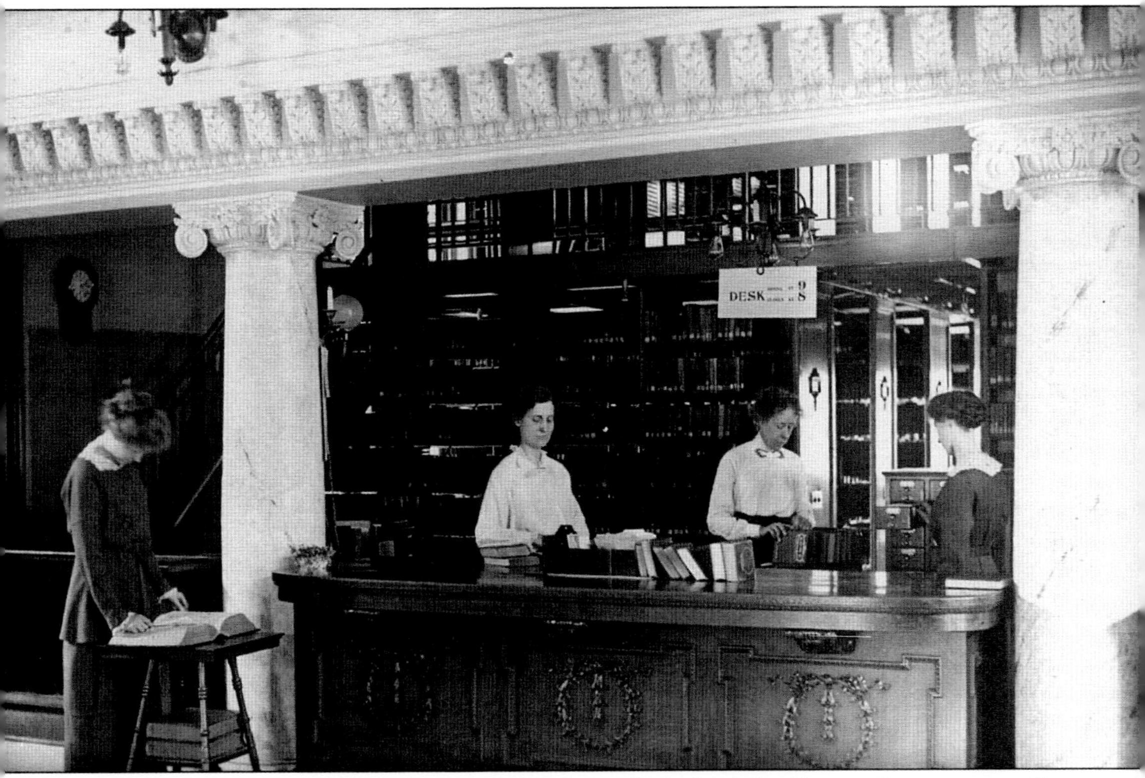

The checkout desk, girded by majestic columns, was the hub of the library. Every aspect of the library's construction and operation was of the highest quality. In 1917, the basement was remodeled into the children's department. Sorting books behind the counter in this 1918 card from left to right are Ella Swartout, Ella Burgett Conn, and Carrie Matthys Torry. The woman on the left perusing the book is unidentified. The Brumback Library system continued to grow, with branches being established in Convoy, Middle Point, Ohio City, Willshire, and Wren. In 1991, the main library was completely renovated and 10,500 square feet of new space was added. (Van Wert County Historical Society.)

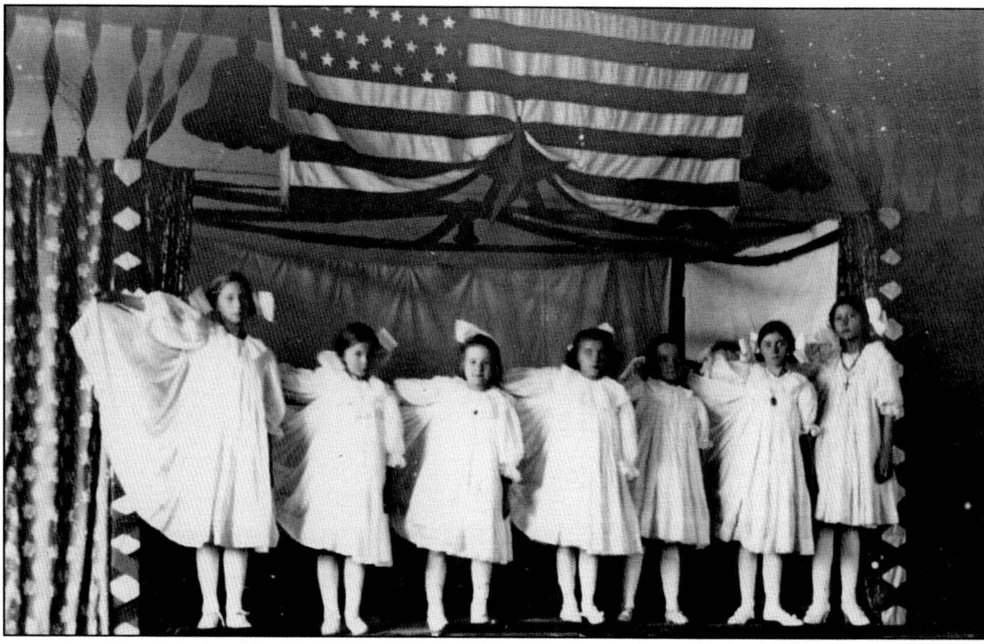

The Butterfly Girls were representative of the choral and dramatic programs presented at many county schools in the early 1900s. Special programs were frequently held at holidays and on the last day of school among the grade levels. Songs, instrumental music, poetry recitations, dramatic readings, and skits were favorite entertainments. (Ken Cripe collection.)

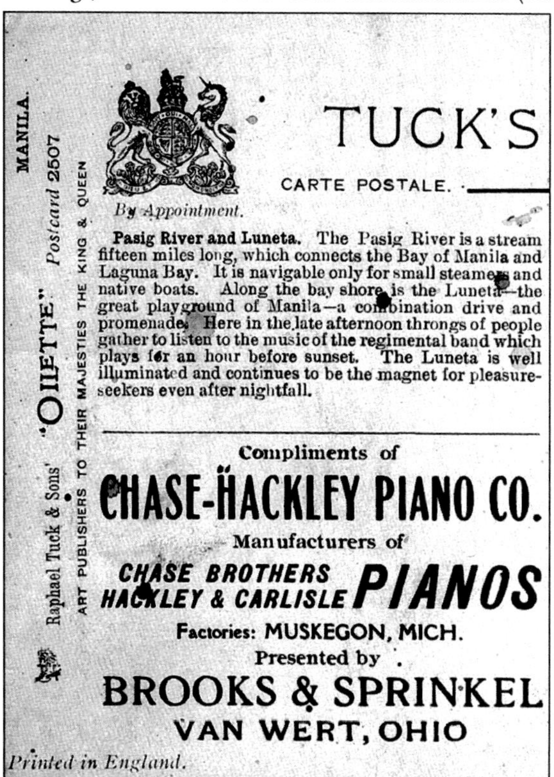

Music in the home became a more frequent form of entertainment as county residents prospered and young ladies were treated to piano lessons. This Tuck's postcard advertises a fine selection of pianos for home enjoyment offered by Brooks and Sprinkel in Van Wert. (Ken Cripe collection.)

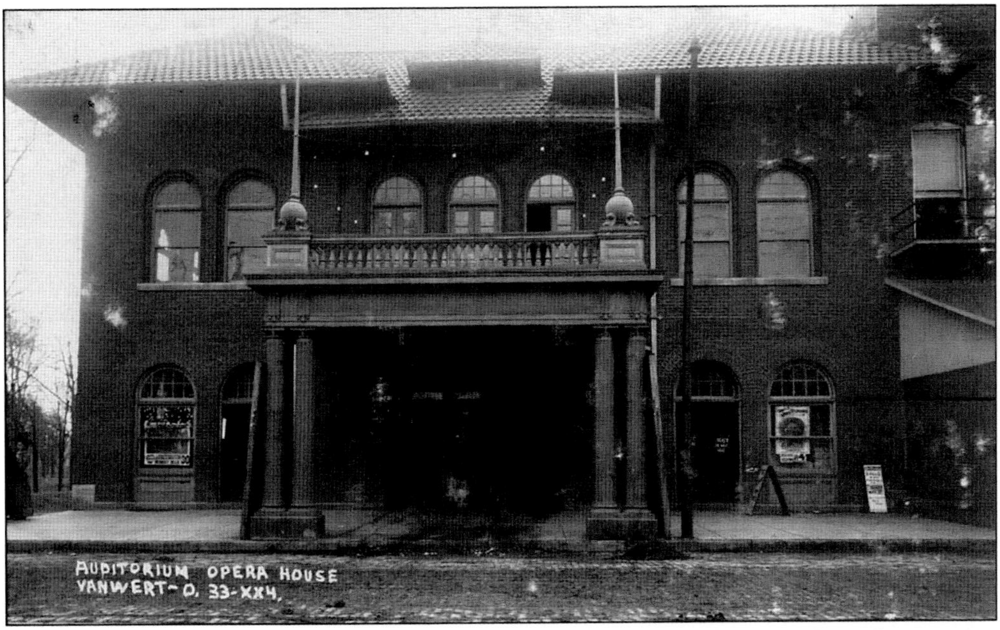

Van Wert opera houses entertained county residents in the late 19th and early 20th centuries. Mr. and Mrs. Tom Thumb appeared at the Grand Opera House on South Washington Street in 1875. The Auditorium Opera House, shown here in 1908, featured talent shows, local theater productions, and plays by traveling repertory companies. Handel's *Messiah*, performed by local people, was an annual treat. (Van Wert County Historical Society.)

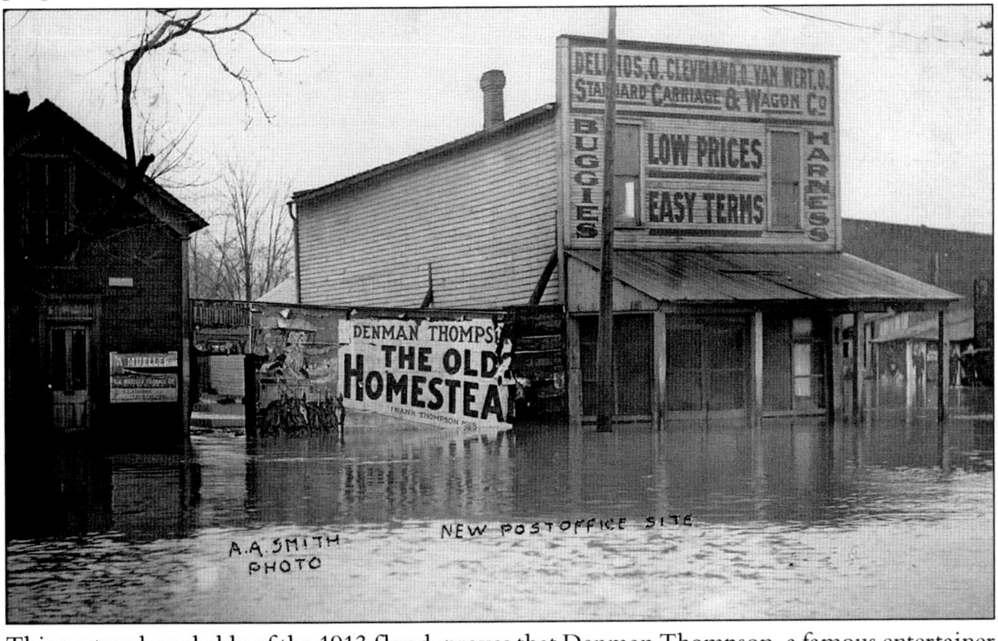

This postcard, probably of the 1913 flood, proves that Denman Thompson, a famous entertainer in the 1880s and 1890s, appeared in Van Wert. Thompson, a New Hampshire comedic actor, became famous as Uncle Joshua Whitcomb in his play *The Old Homestead*. Thompson and his large troupe zigzagged across the country by train, performing in cities as diverse as New York and Van Wert. (Ken Cripe collection.)

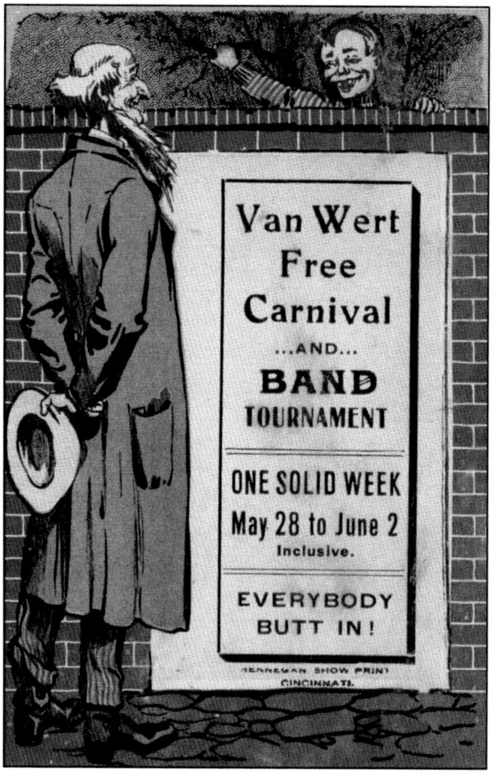

This card was mailed to invite citizens to a weeklong free carnival in 1906. Games, food, entertainment, and a band tournament were all part of the fun in the county seat. (Ken Cripe collection.)

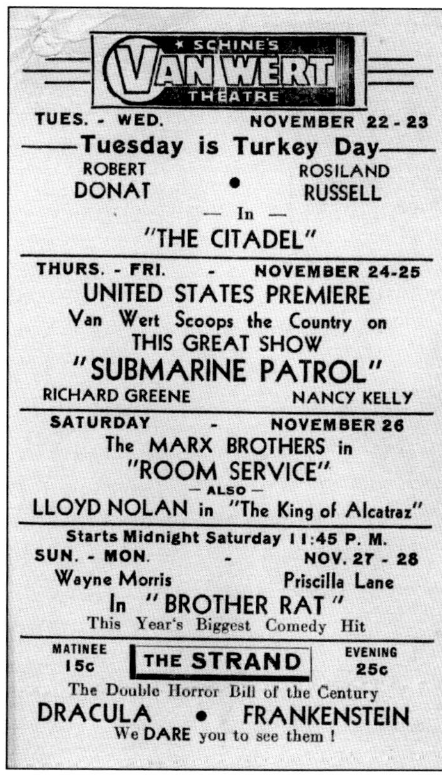

Free turkeys, the national premiere of a film, the Marx Brothers, and *Dracula* enticed movie patrons to visit the Strand Theater on Main Street in Van Wert in November 1938. Movies were popular, inexpensive entertainment for the entire family. Smaller communities also had their own movie theaters in the very early 1900s. Convoy residents enjoyed the Early Habit Movie in their hometown. (Ken Cripe collection.)

Seven

Down on Main Street

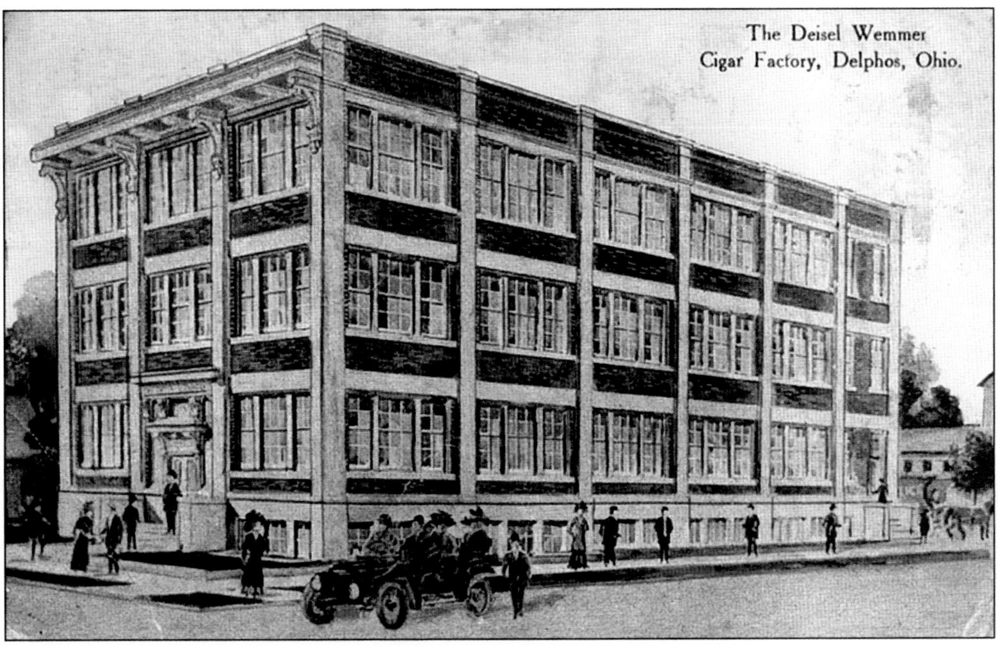

Businesses in Van Wert County over the years have ranged from single-owner shops, to large farms, to nationally known corporations. Some companies with roots in the 19th century still flourish today while others have taken their place in history books. The Deisel Wemmer Cigar Factory of Delphos is one that no longer exists. When this card was mailed in 1911, however, the factory was operating at full speed, manufacturing San Felice and El Verso cigars. The parent company started in Lima in the 1880s, and soon had factories across northwestern Ohio. (Author's collection.)

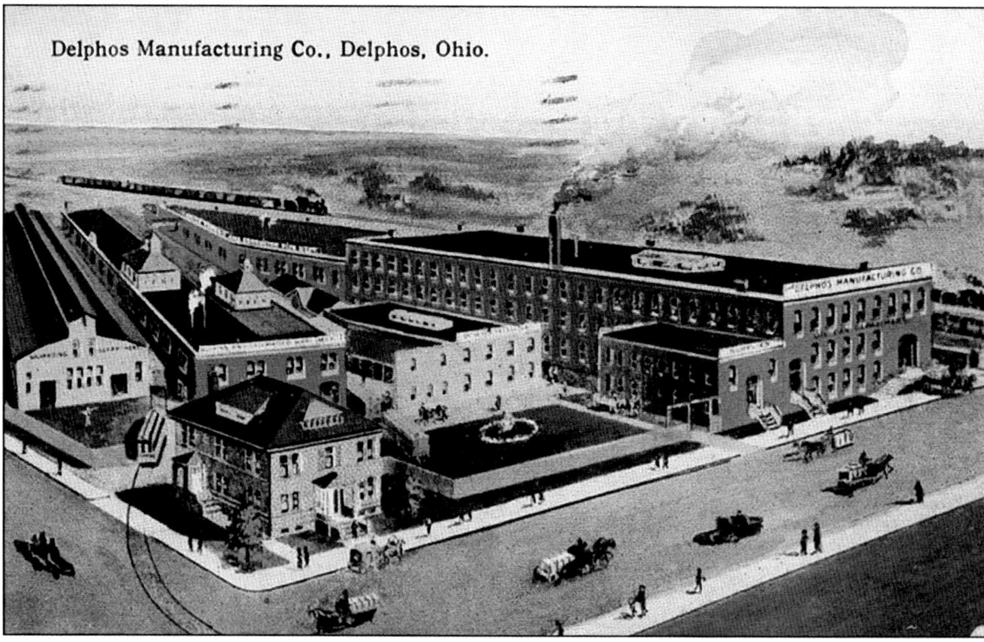

The Delphos Manufacturing Company shipped oil and gasoline cans, gutters, and poultry and hog feeding equipment across the country for decades. Henry Leilich helped start the company in 1898 in Delphos. This card, postmarked 1925, shows the plant in its heyday on Pierce Street. The Pennsylvania Railroad tracks, which moved the company's freight, can be seen off to the right. (Author's collection.)

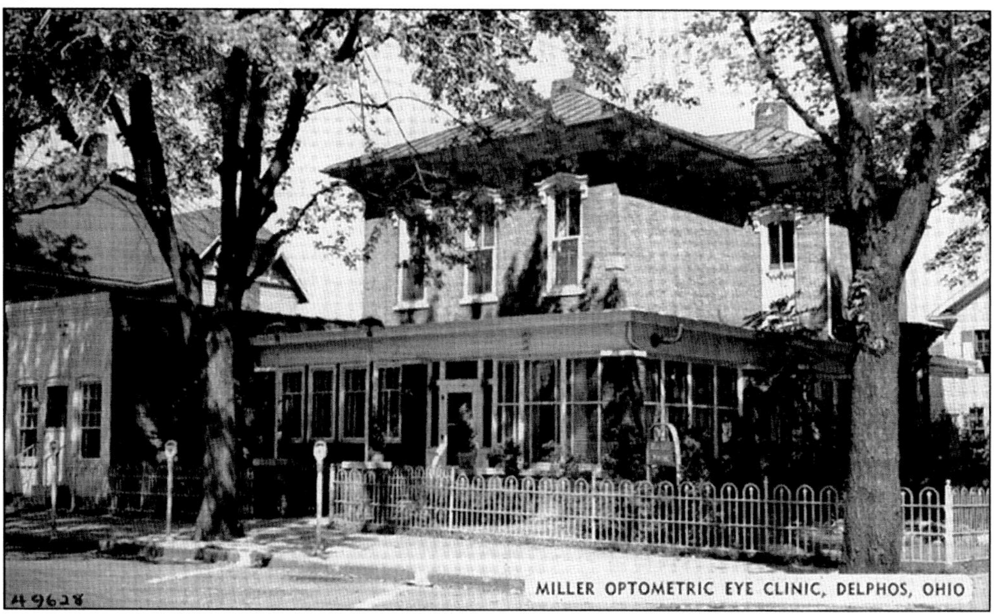

Miller Optometric Eye Clinic in Delphos offered "optometric eye analysis with precision instruments," a selection of frames, and grinding of lenses under one roof. Dr. G. K. Miller and Dr. Clint Miller were in charge when this postcard was mailed in January 1951. Miller's was open until 9:00 p.m. Monday through Saturday, and from 1:00 p.m. to 3:00 p.m. on Sunday, a rarity then. (Author's collection.)

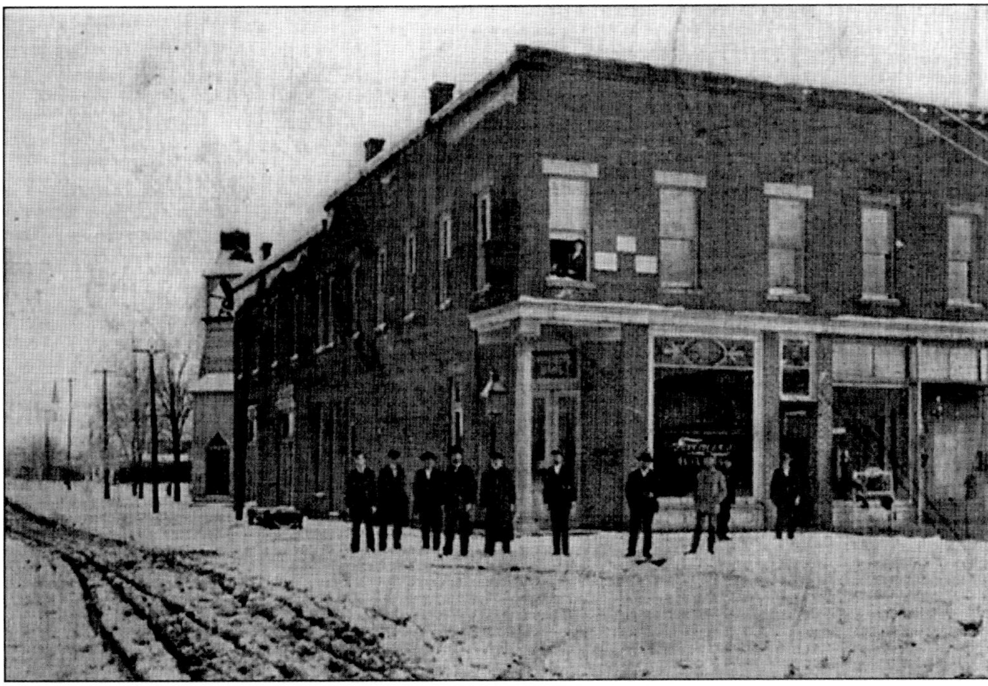

By 1900, changes in federal law and the economy resulted in thousands of state-chartered banks cropping up in small rural communities across the nation. Farmers' Bank of Ohio City played an important role in the local economy, supplying credit to farmers and other entrepreneurs. By the time this card was mailed in 1907, farmland was no longer cheap, but the market for Ohio agricultural products was broadening. (Author's collection.)

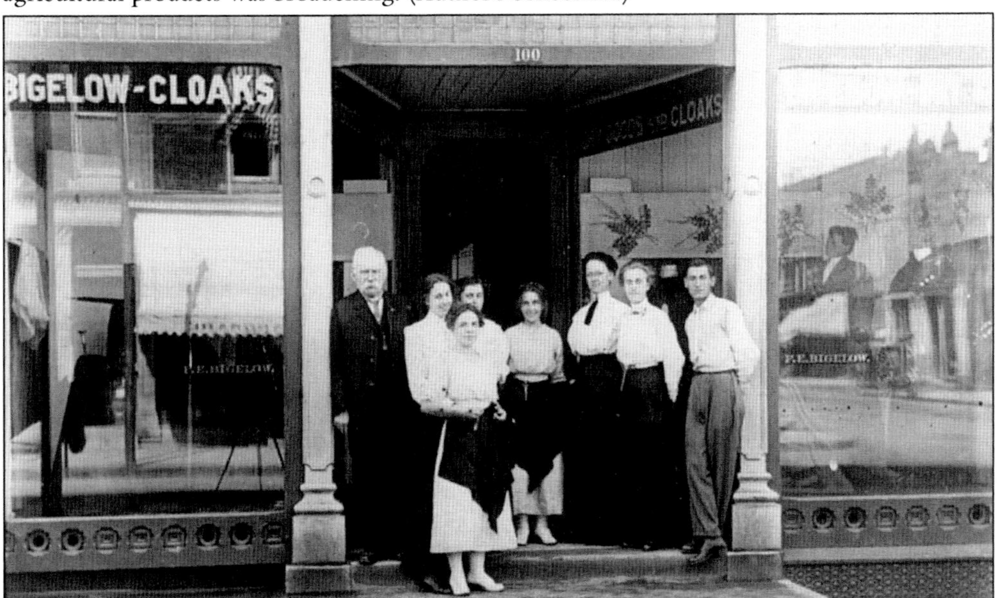

Bigelow's Dry Goods was operated by F. E. Bigelow at 100 East Main Street, in Van Wert in 1910. Dry goods stores provided customers with all sorts of textiles from ribbons to bed linens to overcoats. (Ken Cripe collection.)

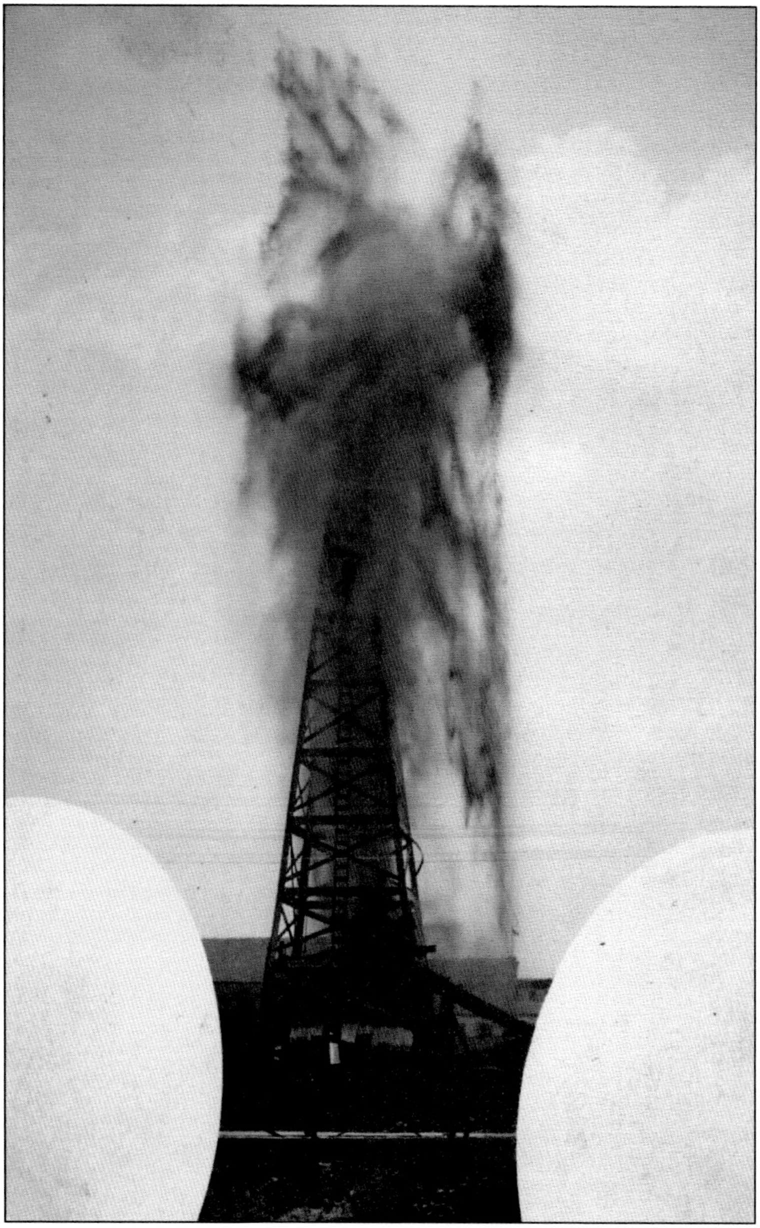

Oil and natural gas wells in the county date back to the late 1880s when a rich pocket of natural gas was found on Lewis Nachbar's Union Township farm. The gas burned day and night for years, providing a source for commercial use. Between 1900 and 1902, oil was found around Ohio City and Liberty Township, Ridge Township, Venedocia, York, and Jennings Townships. This card shows a 1901 gusher at Edmund A. Leathers's Ridge Township farm. A well drilled there provided 250 barrels of oil daily for 33 consecutive days without being pumped. Oil from the Liberty Township fields was received at a Standard Oil pumping station at McKee (later Dull). From there the oil was pumped into pipelines that went from Lima to Chicago. The anticipated boom of the early 1900s never materialized, but moderate quantities of oil continued to be produced until the early 1950s when Gulf Oil of Findlay canceled the last leasing agreement in the county. (Ken Cripe collection.)

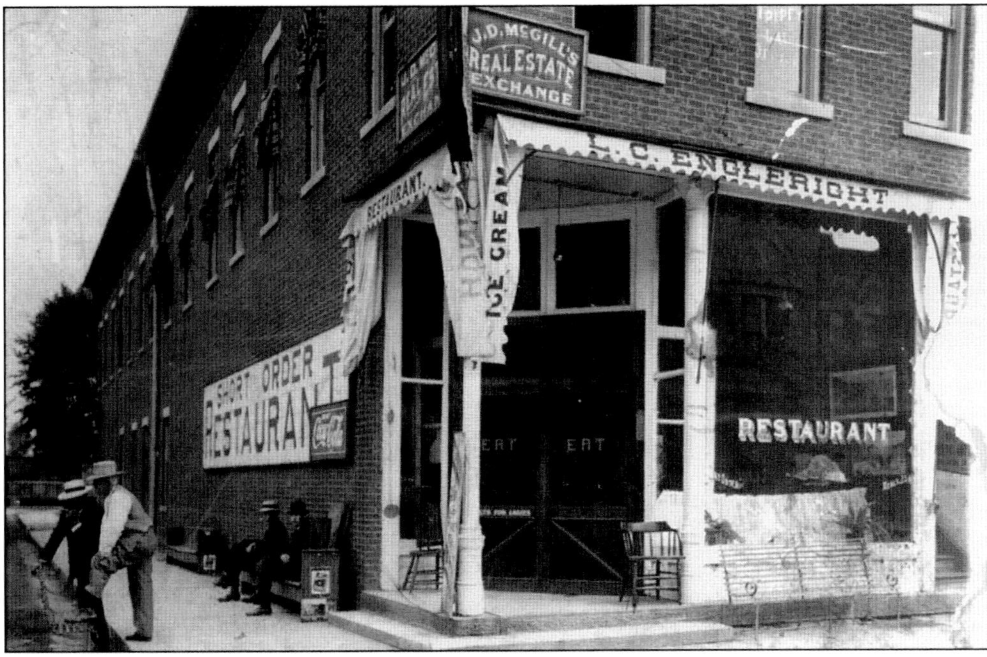

Ice cream and short order lunches were the specialties at L. C. Engleright's restaurant next door to the courthouse. Engleright's was listed at 133 East Main Street in the 1897–1898 Van Wert directory, and was still there in 1910. Balyeat's Restaurant later claimed the location. (Ken Cripe collection.)

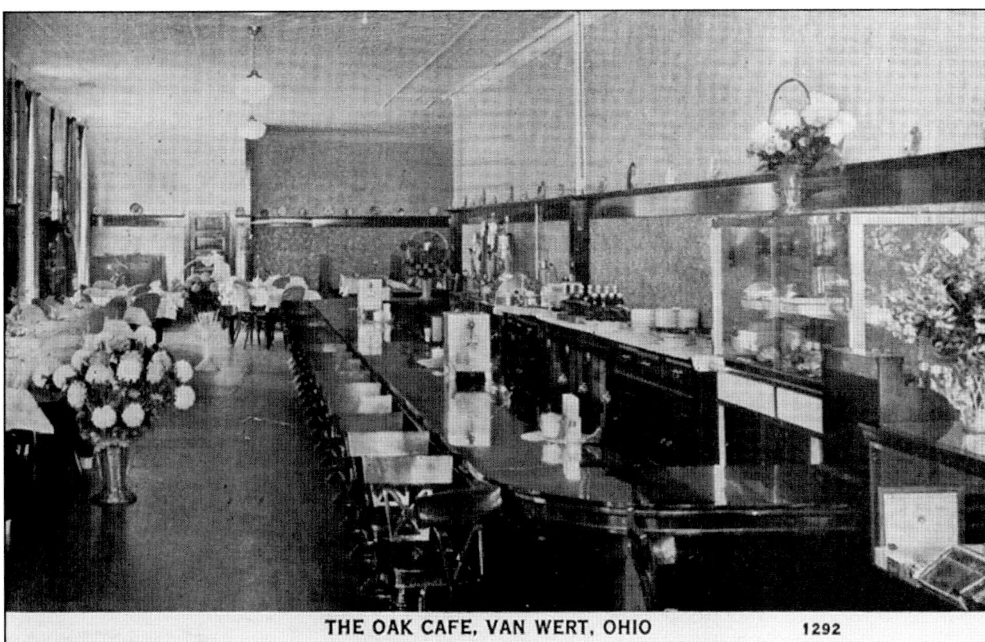

F. F. Rote operated the Oak Café in the 1930s in Van Wert where "all highways pass our door: Routes 17, 30, 116, 118, and 127." Postcards were increasingly used as advertising tools then, and Rote used the back of this postmarked 1933 card to promote the restaurant's quality food, courteous service, and soft hot water in the restrooms. (Author's collection.)

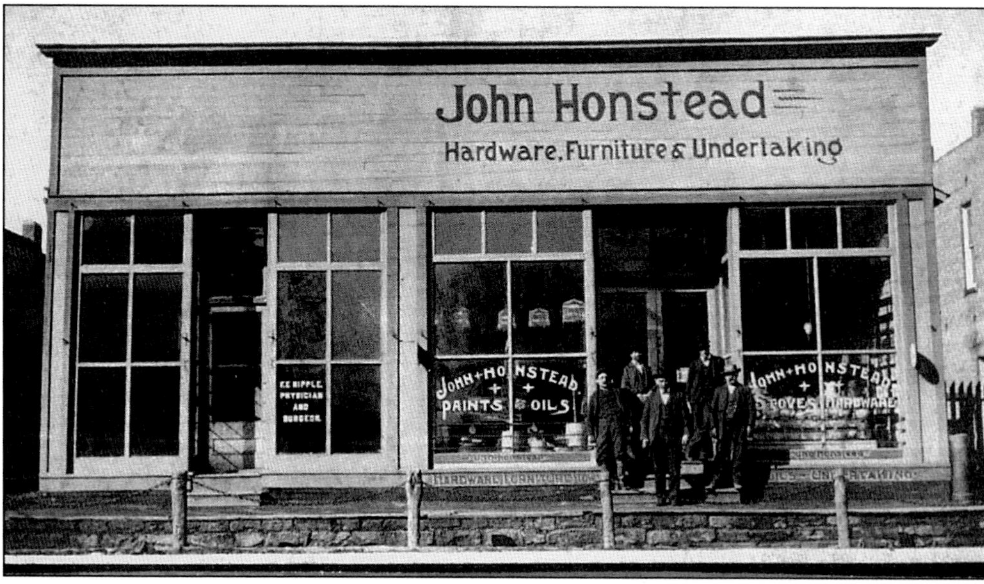

Business combinations of the late 1800s, when this card was probably made, are often perplexing today. John Honstead sold paint, oil, hardware supplies, and furniture at his Crawford Street store in Van Wert, and also provided undertaking services. F. E. Hipple, physician and surgeon, is located rather ominously next door. (Ken Cripe collection.)

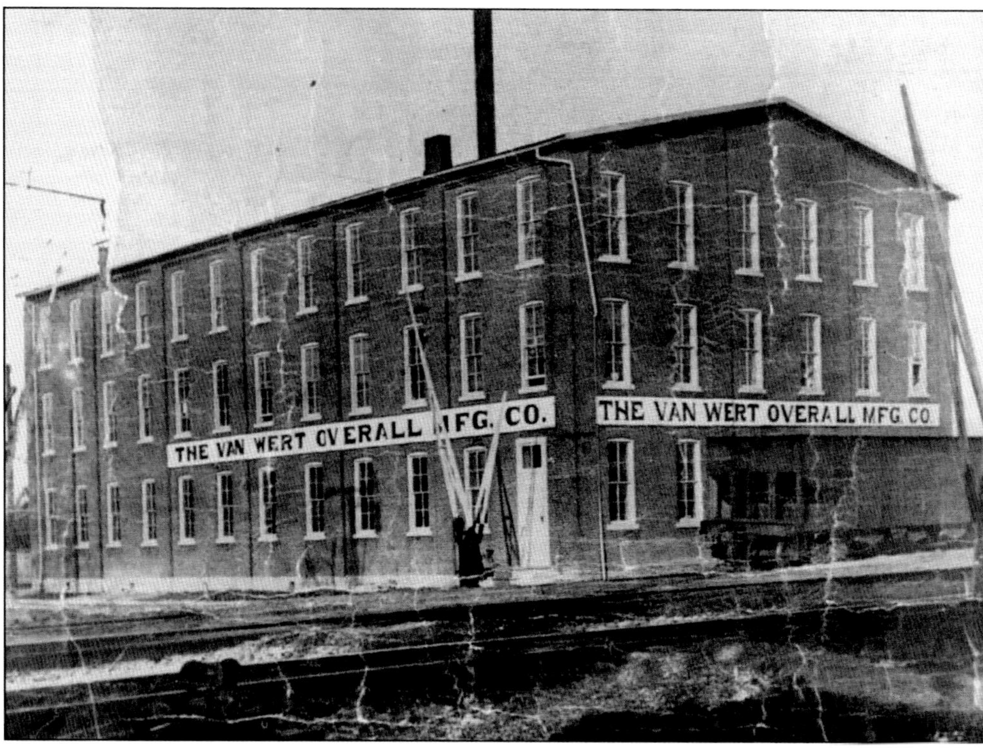

The Van Wert Overall Manufacturing Company employed hundreds of residents over the years, making work clothing and uniforms. The firm started on East Main Street in Van Wert in 1898 and later moved to the Harrison Street location, seen on this postcard. (Ken Cripe collection.)

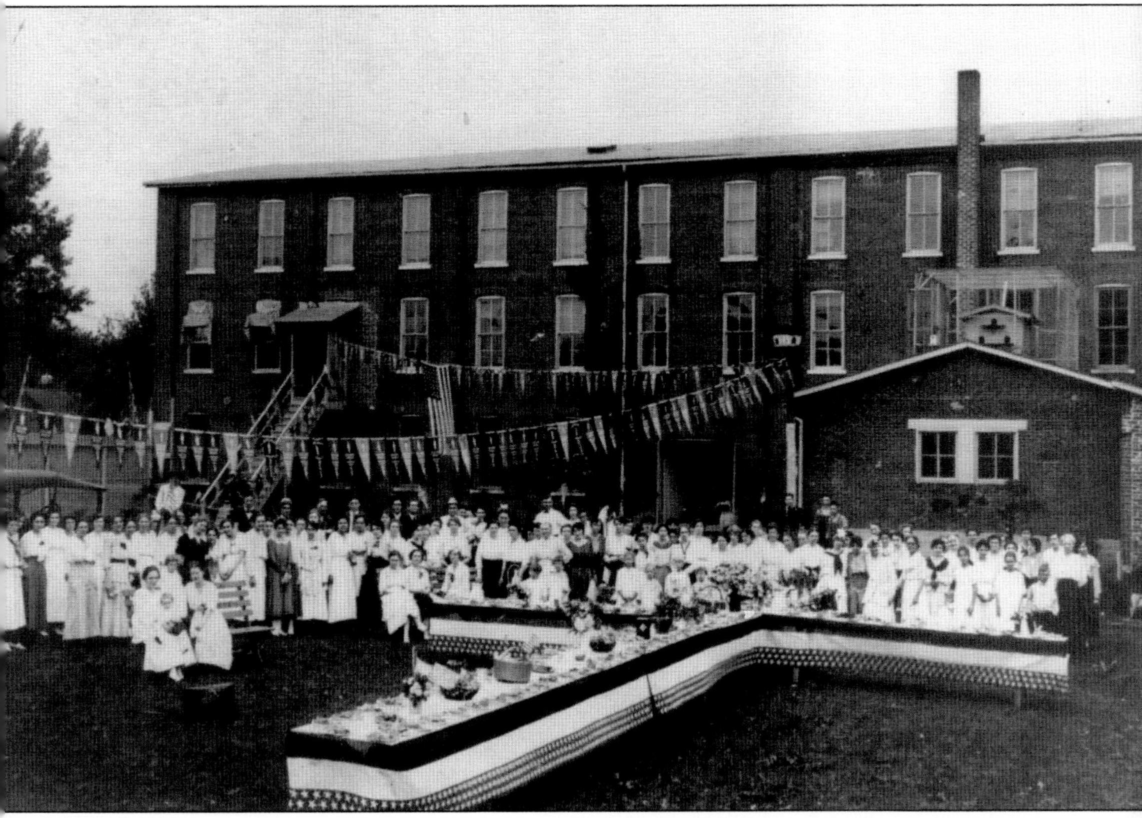

The pennants and table decorations in this *c.* 1920 postcard hint at some sort of patriotic celebration. The location was the rear of Kennedy Manufacturing, on Harrison Street in Van Wert. One of the county's major manufacturers for years, the company was started by Howard Kennedy, a fireman on the Pennsylvania Railroad in the early 1900s. Kennedy got tired of constantly replacing the suitcases he carried on his travels so he made a metal suitcase that was virtually indestructible. His friends soon wanted metal suitcases too, and he found himself in business making the suitcases and metal toolboxes. Howard and his brother Charles started their first factory in Fort Wayne in 1911, moved to Van Wert on the corner of Jefferson and Jackson Streets in 1914, and then on to a more suitable space on Harrison Street in 1919. Kennedy Manufacturing also became known for its window refrigerator units and fishing tackle boxes. (Ken Cripe collection.)

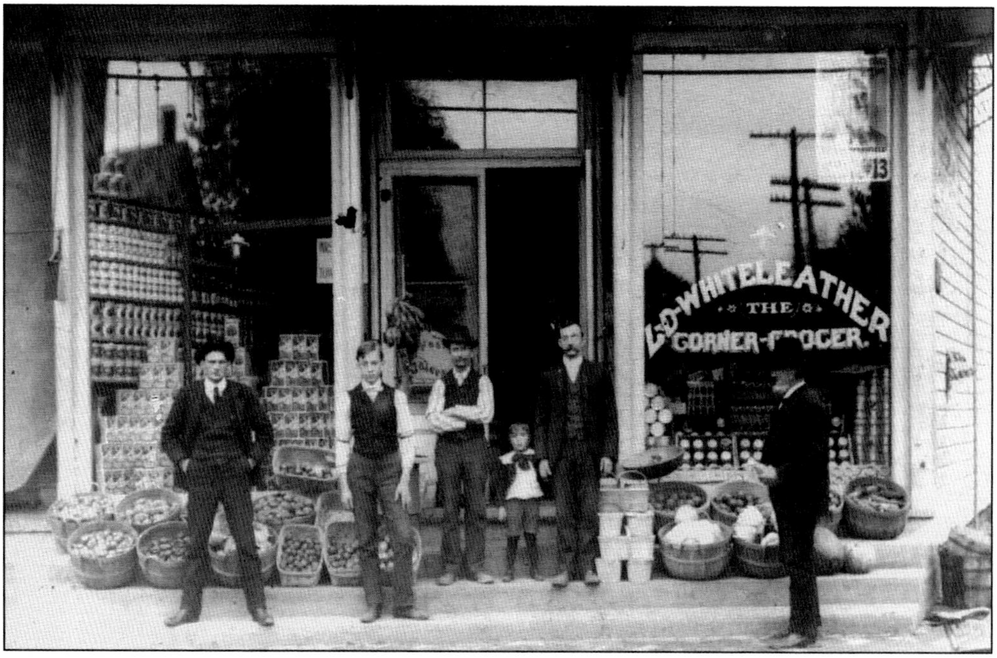

Each neighborhood in every village and town had its own corner grocery in the early 1900s. L. D. Whiteleather ran this store at 252 West Main in 1907. Baskets of locally grown fresh produce, the weekly specials, and neatly displayed stacks of canned food provided a clean and convenient way for homemakers to shop for their families. (Ken Cripe collection.)

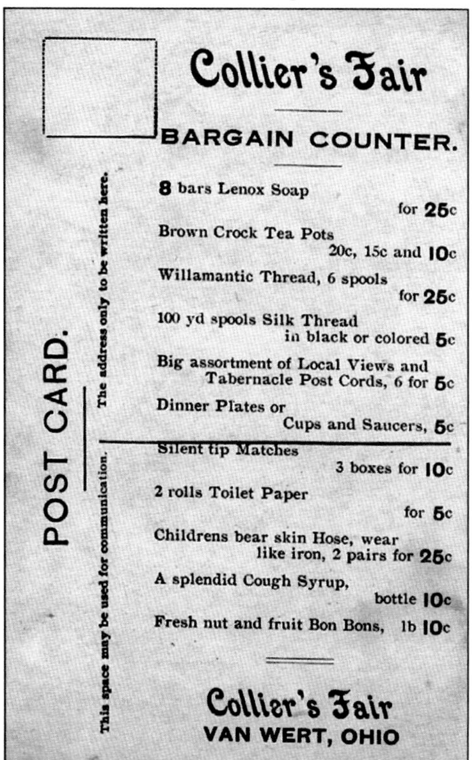

Collier's Fair in Van Wert offered something for everyone in the early 1900s, including six postcards of local scenes for a nickel. The front of this advertising card features a color drawing of a little boy handing a bouquet of red roses to a girl with a "Roses are red" verse. (Author's collection.)

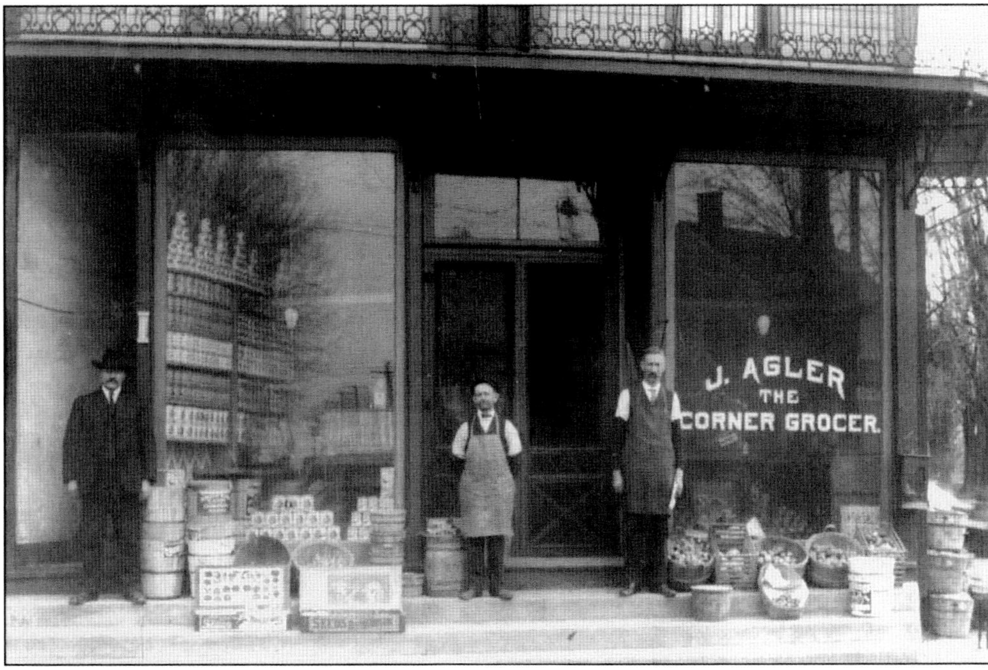

J. Agler's grocery was located on Main Street at Shannon Street in 1910, where L. D. Whiteleather operated his store a few years earlier. A new name on the window was the only change needed. (Ken Cripe collection.)

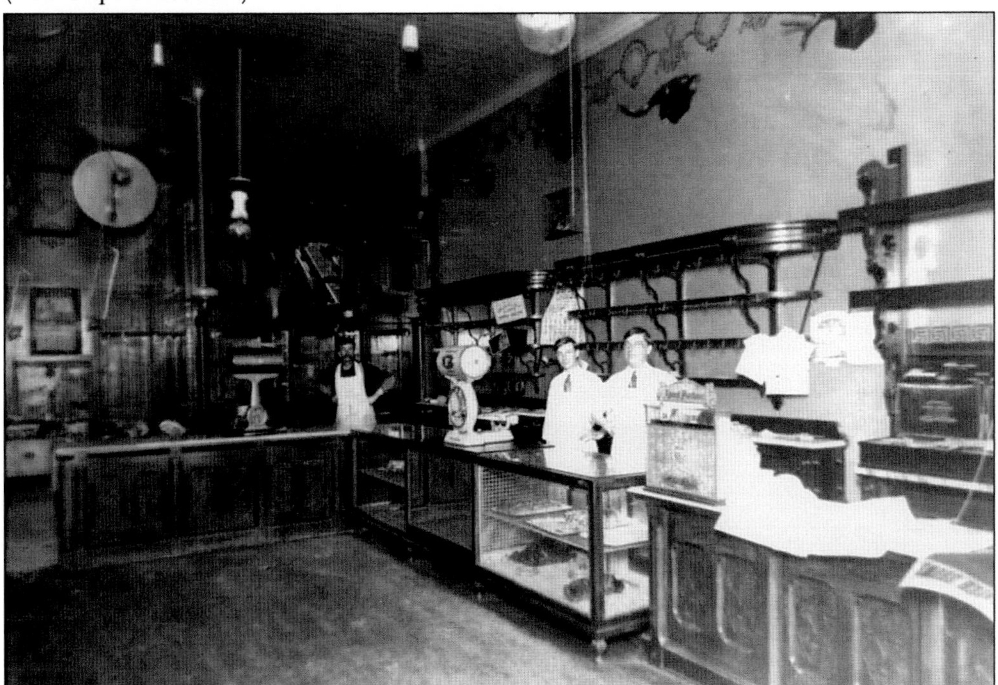

Most people bought their meat from a butcher shop such as Wild's Meats, located at 116 West Main Street, in Van Wert, seen in this early-20th-century postcard. Many meat markets did their own butchering, and some delivered meat door-to-door to customers. (Ken Cripe collection.)

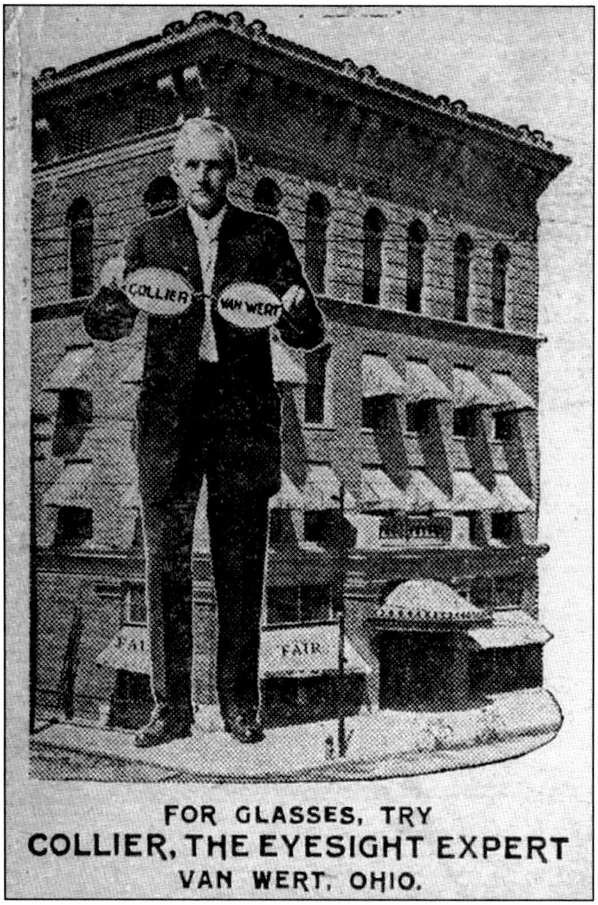

Humor helps sell, and Collier Optician used exaggeration and irony to attract customers with these *c.* 1920 advertising postcards. (Ken Cripe collection.)

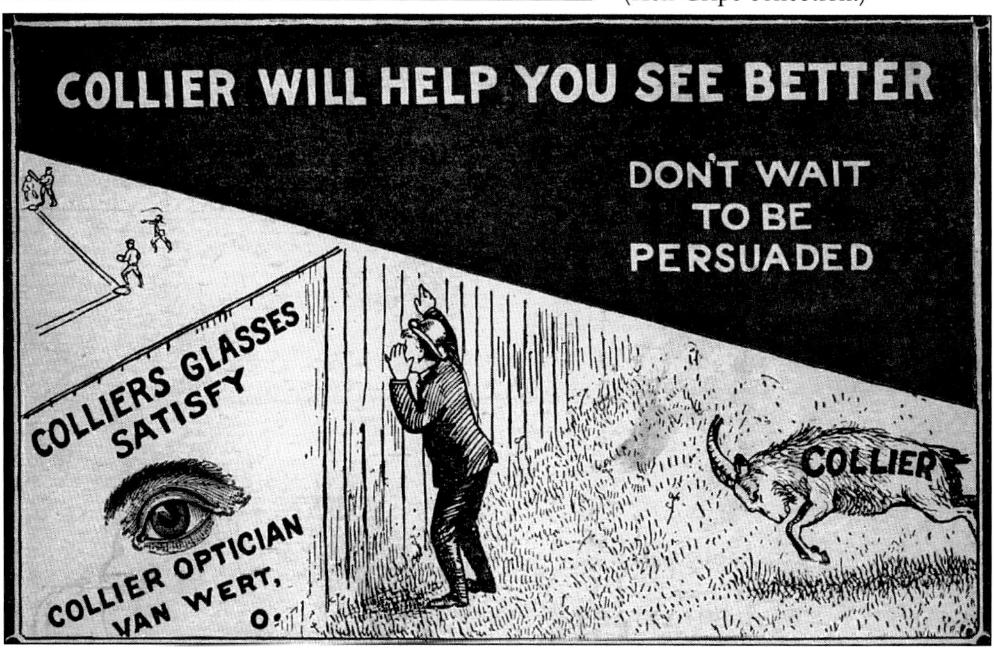

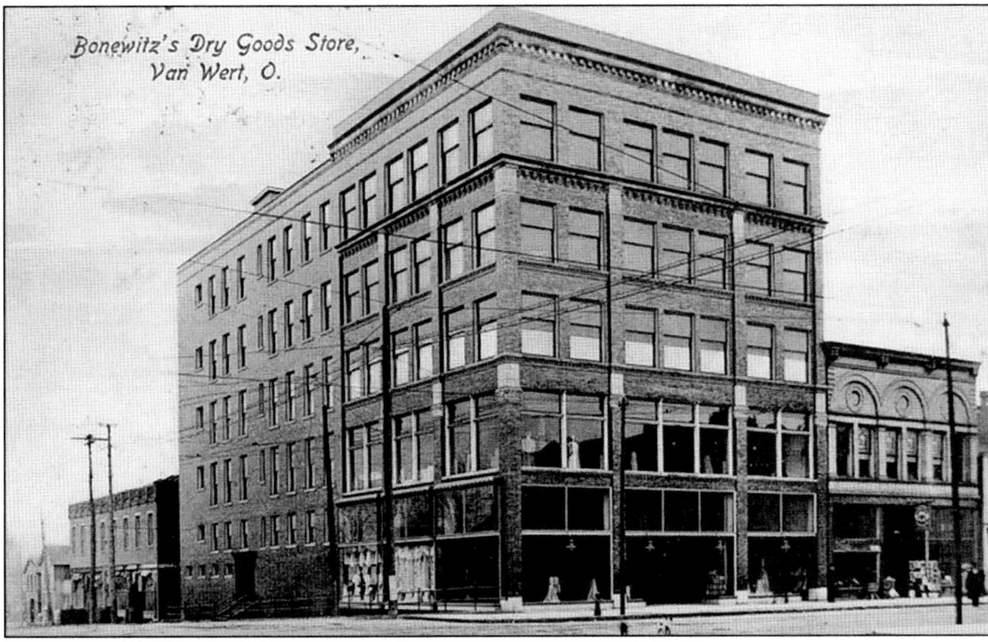

Bonnewitz's Dry Goods at Main and Market Streets was a forerunner of the large department stores where consumers did most of their shopping through the 1950s. Bonnewitz was a popular destination for generations of county residents. The card was mailed October 11, 1909, just a few days after a major fire at the store. (Author's collection.)

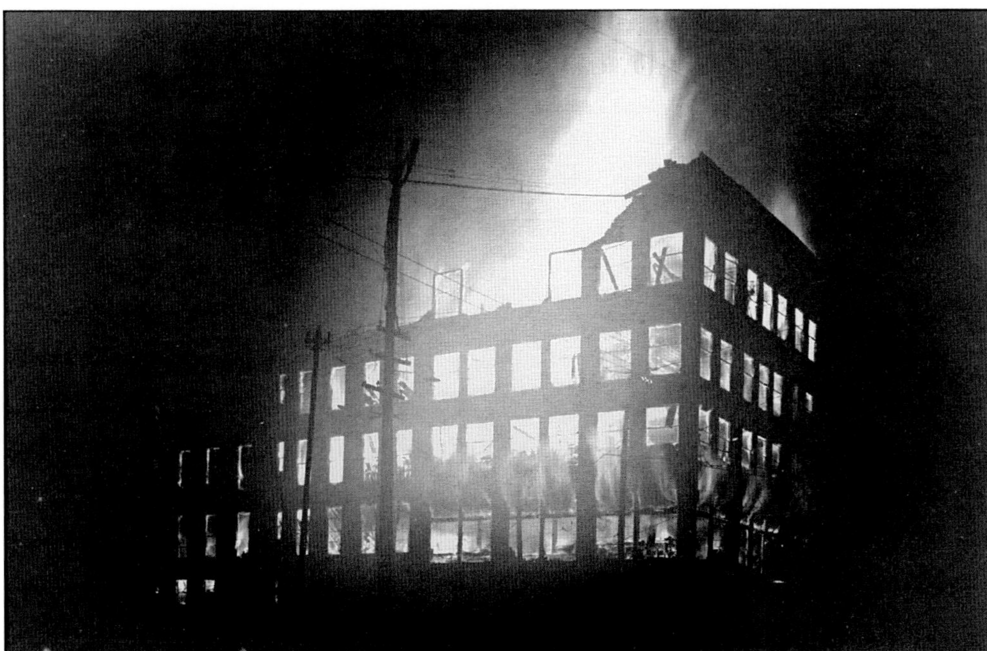

An overnight fire devastated the Bonnewitz building on October 6, 1909. The fire was said to have continued burning for several days, and the building and contents were declared total losses. (Van Wert County Historical Society.)

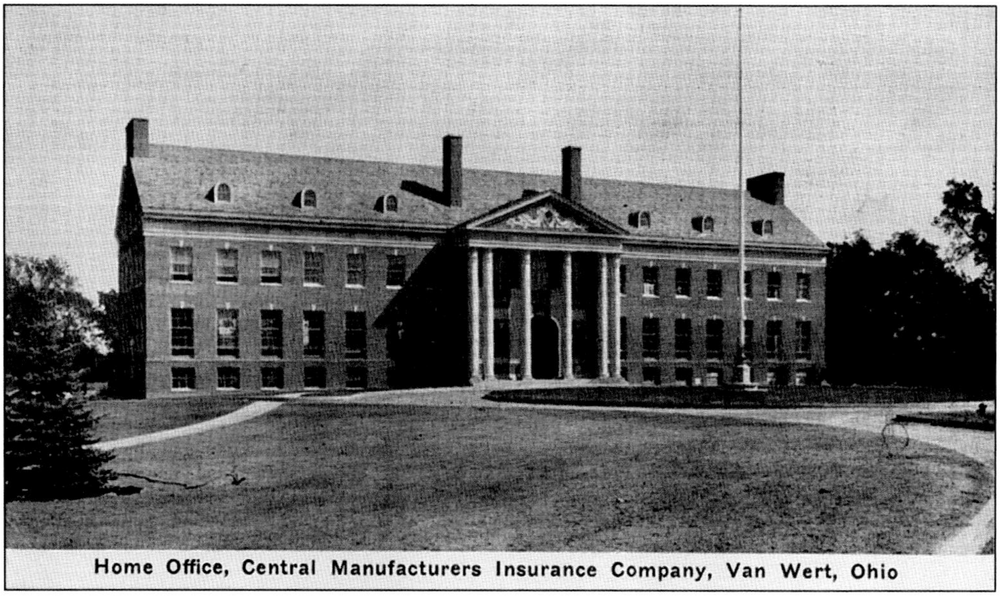

The Central Mutual Insurance Company had its roots in the Van Wert County Mutual Fire Insurance Company, founded in 1876 to insure local residents. By the time this Georgian-Colonial headquarters was built on South Washington Street in 1931, the company was called Central Manufacturers Insurance and it boasted assets of over $3 million with branches in 32 states, the District of Columbia, and Canada. (Author's collection.)

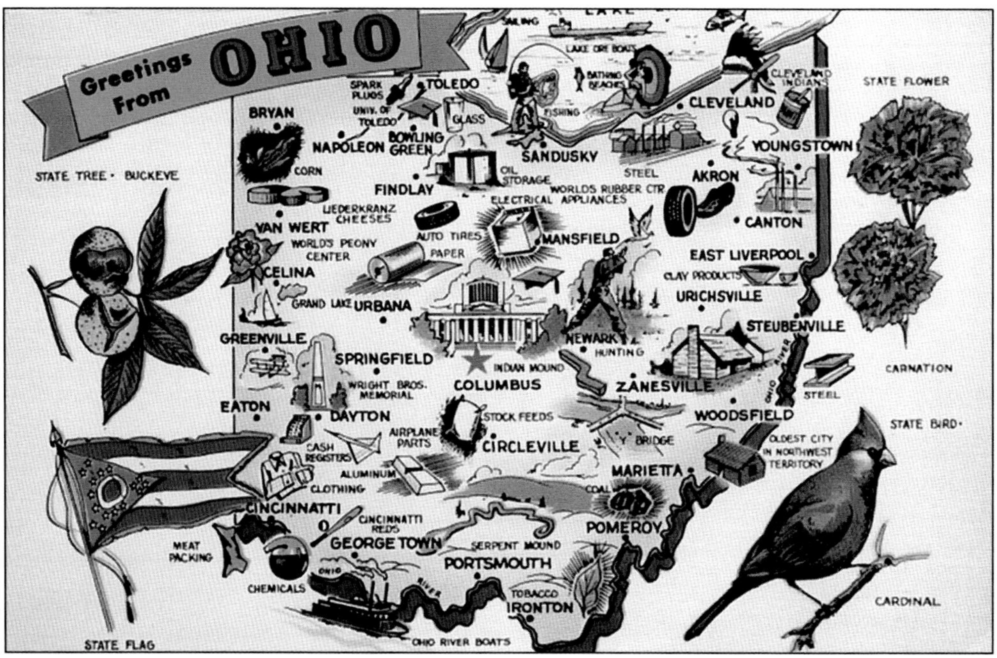

Peonies and Liederkranz cheese put Van Wert on the postcard map. Emil Frey developed the gold-crusted, soft ripening cheese for the Monroe Cheese Company, which opened in Van Wert in 1926. After Borden Company purchased the Monroe Cheese Company in 1929, the plant became the sole Liederkranz producer. The name translates into "wreath of songs," a tribute to the choral group to which Frey's boss belonged. (Author's collection.)

Eight

Community Scenes

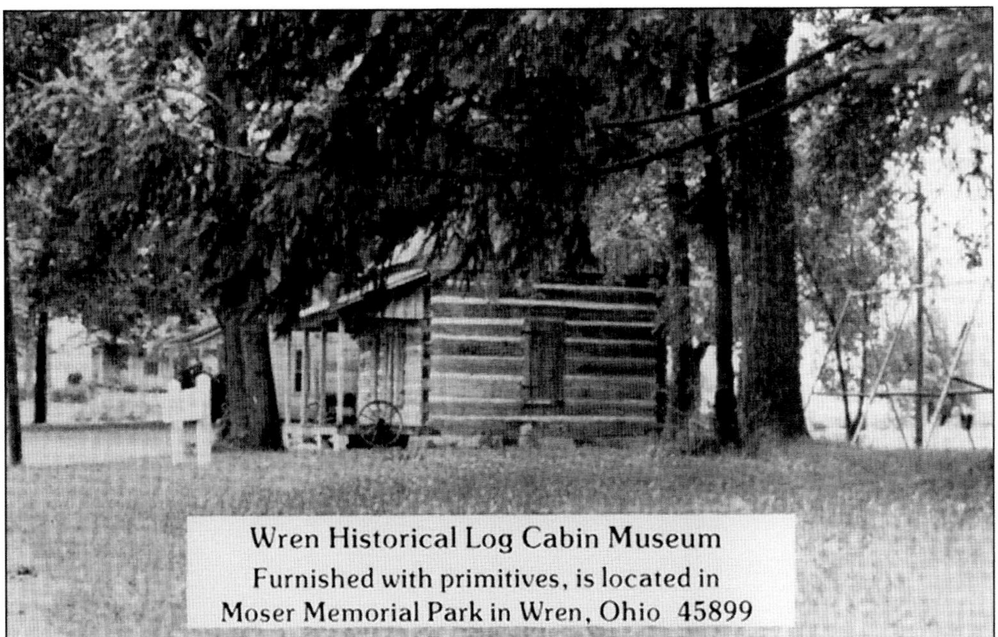

Hundreds of folks lived in log cabins similar to this one in the 1820s and 1830s while the county was being surveyed and settled. Before the community of Wren existed, an African American community was created in 1837 and 1838 in Willshire Township. Between 30 and 40 people, formerly enslaved by John Randolph of Virginia, were granted deeds for farms of 40 to 60 acres. The men arrived first to clear the land and build cabins, and then sent for their families. The Wren cabin is in the community park, deeded to the village by the Jason L. Moser family for $1 in 1924. (Author's collection.)

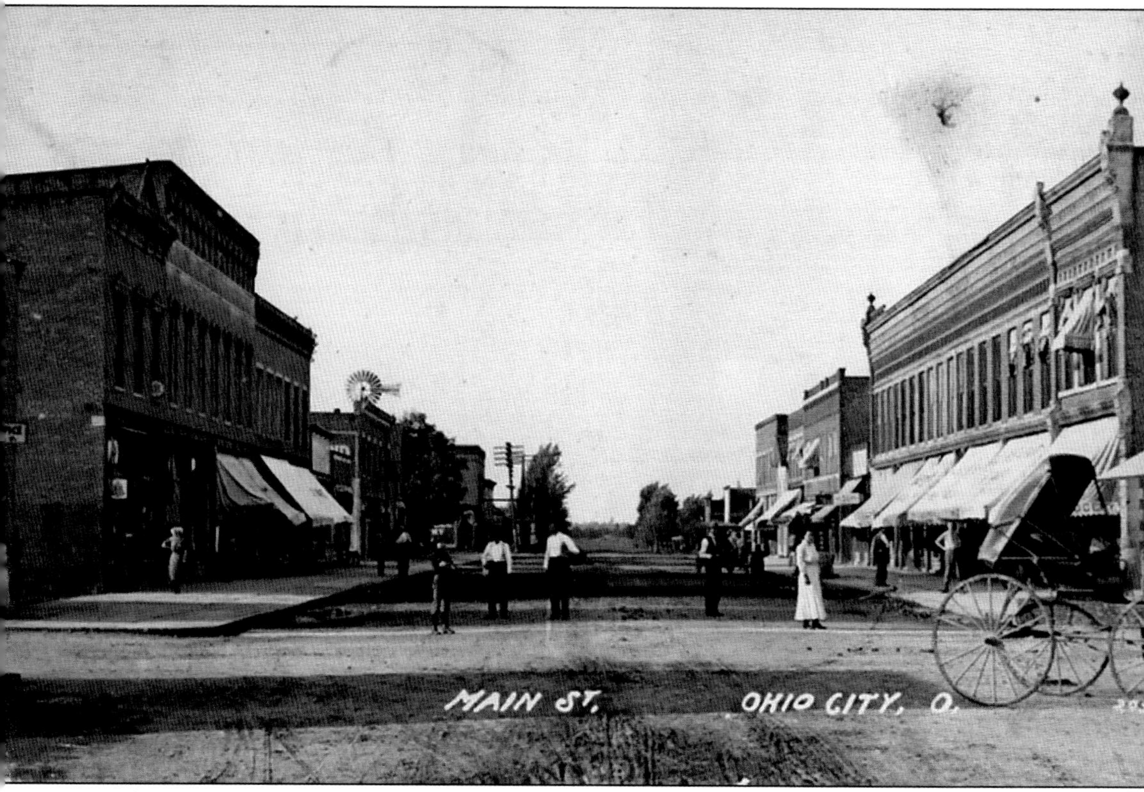

Ohio City residents pose like actors on a movie set for this *c.* 1910 postcard view of Main Street. The community had already gained fame as the early home of John W. Lambert, the automotive pioneer who is credited with building the first gasoline-powered car in the United States in 1891. Ohio City's history dates back to 1840 when white settlers arrived in Willshire Township. The Koogle Post Office started to serve local residents, and the community of Enterprise grew up around it. The discovery of another Enterprise in the state led to the Ohio City name change by 1900. Village businesses provided for citizens' needs. Peter Putnam sold cement and coal. George L. Moore dealt in real estate and insurance. Citizens went to Swoveland Drug Store when they were sick, D. H. Heiby's Butcher Shop and W. M. Gossette's Bakery when they were hungry, and to the Farmers' Bank when they needed a loan. Blacksmiths and buggy suppliers coexisted with automobile mechanics. (Author's collection.)

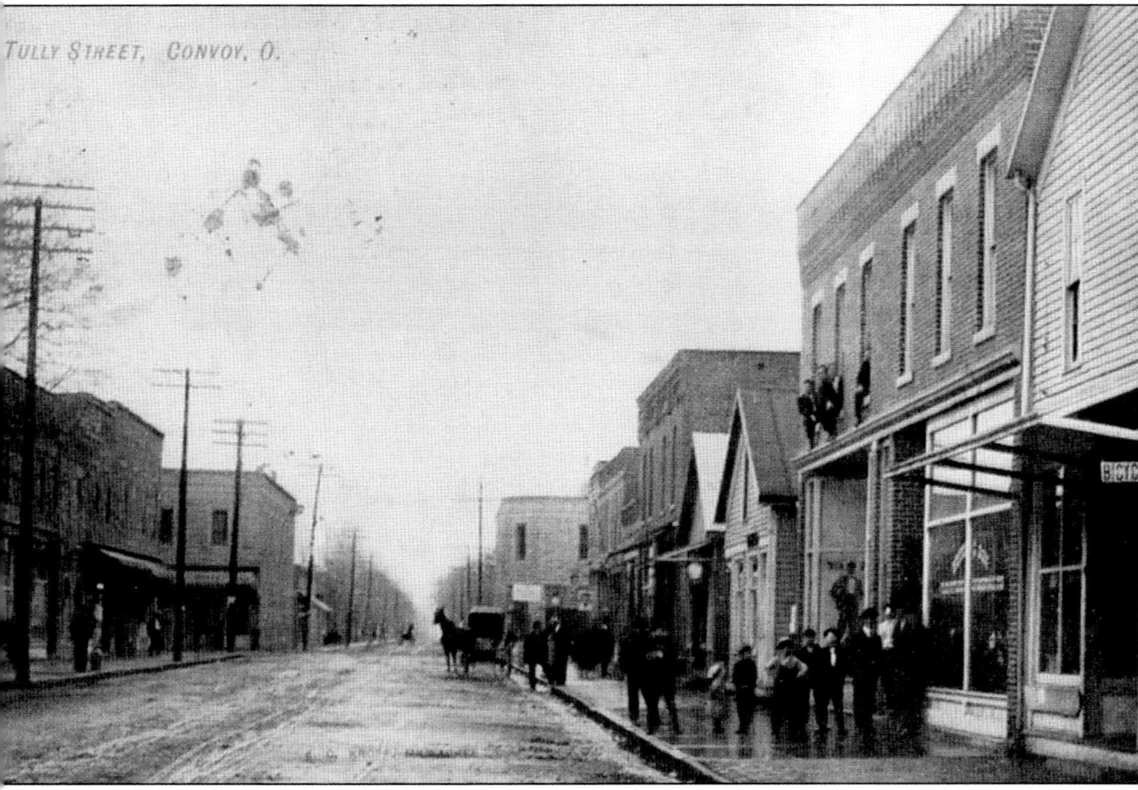

Convoy residents also turned out for the photographer for this *c.* 1916 postcard. James Pettit and Robert Nesbit laid out the Tully Township village in 1854. Nesbit, an Irish immigrant, had been sent to the township in his job for the Pennsylvania Railroad. The area was the last part of the Black Swamp region to be settled. Land was still relatively inexpensive there, and early settlers helped clear the timber and drain the land to establish homesteads. Nesbit named the village after his hometown of Conmhagh, Ireland. Pettit opened a dry goods store, and later a hotel, used by visitors who arrived via the railroad. Many of the new residents were Irish, and in 1860, St. Mary's Catholic Church began holding services on the west edge of town, served by a priest from Delphos. Convoy incorporated in 1874 with a population of 400. A. B. Penny was the first mayor. (Author's collection.)

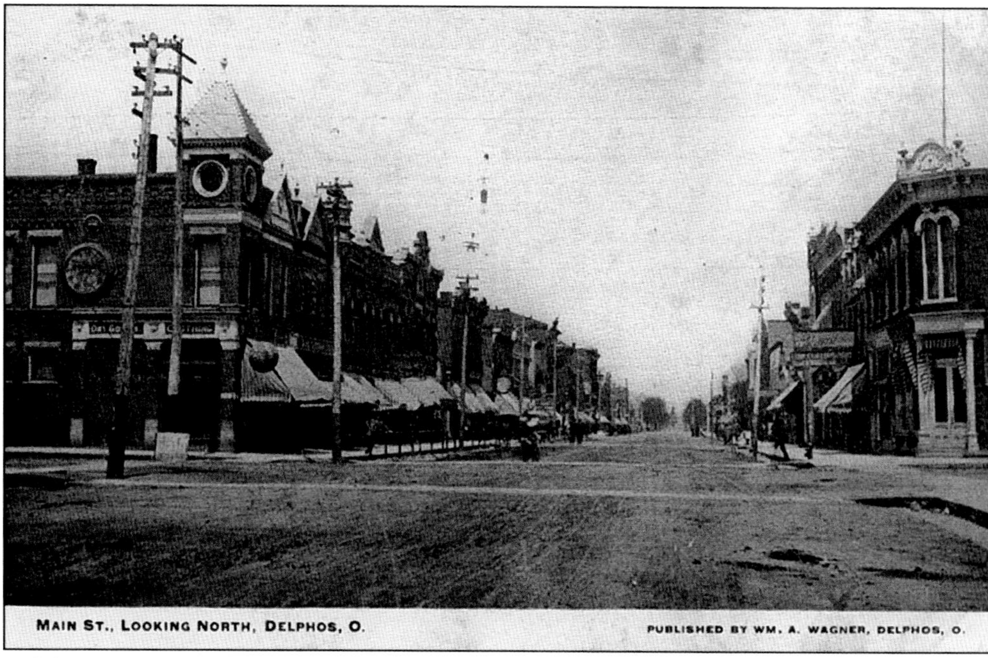

Delphos's Main Street shows a growing downtown area in this *c.* 1910 photograph. The Miami and Erie Canal, completed in 1845, created the community, first known as Section 10 for its location on the canal. The west towpath of the canal is the divider between Van Wert and Allen Counties. The town was incorporated in 1851 as Delphos, based on the Greek city of Delphi. (Author's collection.)

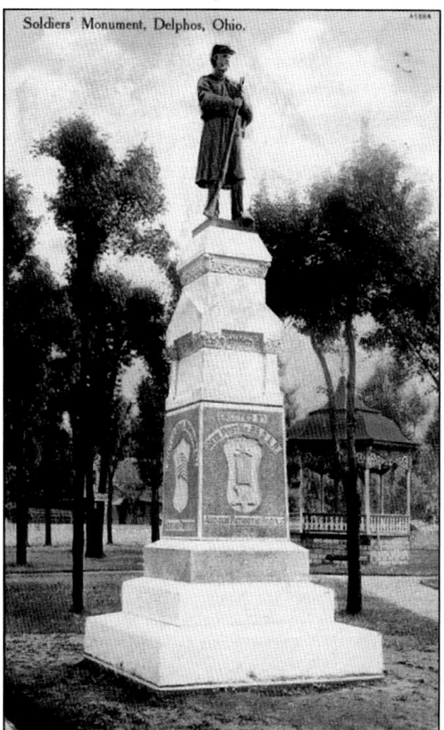

This memorial to the soldiers of the Civil War was erected by Post No. 85 of the Grand Army of the Republic in 1909 in Delphos. The GAR, composed of veterans of the conflict, erected similar monuments nationwide to commemorate the sacrifices made in the bloody war. The card is postmarked August 24, 1911. (Author's collection.)

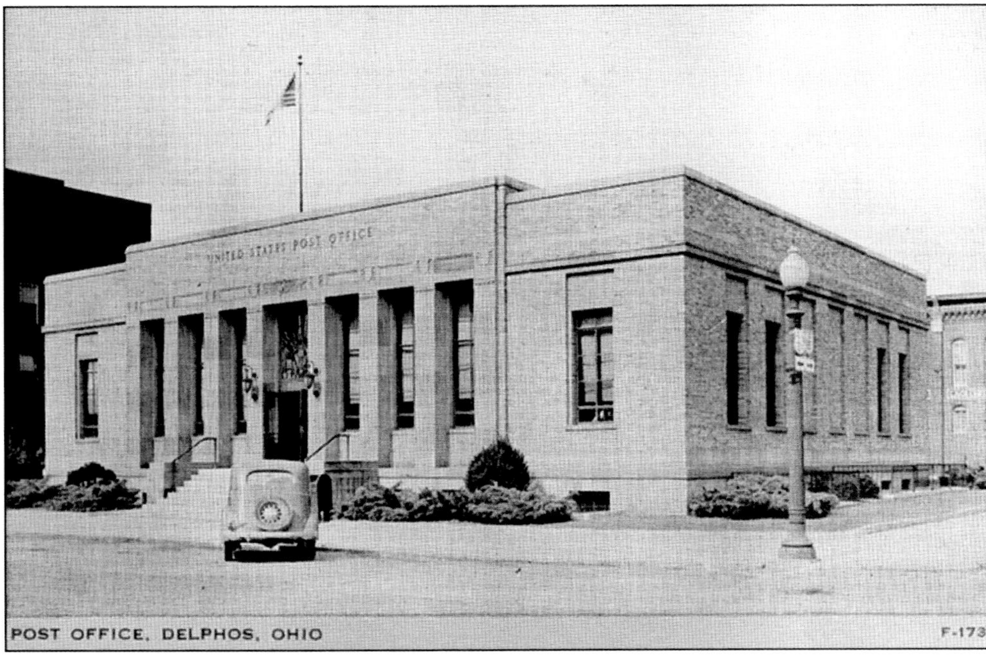

"Just had a soda. Nice and warm here," the sender wrote on July 29, 1947, to a friend in Cleveland. Delphos's large, modern post office is shown. (Author's collection.)

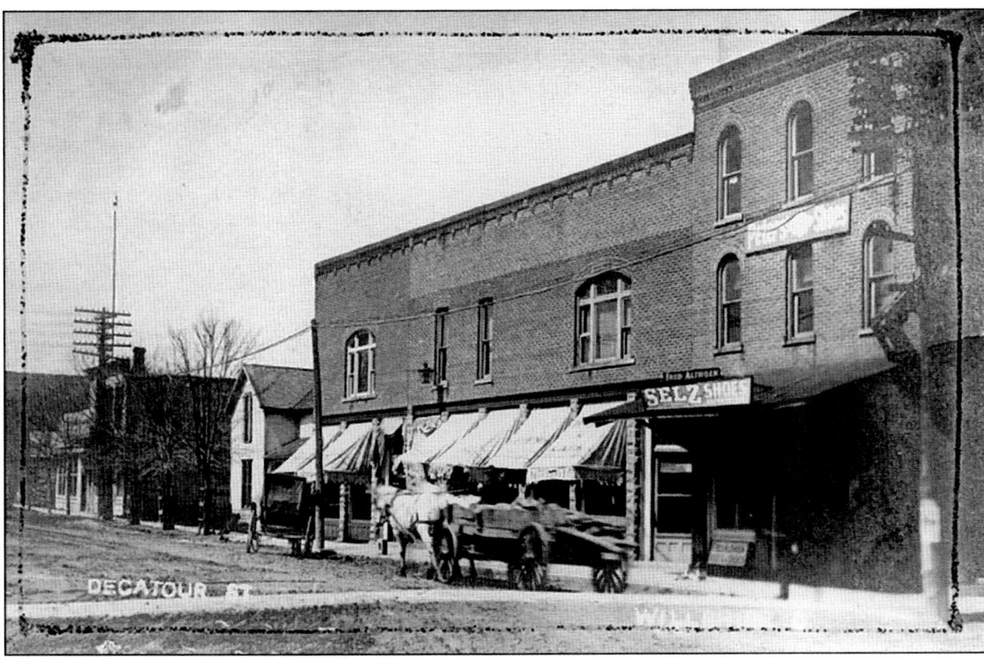

A team pulls a wagon of lumber down Decatur Street in Willshire in this *c.* 1910 postcard. Businesses in town at the time included three blacksmiths, a harness shop, two buggy shops, a livery barn, and a grain elevator. Agriculture was still king but new businesses were also evident including a canning factory, stone quarry, and photograph gallery. (Author's collection.)

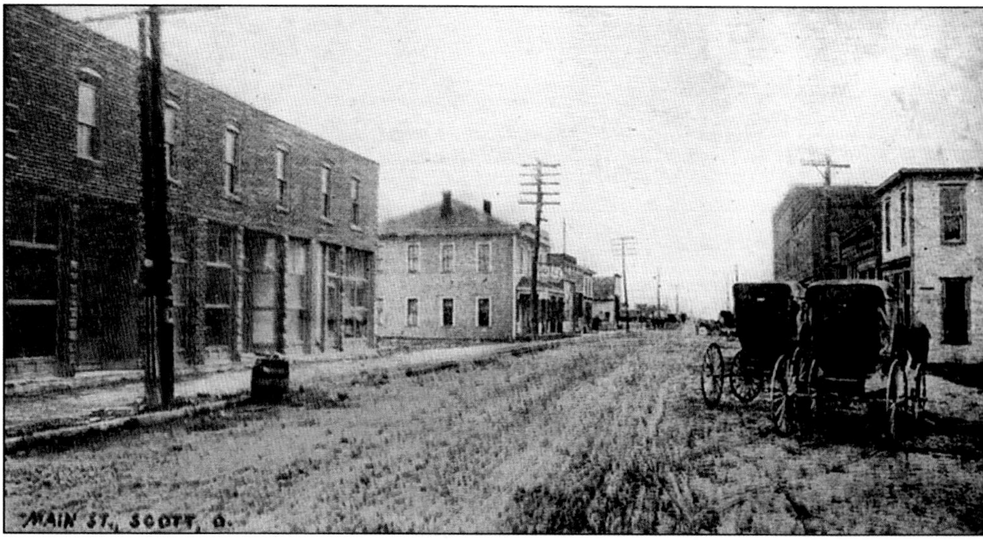

Scott, on the Van Wert/Paulding County line, had many sawmills and farms. Cincinnati Northern Railroad's depot sent out carloads of grain, timber, hoops and staves. In 1911, when this card was mailed, the village boasted a bank, real estate agent, two doctors, a restaurant and poolroom, a hotel, a drugstore, and a hardware store in addition to the usual businesses. Most stores were on Blaine Street. (Author's collection.)

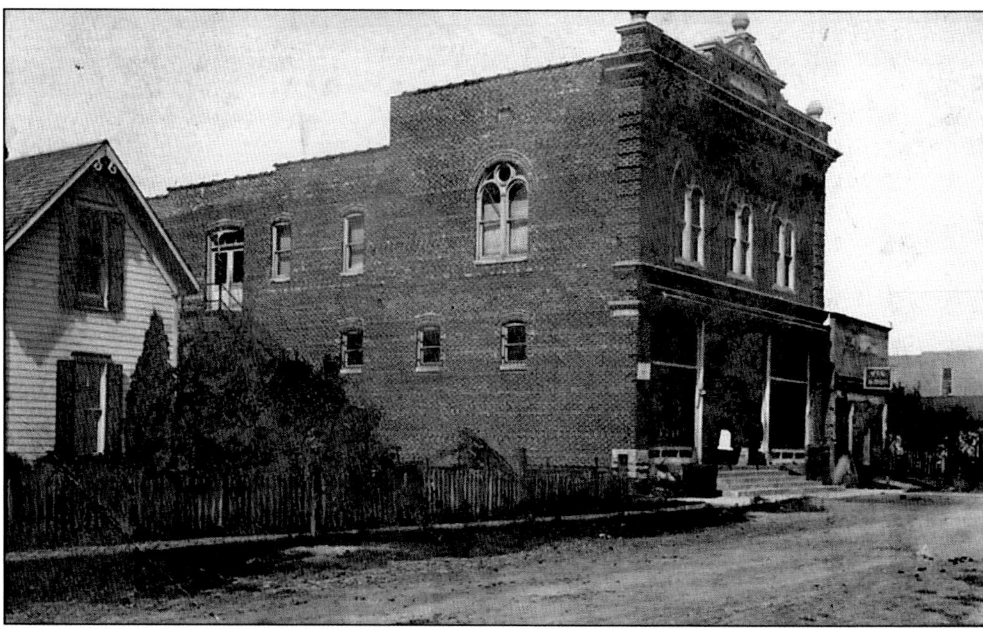

Welsh relatives of former Ohio governor William Bebb settled Venedocia in 1848. The Toledo, Delphos and Burlington Railroad connected the village to the region. A general store and tin shop are pictured in this card, postmarked July 31, 1908. The 1910 county directory listed a barbershop, a drug and hardware store, a dry goods store, a harness and robe shop, an elevator, a meat market, and a doctor in town. (Author's collection.)

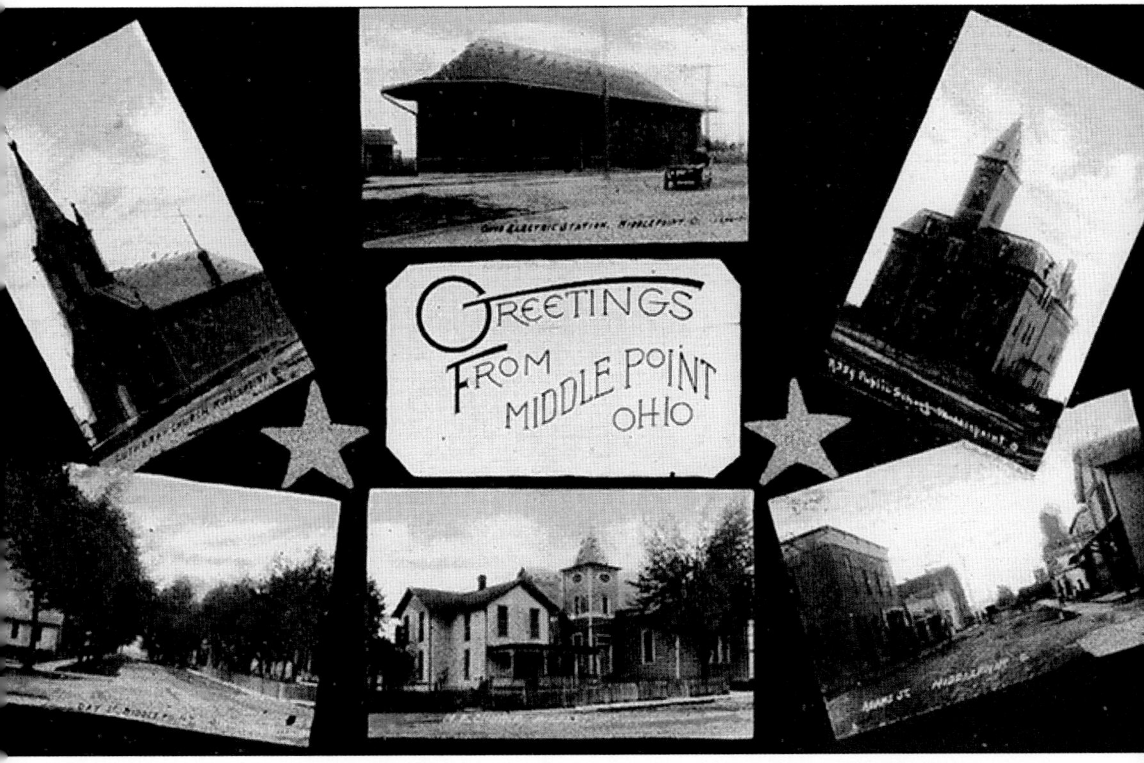

Mid-way between Van Wert and Delphos, the Washington Township town of Middle Point came into its own in the 1880s. The railroad came to town in the 19th century and the interurban electric railroad arrived early in the 20th century. Remnants of concrete bridges that were part of the interurban system can still be found on Middle Point Road. This *c.* 1910 photograph collage was the village's calling card to potential residences and businesses. Middle Point had all the amenities: tree-lined residential neighborhoods, a good public school, numerous houses of worship, modern transportation facilities, and a growing downtown business district. In addition to agriculture, the other main industry in the area was a stone quarry. The town continued to thrive for decades, reaching a population of 586 in 1940. (Author's collection.)

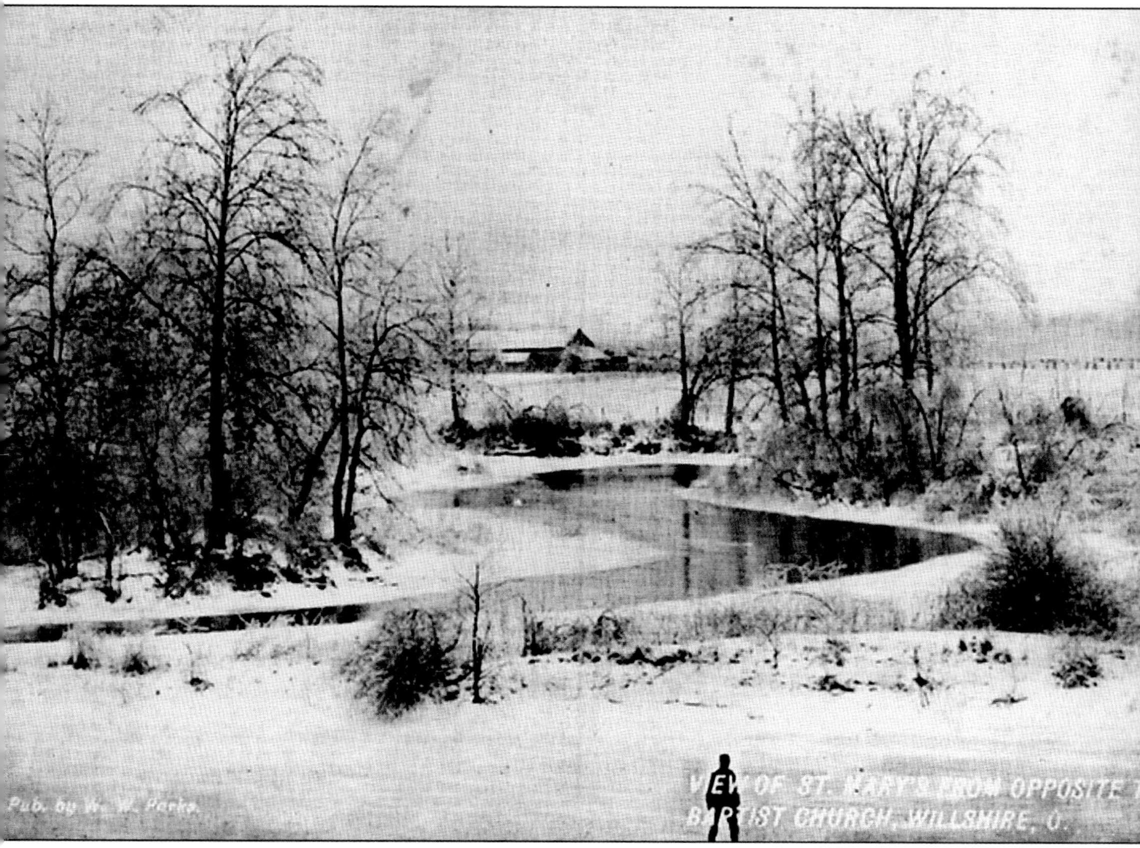

Hungry wolves and the threat of violence from Native Americans prompted James Riley to nickname Willshire the Devil's Race Ground in 1821. But Riley was convinced that the curving St. Marys River would bring prosperity to the region once the proposed Miami and Erie Canal was built. A serious malaria epidemic in the spring and summer of 1854 killed many residents. With little treatment available, the ill were sedated with whiskey and the dead were wrapped in sheets and buried in yards and gardens. But the pioneers persisted, establishing churches and a school, conducting public business in a log courthouse, and building shops and stores to serve the growing population. Many of Riley's dreams for the community had been realized by the time this idyllic winter scene was photographed from the vantage point of the Willshire Baptist Church. The postcard was mailed from Willshire to Irene Yochum of Marion on August 11, 1916, by two girls—Geraldine and Ileen—who were visiting their grandmother. (Author's collection.)

Convoy's brick city hall and fire station on South Main Street was a local landmark when this postcard was mailed on January 29, 1910. Thomas Salmon was mayor at the time. William Dressel was village clerk, Joseph Kreischer was treasurer, and Charles Engemire was town marshal. (Author's collection.)

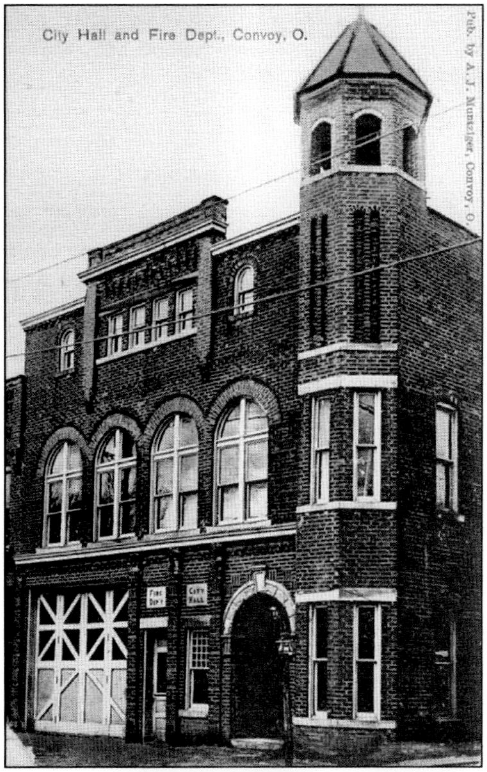

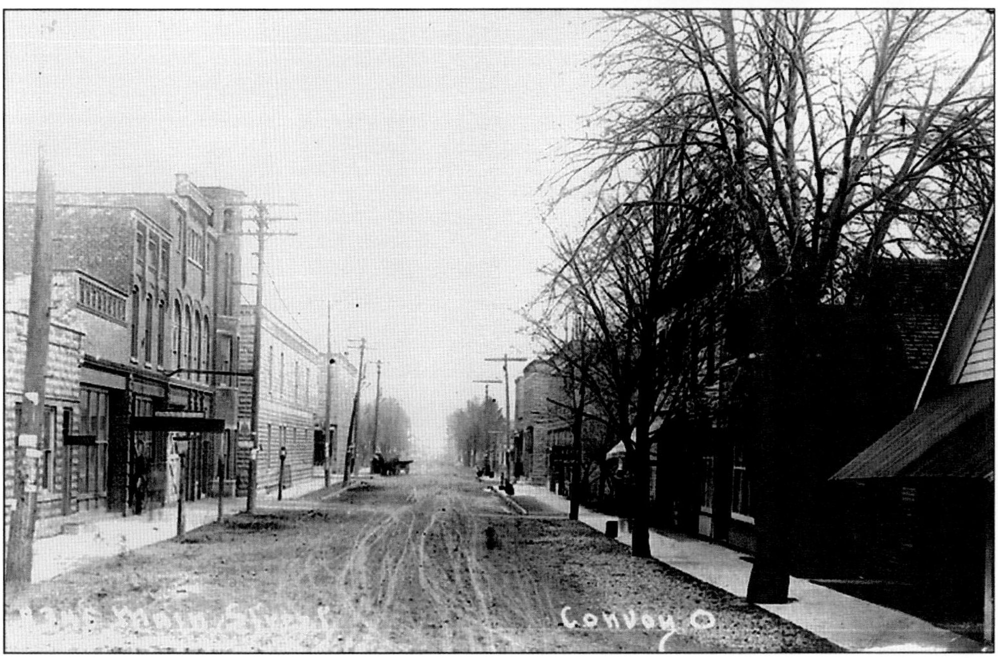

This early photograph card of South Main Street in Convoy showed the proximity of the town hall, businesses, and homes. J. T. Edwards's Livery and Feed Barn was visible on the right. Horses were still a big part of daily life, and Convoy offered two harness shops, a hay and straw dealer, two buggy shops, and four blacksmiths. (Author's collection.)

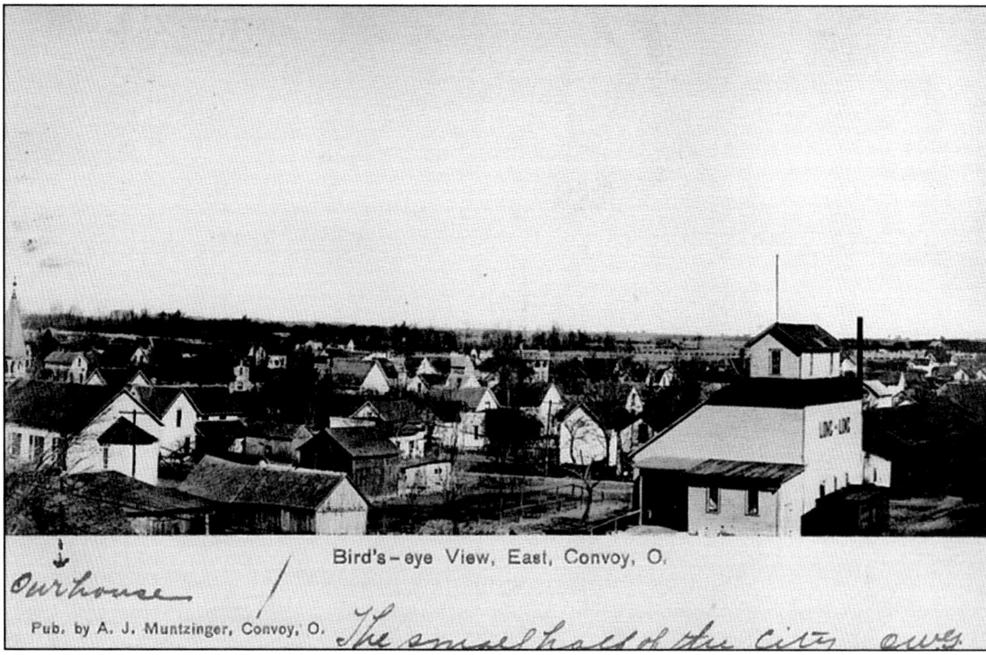

"The small half of the city," wrote the sender of this Convoy scene on July 19, 1909. Despite two serious fires in the downtown area in the first decade of the 20th century, residential and commercial growth continued. Long and Long Grain Company is visible in the right foreground. (Author's collection.)

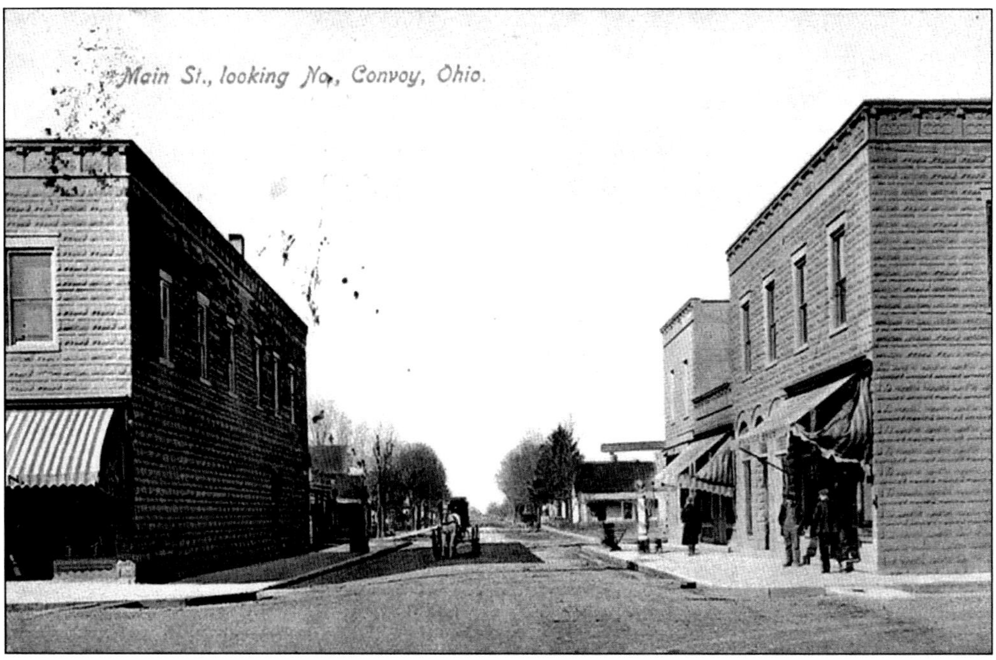

Room for growth is displayed in this *c.* 1902 postcard of Convoy's North Main Street. The barber's pole of Sprowl's Barber Shop on the right and the horse and buggy in the street conveyed 19th-century charm, but Convoy was moving into a new era of progress and growth. (Author's collection.)

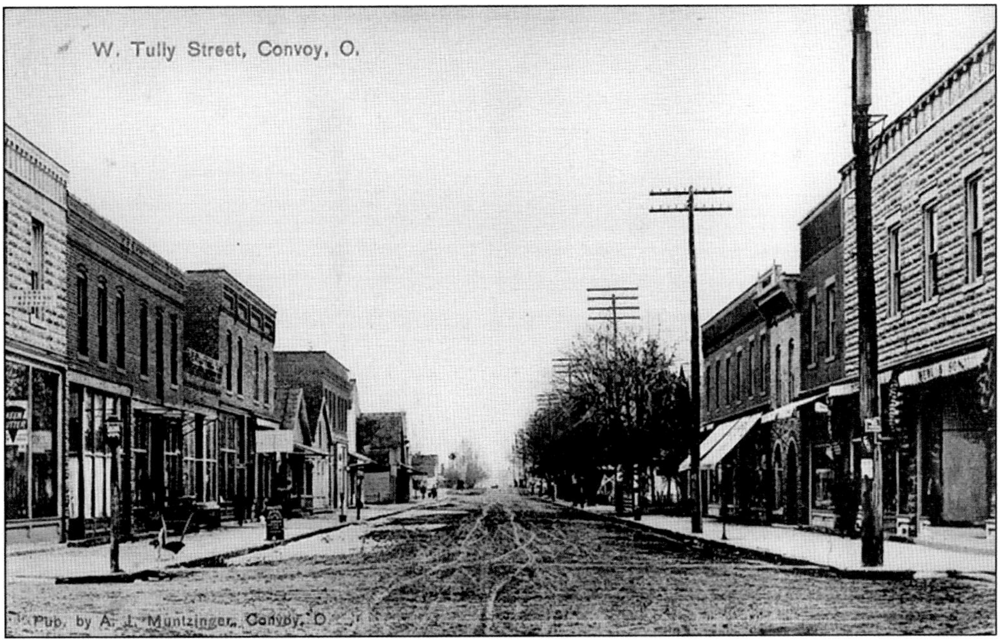

A. J. Muntzinger, listed in the 1910 county directory as a salesman and proprietor of the Polish Company, published this postcard of West Tully Street in Convoy. By the time the card was mailed in Dixon on May 18, 1914, Convoy was a bustling town of more than 60 businesses and hundreds of families. The Hotel Convoy, operated by J. F. Brown, was one of two hotels in the village. (Author's collection.)

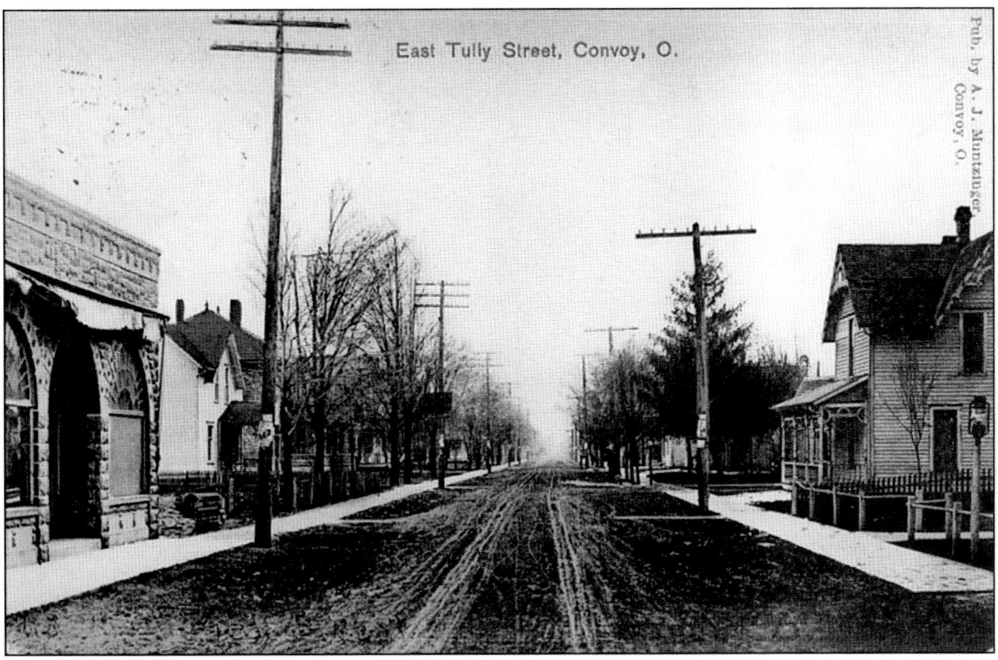

This photograph of East Tully Street was from the same postcard series, and was also postmarked 1914. Rows of houses seemed to stretch into infinity. Some of the houses on the right side of the street were torn down to build the Evangelical Lutheran Church, beginning in 1912.

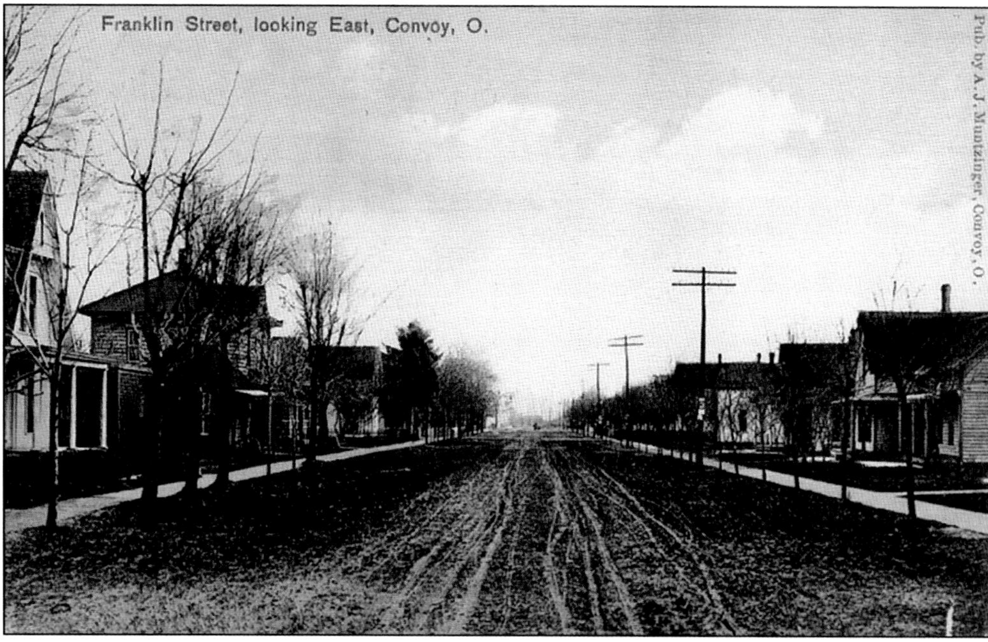

Wide residential streets like Franklin in Convoy saw more automobile traffic by the time this card was mailed in 1918. Rummel and Freck of Convoy placed a full-page advertisement in the 1910 county directory announcing themselves as the exclusive agents in the county for Reo automobiles, "the strongest, most endurable and simple constructed machines on the market." A touring car cost $1,000 in 1910, and a runabout, $550. (Author's collection.)

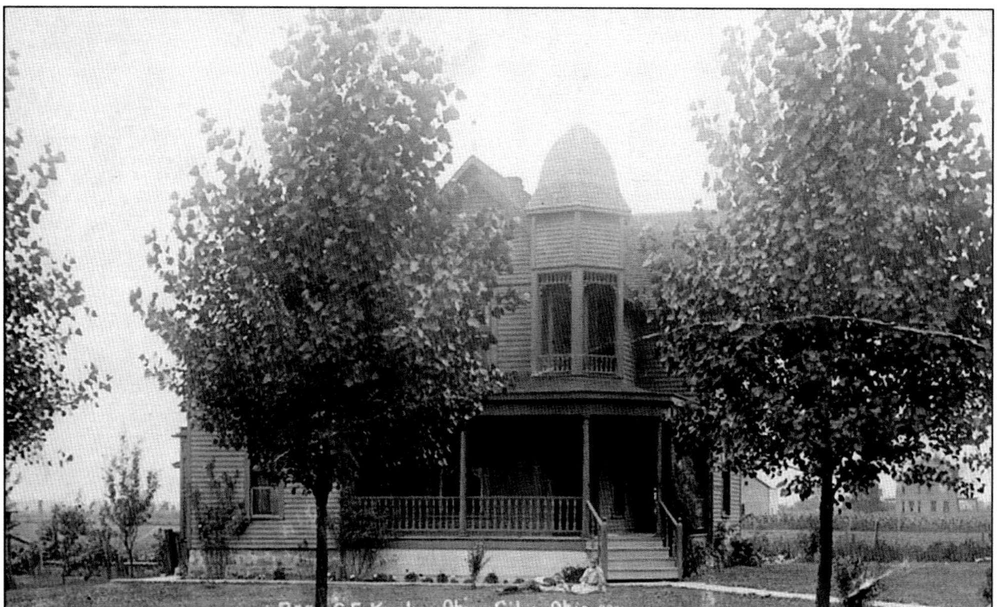

As county residents became more prosperous, some of them had photograph postcards made of their homes to send to friends and relatives. This view of the C. F. Koch residence in Ohio City was postmarked November 20, 1888. (Author's collection.)

Nine

The County Seat

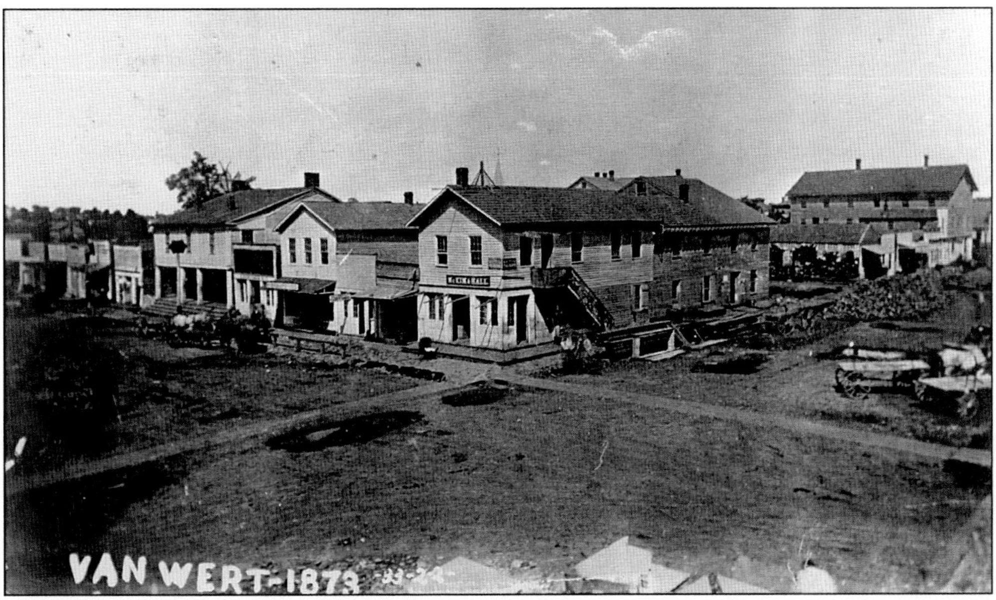

Van Wert was laid out in 1835, chosen as the county seat in 1839, and incorporated in 1848. This rare postcard view shows the downtown area in 1873. Van Wert grew rapidly in the mid-1800s. By 1882, the town had 27 grocery and provision stores, six dry goods stores, six sewing machine shops, six boot and shoe stores, five bakeries, five millinery shops, five drugstores, four hotels, three newspapers, three saddle and harness shops, three hardware stores, two furniture stores, two undertakers, two jewelers, two dressmakers, one fruit store, one boot store, and one hair store. (Ken Cripe collection.)

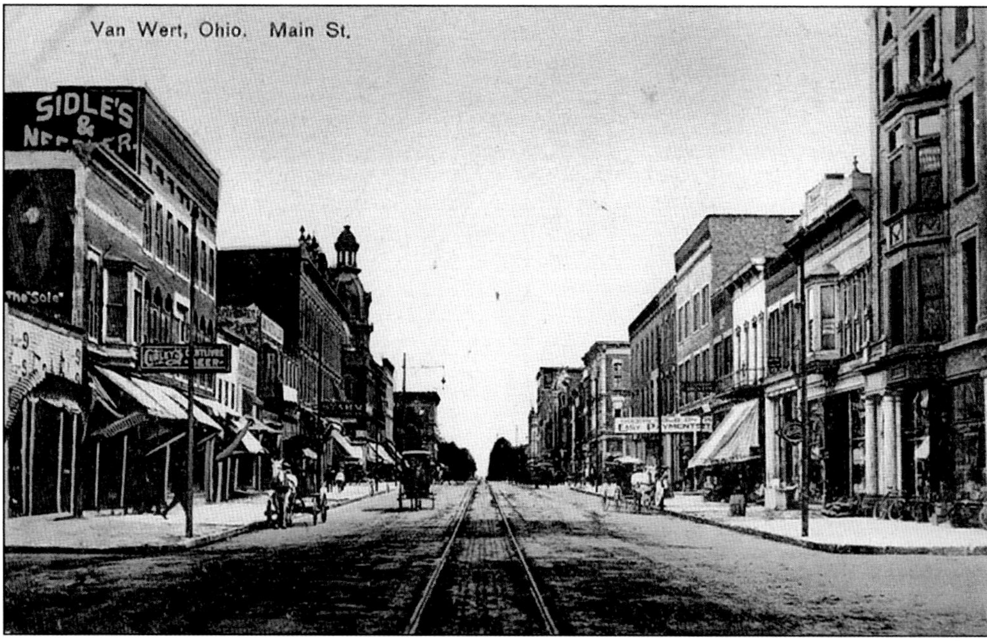

When this card was mailed in 1910, horses and buggies shared Main Street in Van Wert with traction lines and a few automobiles. Residents and visitors could take care of all their professional and personal needs by walking up and down Main Street. Bankers, attorneys, real estate agents, physicians, blacksmiths, and the occasional pool hustler could all be found there, along with an assortment of shops. (Author's collection.)

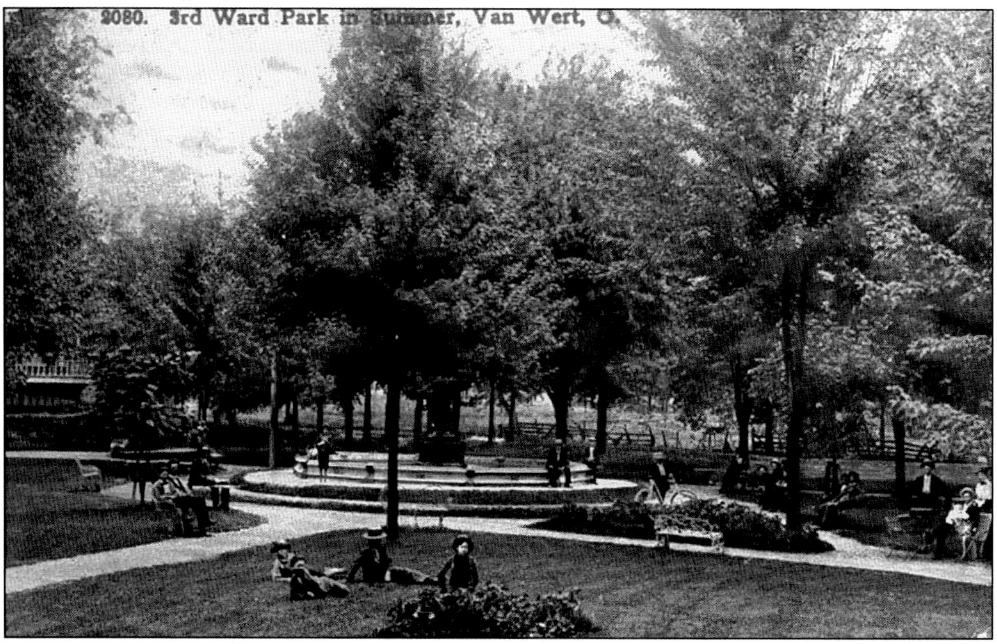

William Jennings Bryan lost three presidential campaigns between 1896 and 1908, but was warmly welcomed by Van Wert County residents when he spoke at Third Ward Park in Van Wert on May 9, 1912. The Democrat, who worked to influence economic policy, became Pres. Woodrow Wilson's secretary of state in 1913. This card was mailed August 8, 1919. (Author's collection.)

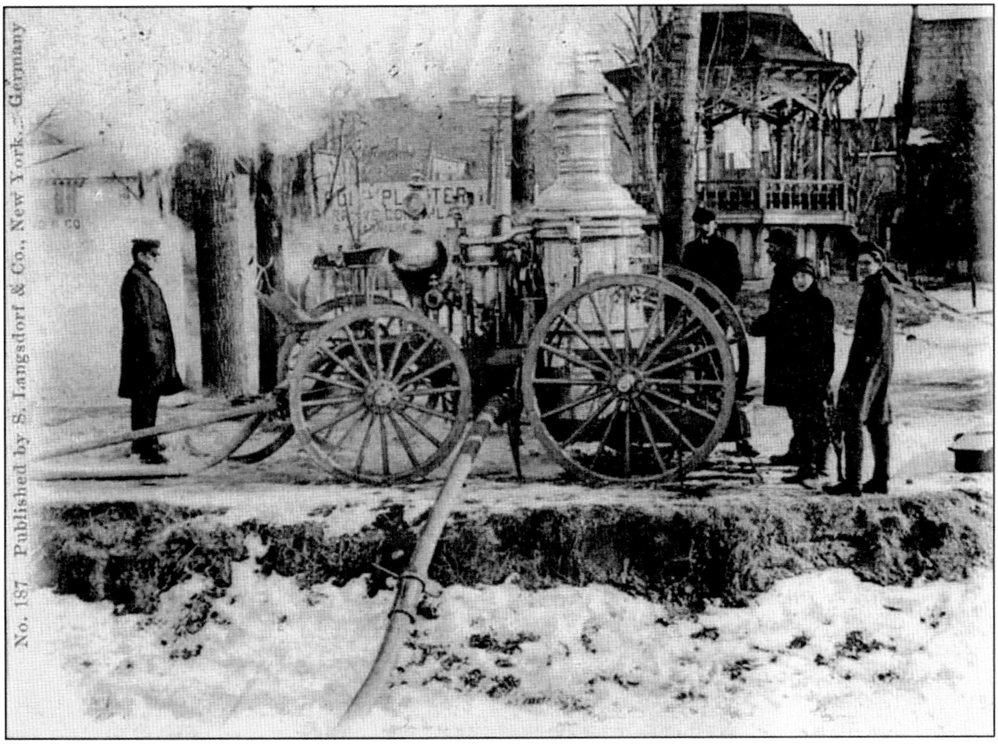

Youngsters stand by expectantly while firemen pumped water from Town Creek to create a skating rink in Third Ward Park. "This is dandy skating here every evening. Large crowds," wrote one postcard correspondent. This card was mailed December 9, 1906. (Ken Cripe collection.)

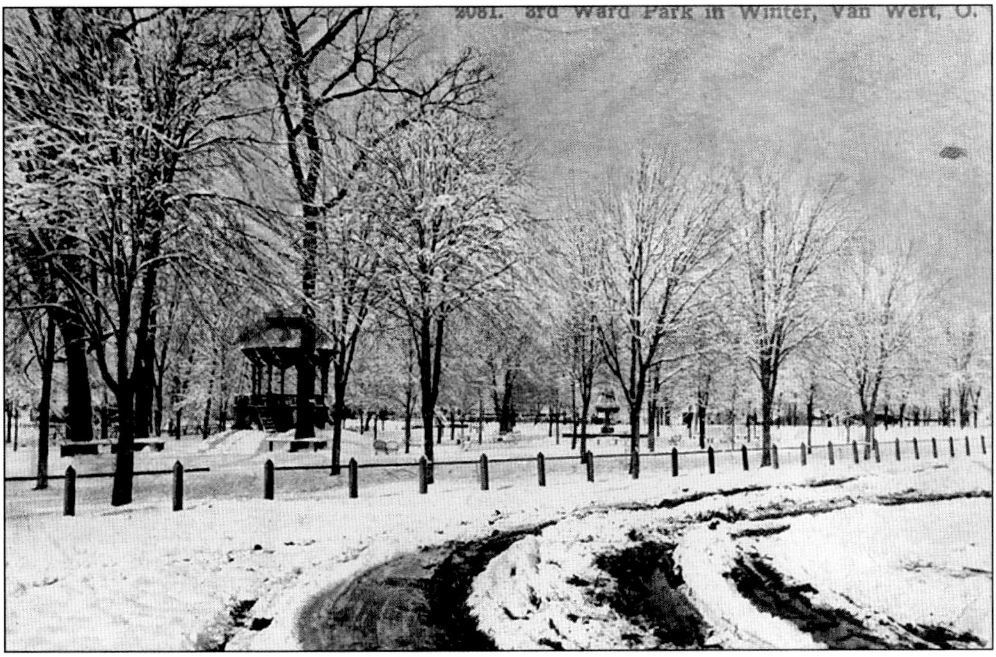

Also called Fountain Park because of its lovely fountain, Third Ward Park was—and is—enjoyed by residents in every season. The postcard was dated 1911. (Author's collection.)

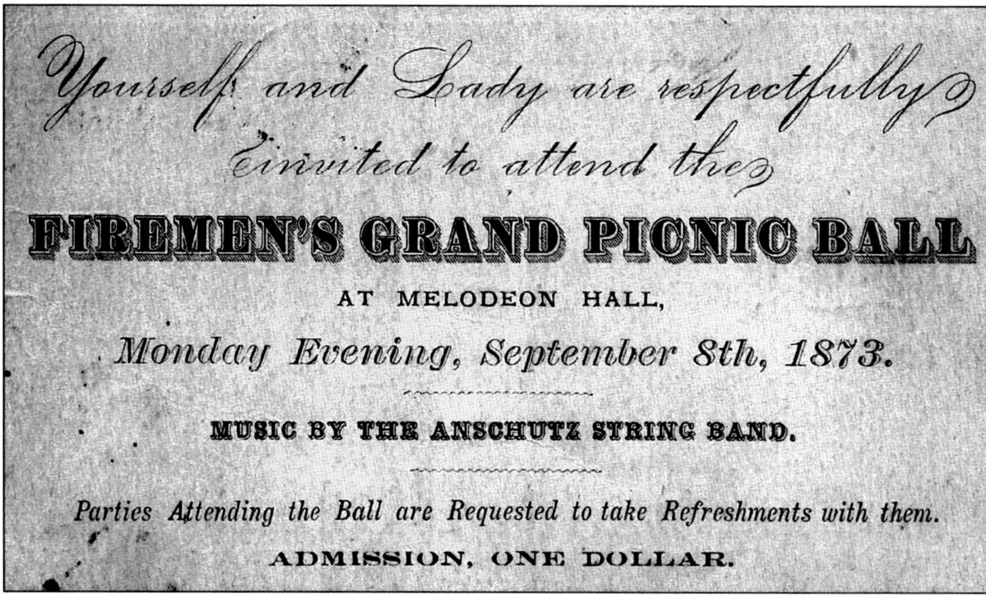

Yourself and Lady are respectfully invited to attend the

FIREMEN'S GRAND PICNIC BALL

AT MELODEON HALL,

Monday Evening, September 8th, 1873.

MUSIC BY THE ANSCHUTZ STRING BAND.

Parties Attending the Ball are Requested to take Refreshments with them.

ADMISSION, ONE DOLLAR.

The Anschutz Band provided the music, and partygoers provided their own (liquid) refreshments at the 1873 Firemen's Grand Picnic Ball. By 1873, Van Wert residents had a professional fire department, but independent firefighters such as the Buckeye Hook and Ladder Company also offered fire protection. (Ken Cripe collection.)

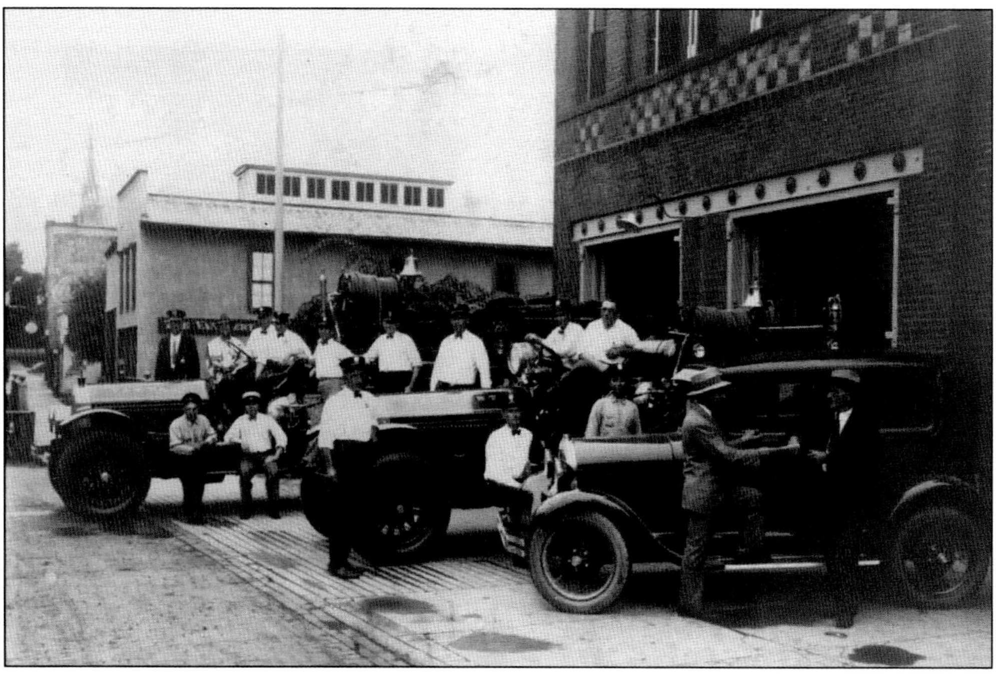

Van Wert City firemen proudly displayed their vehicles in this *c.* 1930 postcard photograph. The department began in 1872, replacing volunteer bucket brigades. Most of the surrounding communities were served by volunteer firefighters at the time. (Ken Cripe collection.)

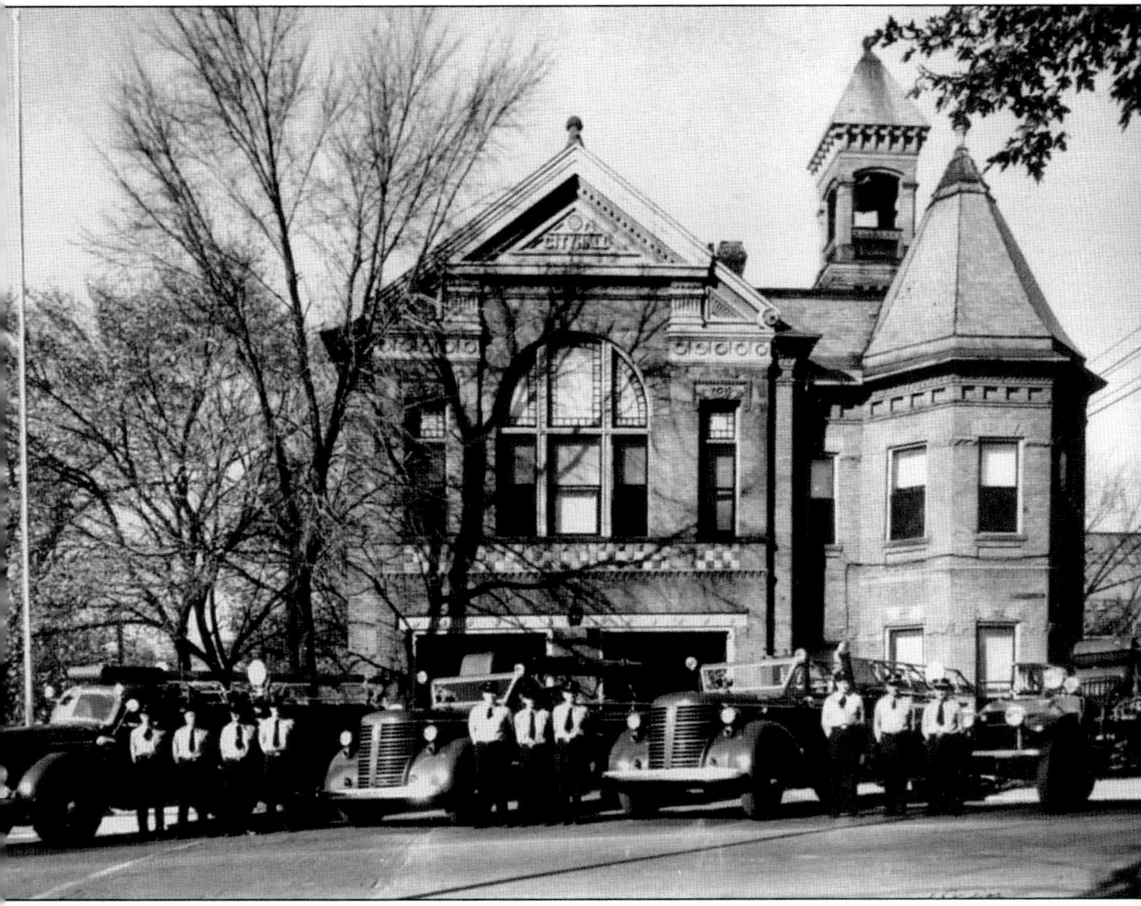

City firefighters pose with their fire engines lined up outside Van Wert City Hall in this *c.* 1920 postcard. With the improvement of gas-powered vehicles, Van Wert and other smaller fire departments enjoyed a major improvement—from horse to horsepower—in the form of better fire trucks. Funded by public revenue, the municipal fire department began in 1872 under the leadership of J. H. Foster. That first city fire department operated with a hand pumper and two wagons plus some reels and hose. When the Buckeye Hook and Ladder Company disbanded, they sold their equipment to the city, and administrators continued to upgrade equipment over the decades. Firefighters shared space with other municipal departments in an impressive stone and brick building at Central Avenue and Washington Street. The city hall was built in 1886 and razed in 1952. (Ken Cripe collection.)

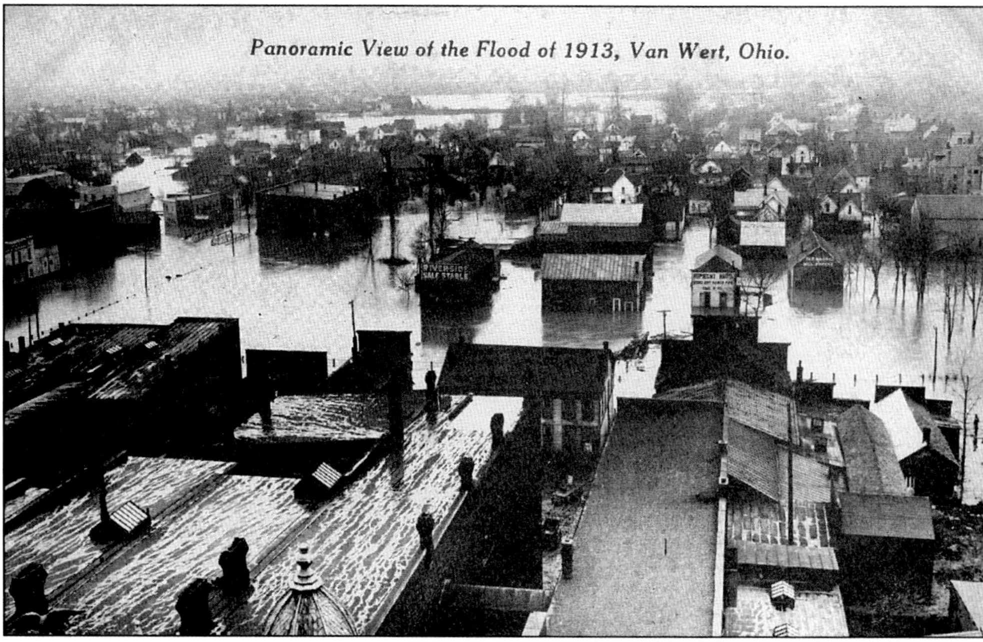

One of Van Wert's greatest challenges was the 1913 flood, a disaster that hit many communities in the region that year. People who lived through the flood never forgot the impact of the terrible natural event. This card shows an overview of Van Wert during the flood. (Ken Cripe collection.)

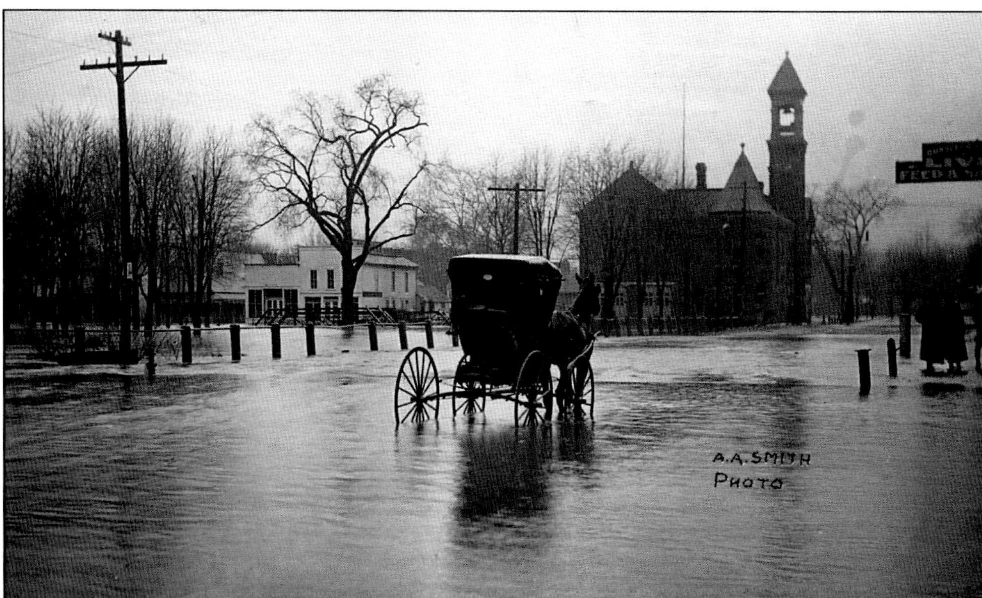

The horse and buggy trudging through flooded streets was reminiscent of Van Wert's first major flood, which occurred in 1883 and damaged homes and businesses. (Ken Cripe collection.)

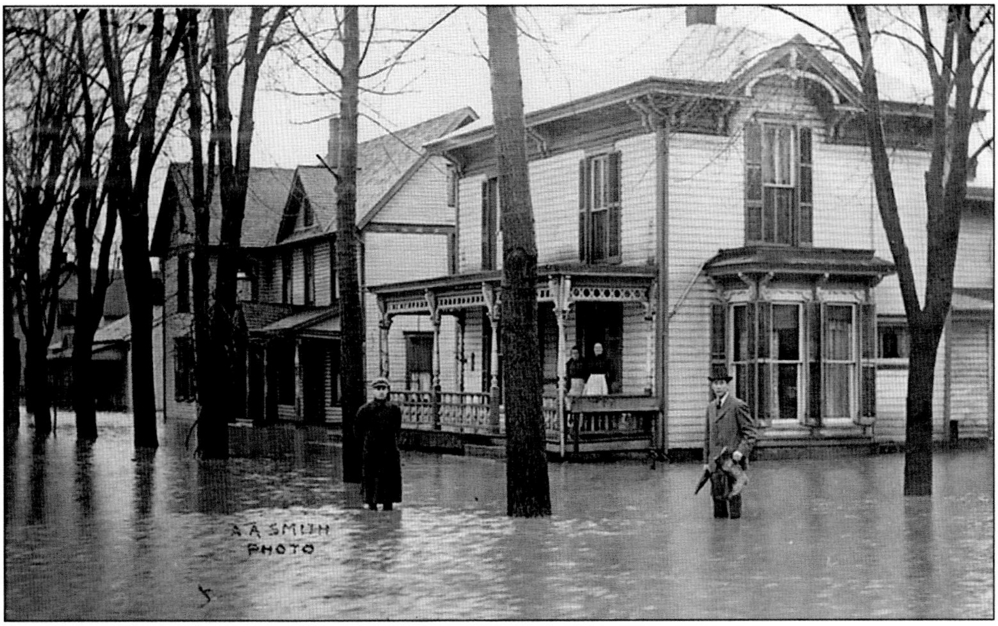

This photograph, taken in March 1913, at the corner of Cherry Street and Central Avenue in Van Wert, illustrated the difficulty of getting around town and the certainty that many basements and first floors would need to be dried out and cleaned. (Author's collection.)

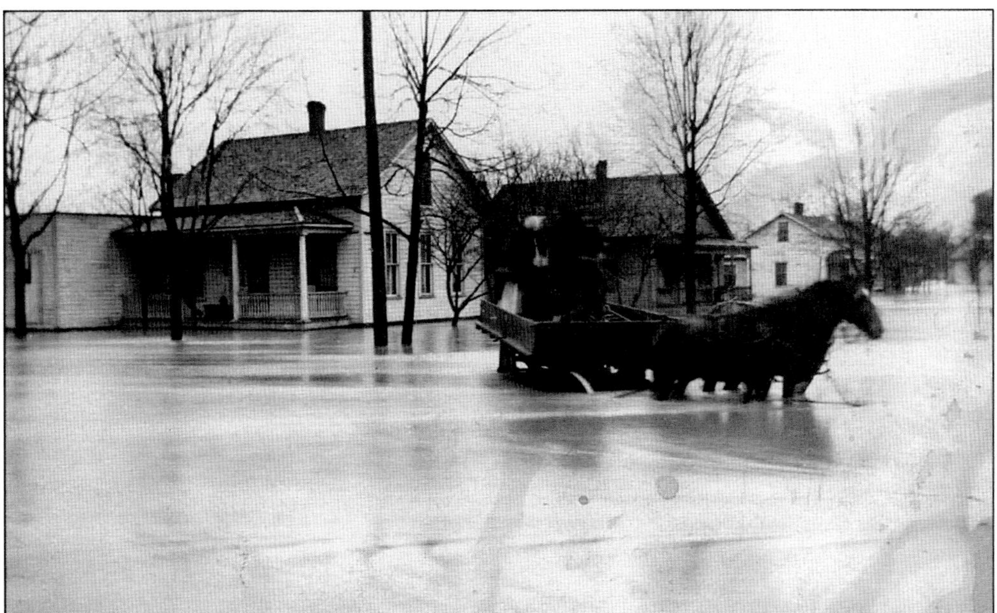

Even horse-drawn carts were stuck in the deep water, as this postcard demonstrates. The photograph was taken from the corner of South Market Street, looking east. (Ken Cripe collection.)

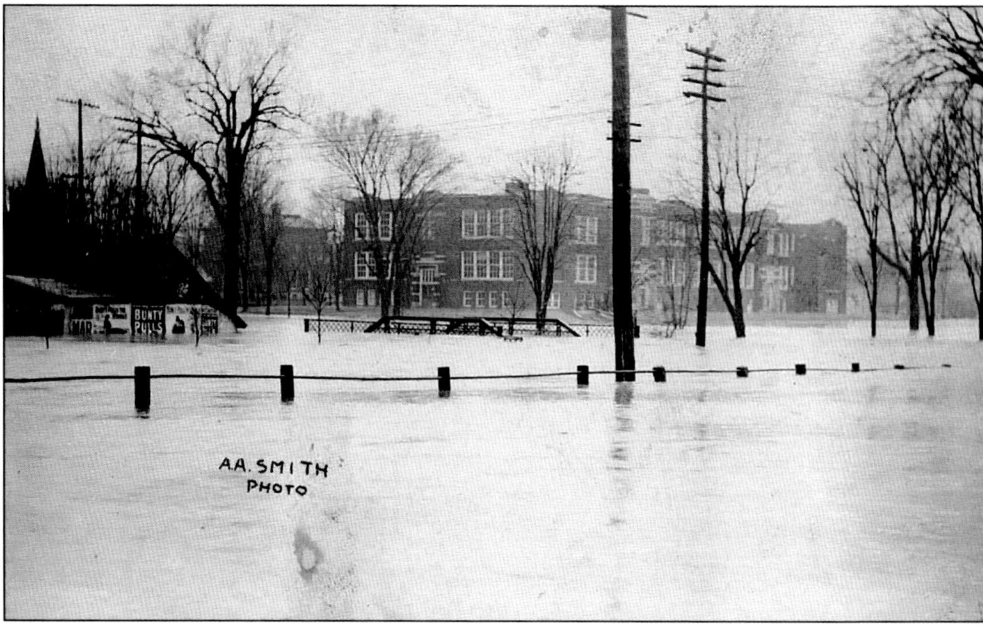

Van Wert High School appears surrounded by a wide moat in this photograph. The Jefferson Street Bridge pokes above floodwaters. (Ken Cripe collection.)

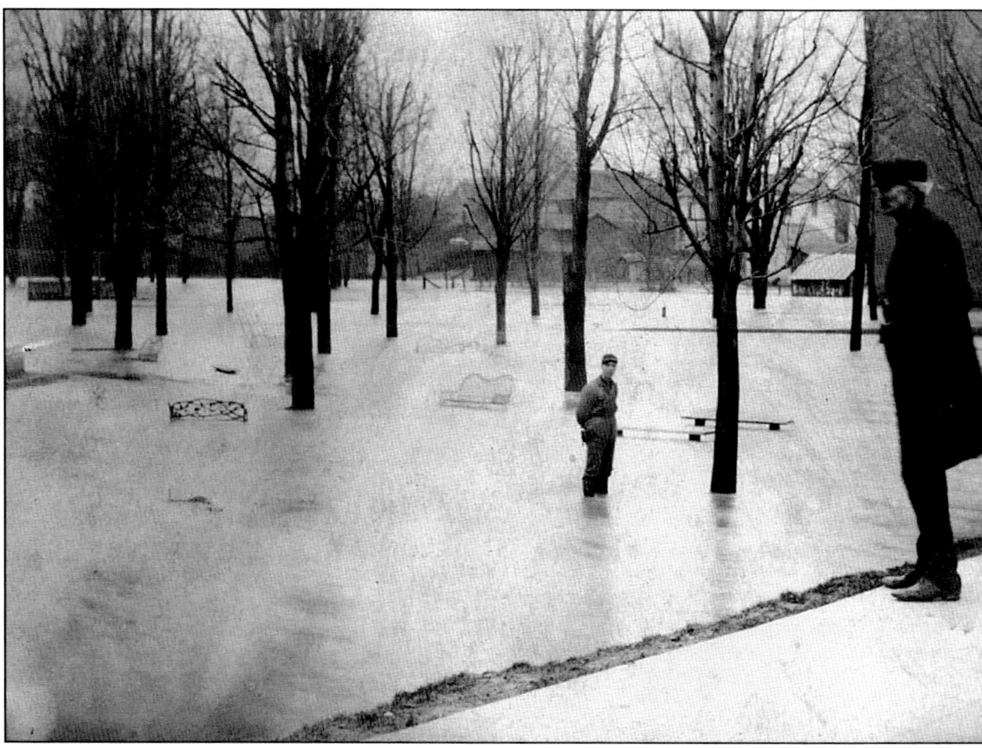

Two residents examine conditions in Third Ward Park where Town Creek spilled over to create a mini reservoir during the 1913 flood. (Ken Cripe collection.)

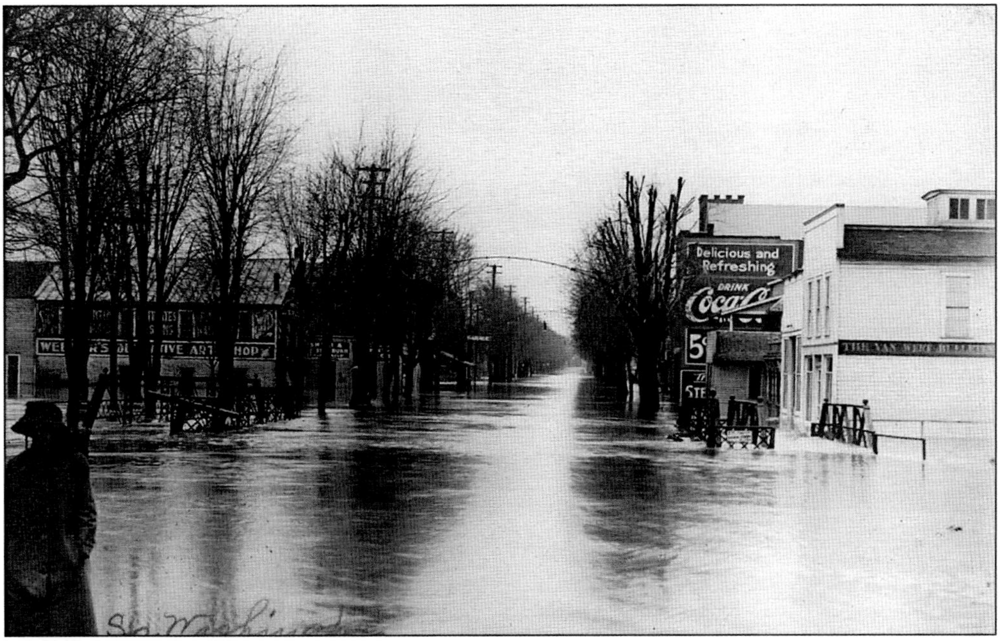

As floodwaters slowly receded, residents ventured out to buy groceries and check on friends. This postcard shows South Washington Street, looking south from Central Avenue. (Ken Cripe collection.)

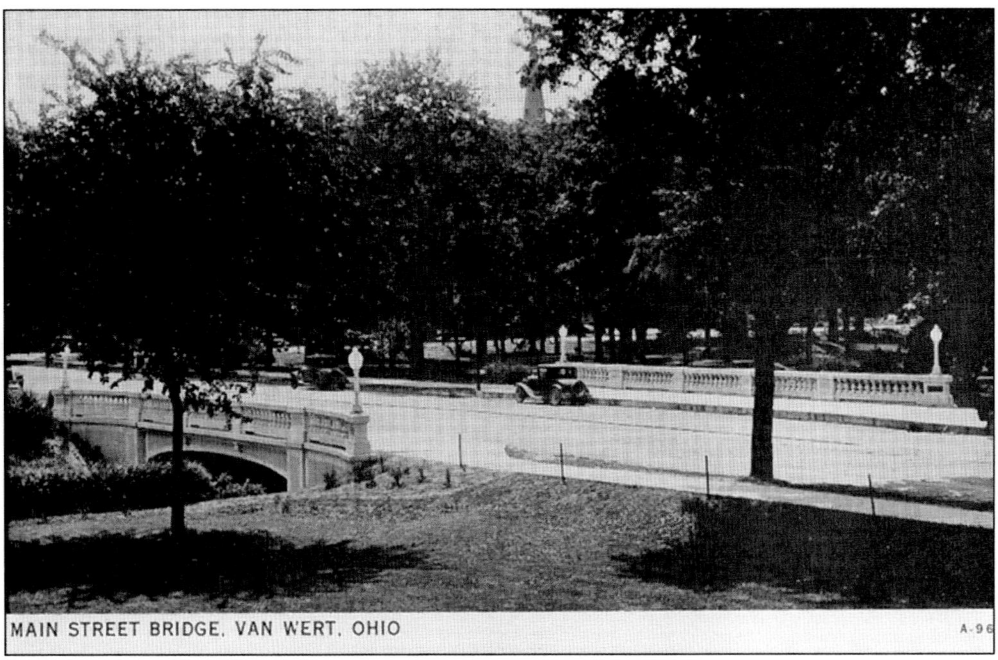

A graceful, strong concrete bridge was built in 1929 to allow residents to travel over Town Creek. City leaders hoped that the bridge would be more resilient during future floods. (Author's collection.)

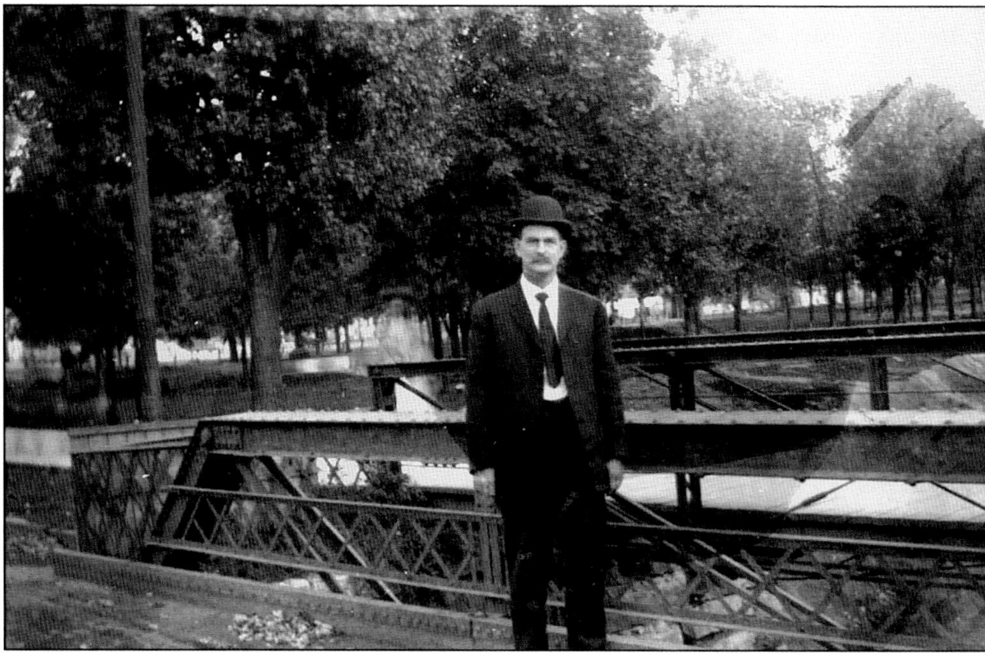

An unidentified man poses on the old Town Creek Bridge before it was replaced. Van Wert had grown tremendously since 1835, and city leaders realized that good streets and bridges were vital to the city's continued success. (Ken Cripe collection.)

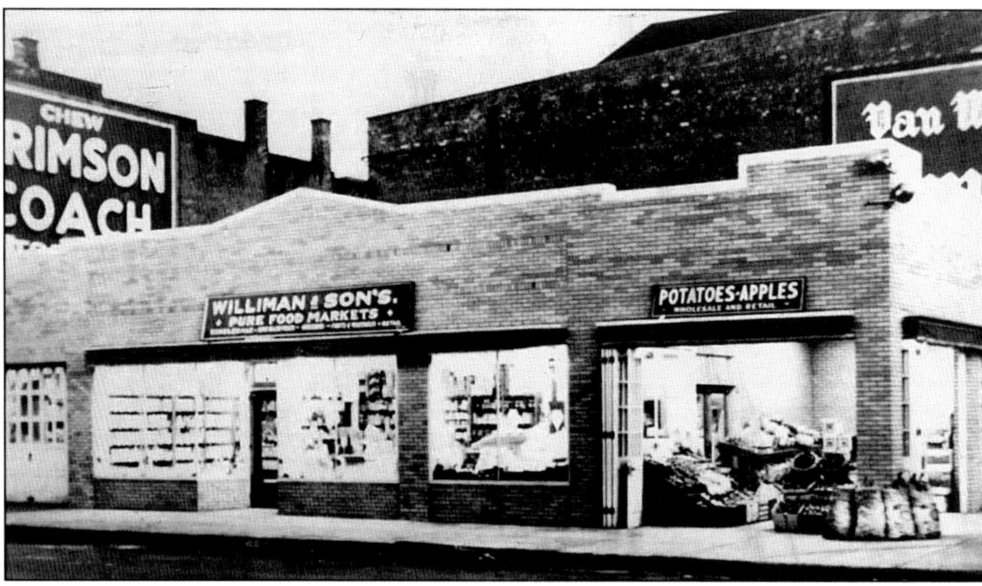

Van Wert residents recovered from the flood to build new homes and start businesses in the 1920s and 1930s, despite some tough economic times. Local shopkeepers like Clarence Williman and sons, Charlie and Phil, grew successful by providing quality goods and services with a personal touch. The exterior of Williman and Sons Grocery at Central Avenue and Market Street is shown in this *c.* 1940 card. (Ken Cripe collection.)

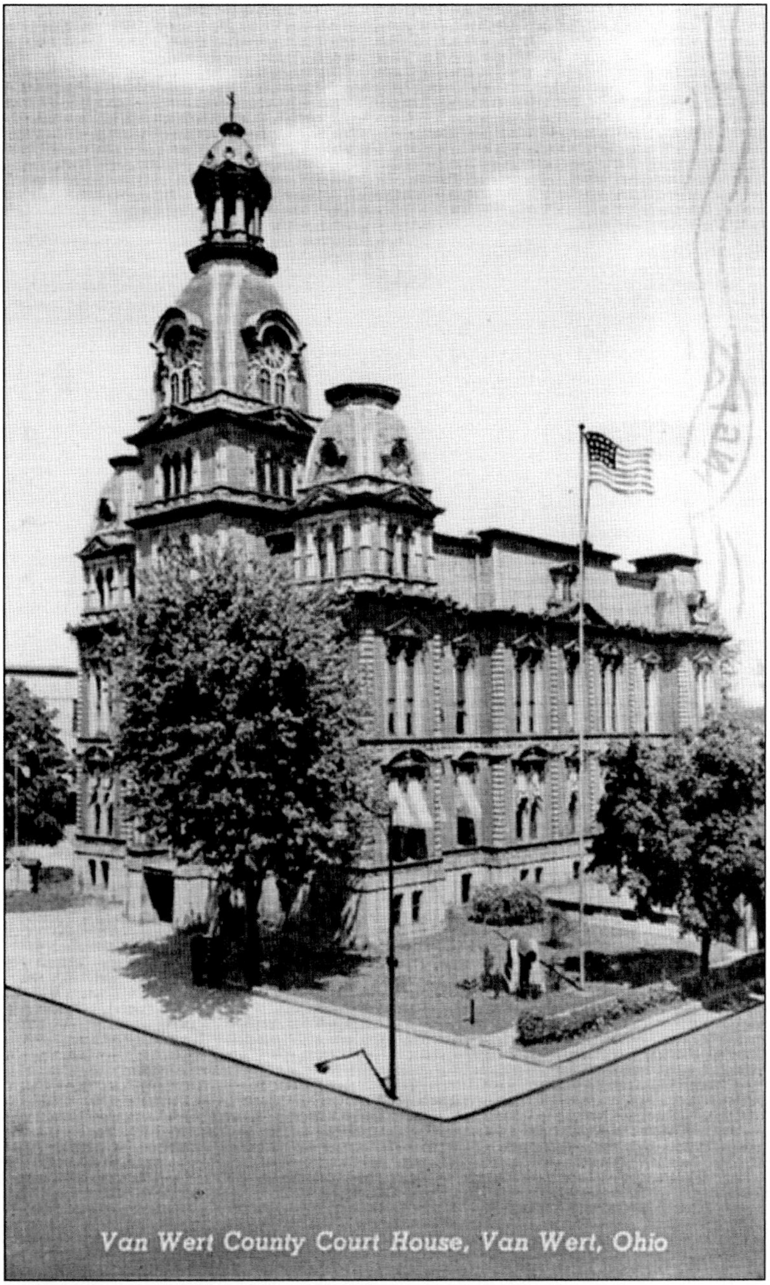

The Van Wert County Courthouse was designed by architect T. J. Tolan and completed in 1876 for around $110,000. A clock and bell, made by the Boston Clock Company, was also installed for about $2,000. The structure was the county's fifth courthouse; smaller structures in town had been used previously. The very first courthouse was a small log house built in Willshire in 1824. When the county seat moved from Willshire to Van Wert in 1839, E. R. Wells, a county official, carried all of the county's official papers in his coat pocket to the new location. This postcard, postmarked May 23, 1941, was mailed by a collector in Virginia to another in Kentucky. Postcard collections were popular at the time, with many collectors specializing in specific topics, such as courthouses, or churches, or movie theaters. (Author's collection.)

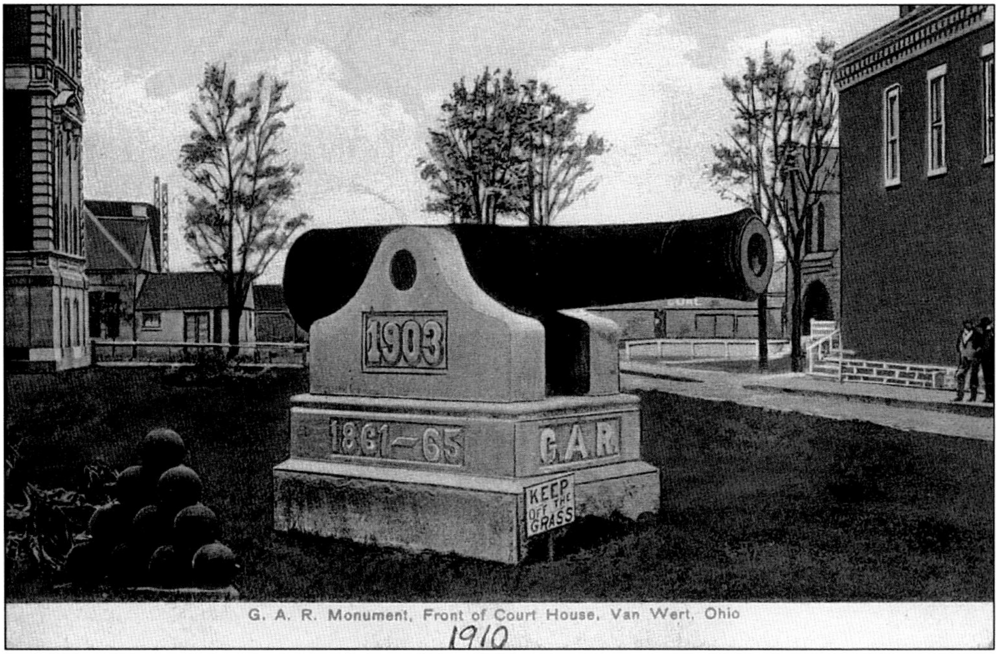

The local chapter of the Grand Army of the Republic placed this cannon on the courthouse lawn in 1903 as a memorial to soldiers who served in the Civil War. (Ken Cripe collection.)

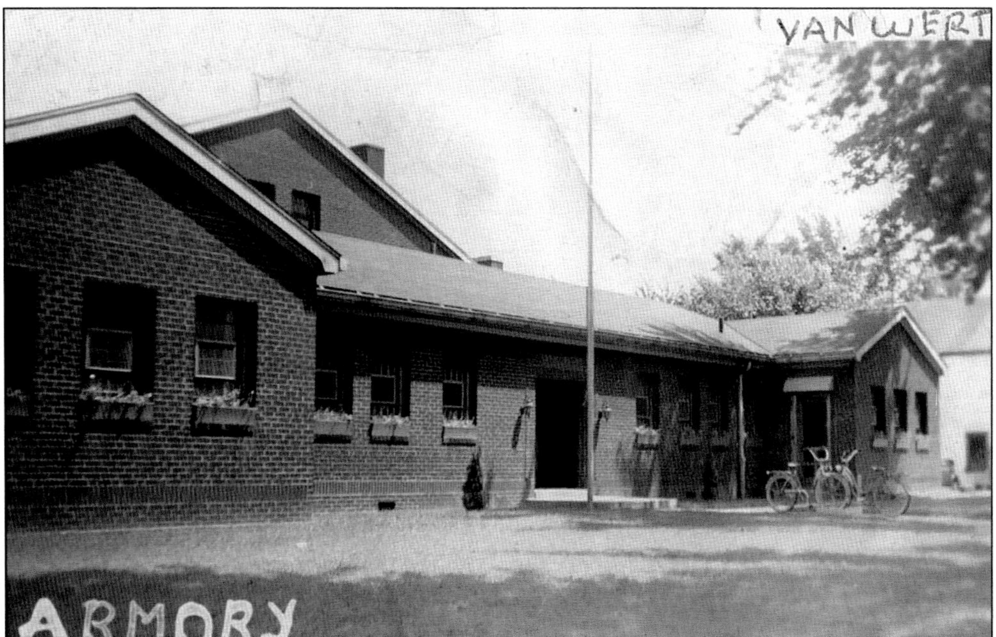

The Armory building in Van Wert is shown in this 1930s postcard. Such small-town Ohio armories often doubled as meeting halls, serving not only the hosting military units, but school groups and other local organizations as well. (Ken Cripe collection.)

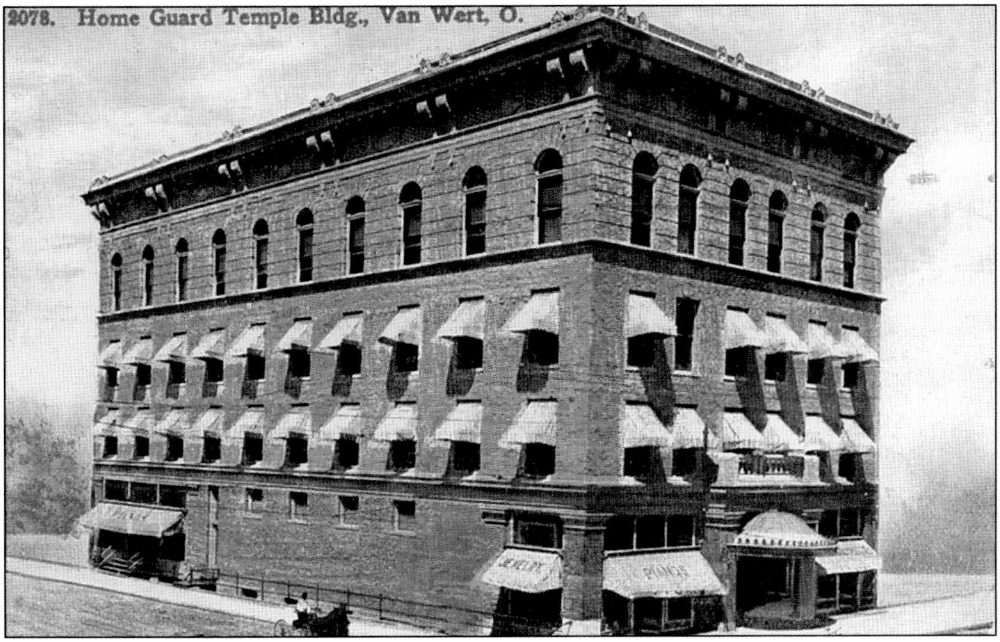

The Home Guard Building at Main and Market Streets was used for many different purposes over the years: manufacturing, office space, and social gatherings. The Trew Nav social club held formal dances on the top floor in the early 1900s. The club's name is Van Wert spelled backwards. The postcard is postmarked 1911. (Author's collection.)

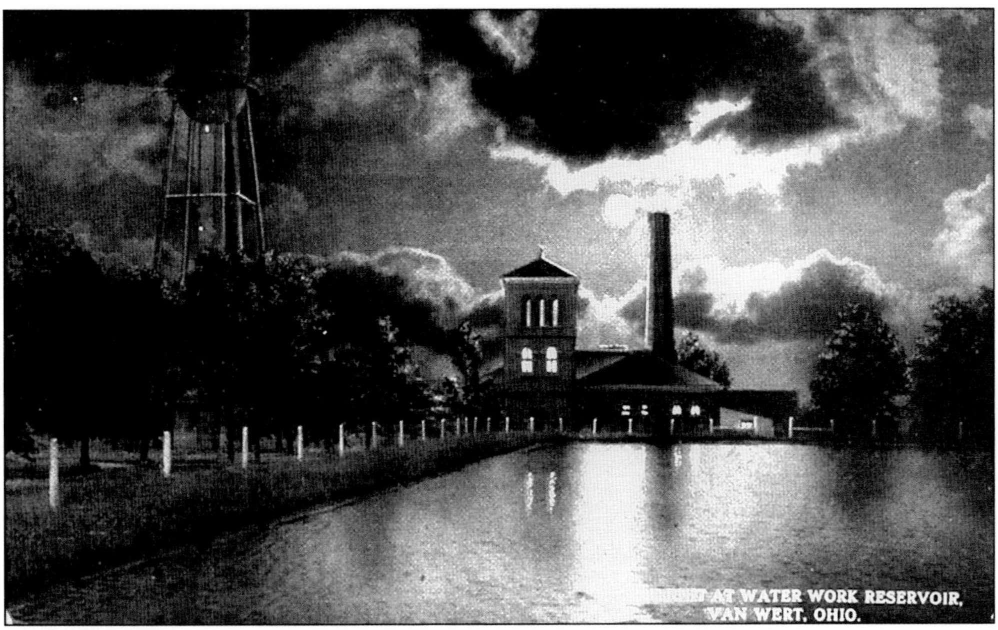

A talented postcard artist could take a black and white photograph of the water works reservoir and make it look romantic by adding some moody clouds and a full moon. In 1911, the sender wrote to his family in Cincinnati that Van Wert was "a nice town, level as a floor" but bemoaned the lack of watering holes of another sort. (Author's collection.)

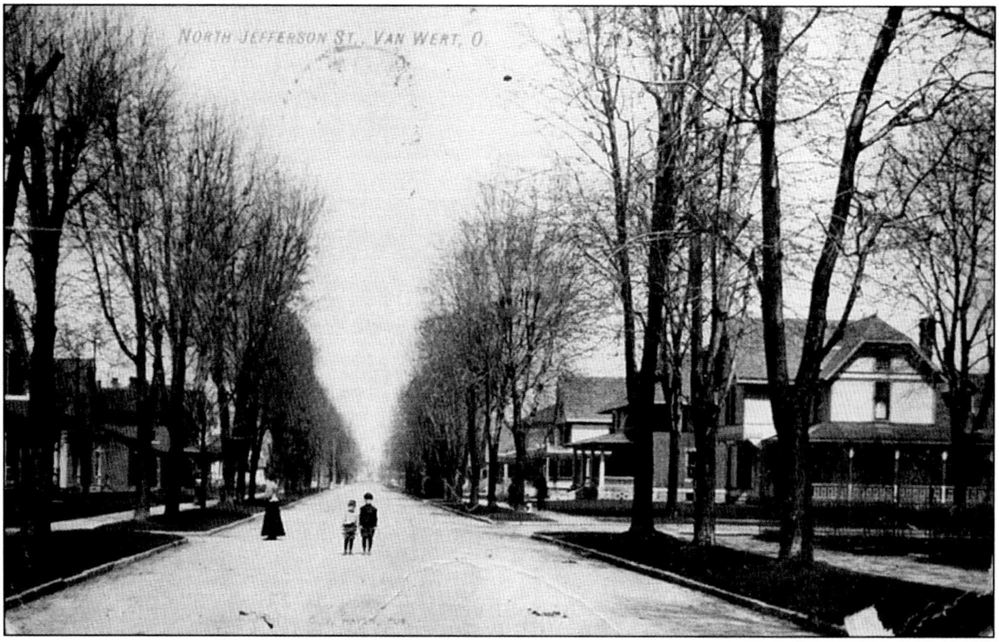

Wide, tree-lined streets and large, comfortable homes beckoned postcard recipients to come to Van Wert, either for a visit or to live there. The postcard of North Jefferson Street (above) is postmarked 1908. The Washington Street card is undated, but of the same era. (Author's collection.)

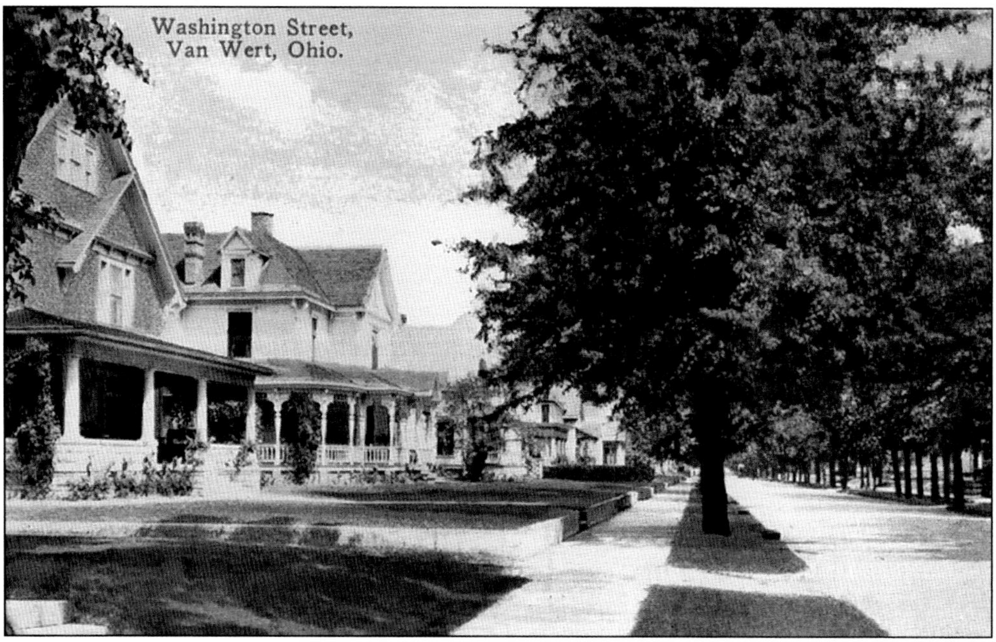

Ten

FRIENDS AND NEIGHBORS

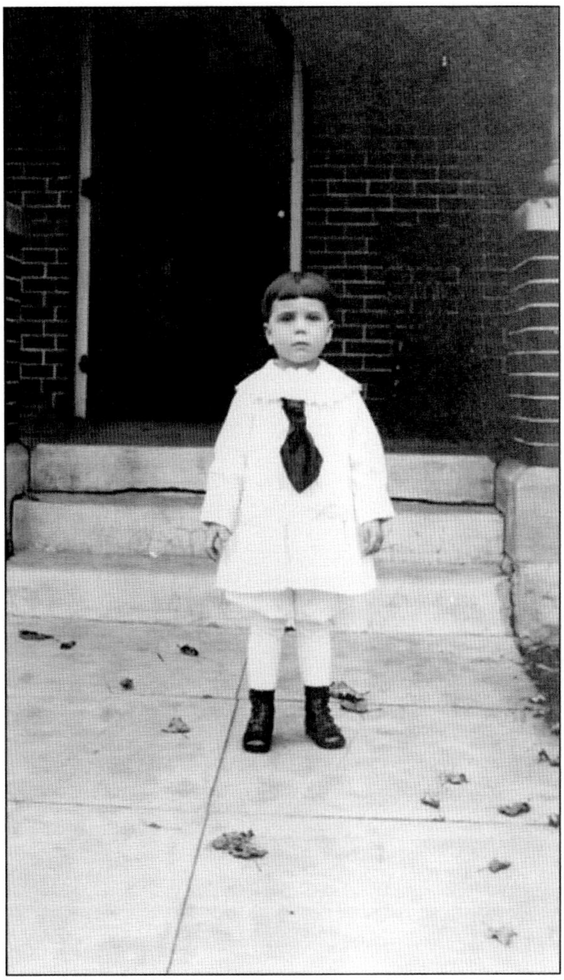

Portrait postcards were extremely popular in the first two decades of the 20th century. Even a farmer's son could dress as a small Edwardian gentleman for his portrait. Frederick Edwin Bauer was three years old in 1917 when this photograph was taken at the home of a Convoy relative. Frederick was the son of Frederick J. Bauer and Elizabeth Bauer (née Steinbauer) of Tully Township, and the author's father. (Author's collection.)

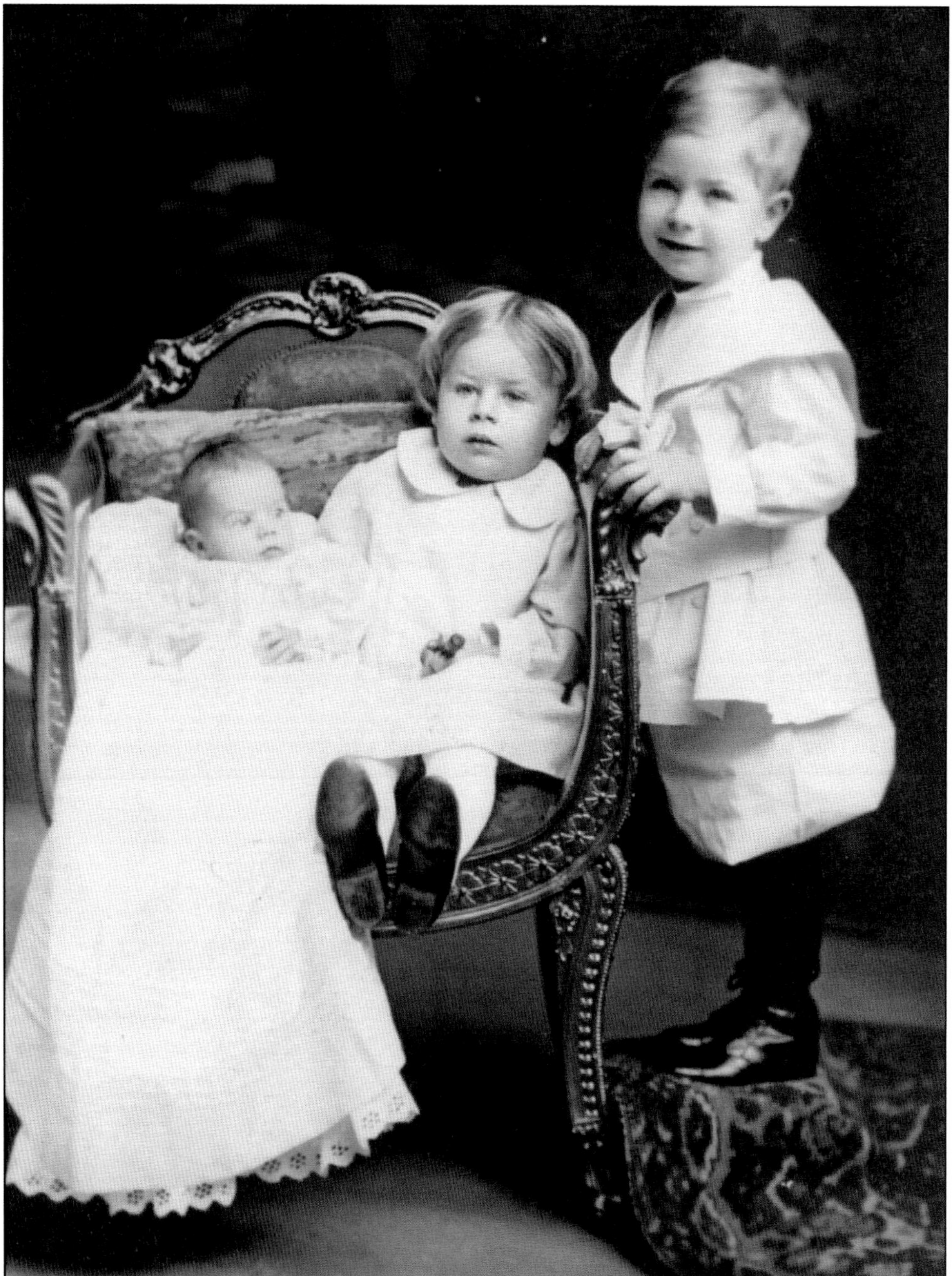

The Yoh family of Van Wert commissioned a beautiful portrait of their children around 1912. Loyal was just an infant, Dorothy was two, and Herman was four when the photograph was taken. Dorothy grew up to become Dorothy Yoh Anderson and the future mother-in-law of postcard collector Ken Cripe. Such photographs of children were typically taken for special occasions: baptisms, first communions, confirmations, and graduations. The cards might be sent as invitations to an event, announcement of a milestone, or a cherished keepsake for loved ones. (Ken Cripe collection.)

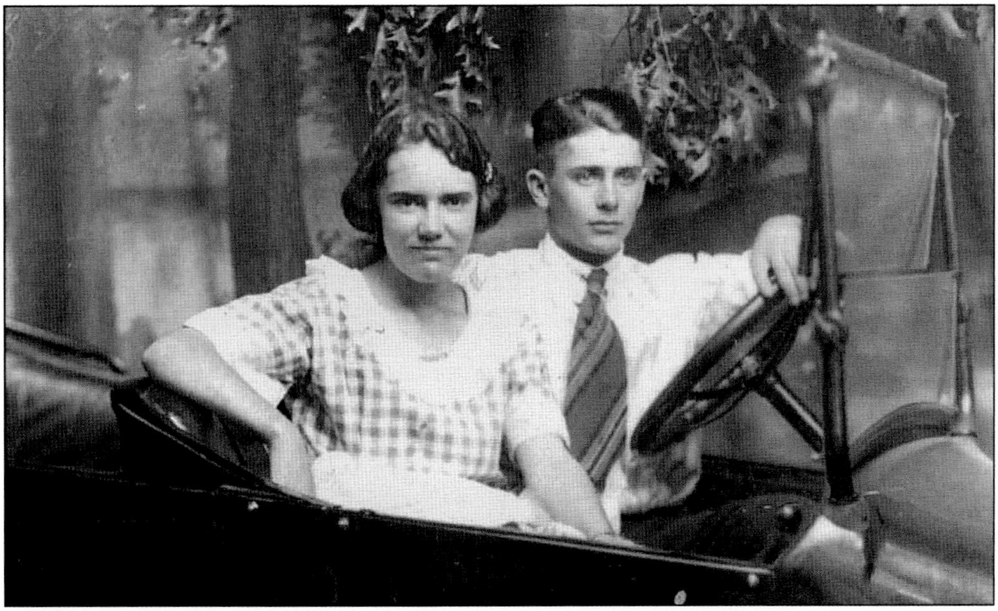

Marjorie Fackler Wollenkaupt, seen here, kept this postcard as a souvenir of the day she and her friend Homer DeCamp spent at the Van Wert County Fair. Wollenkaupt was a sophomore in high school at the time. The photograph was taken at the old Art Hall on the fairgrounds. (Ken Cripe collection.)

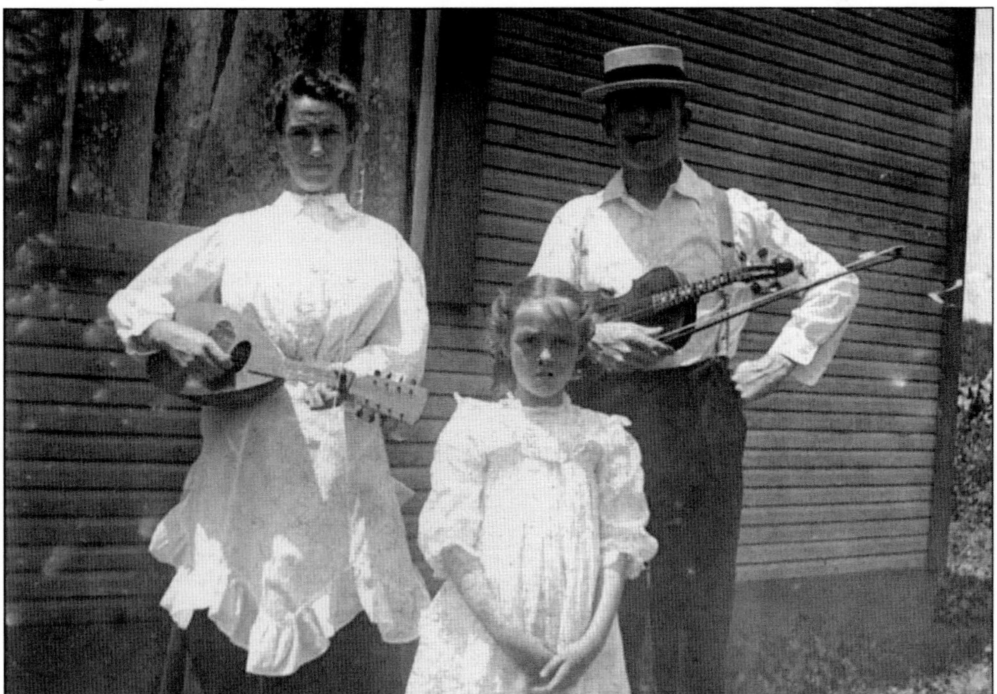

Charlie and Leona Griffith display their musical instruments for this photograph in 1907. Charlie played the fiddle, Leona the mandolin, and daughter Nellie sang along. Charlie Griffith was a barber, and the family lived at 317 North Walnut Street in Van Wert. (Ken Cripe collection.)

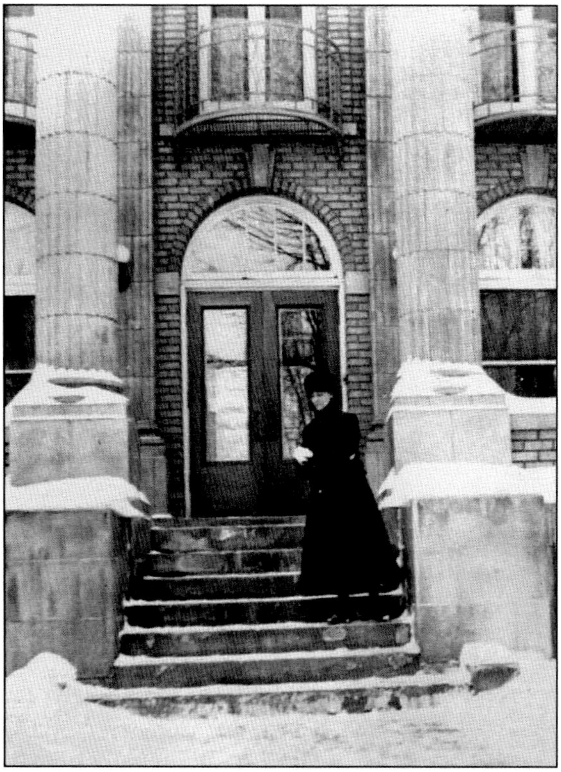

Despite her dignified appearance, the unidentified woman in this *c.* 1917 postcard appears to know how to pack a snowball. The setting was the new YWCA in Van Wert. Could the intended victim have been the photographer? (Ken Cripe collection.)

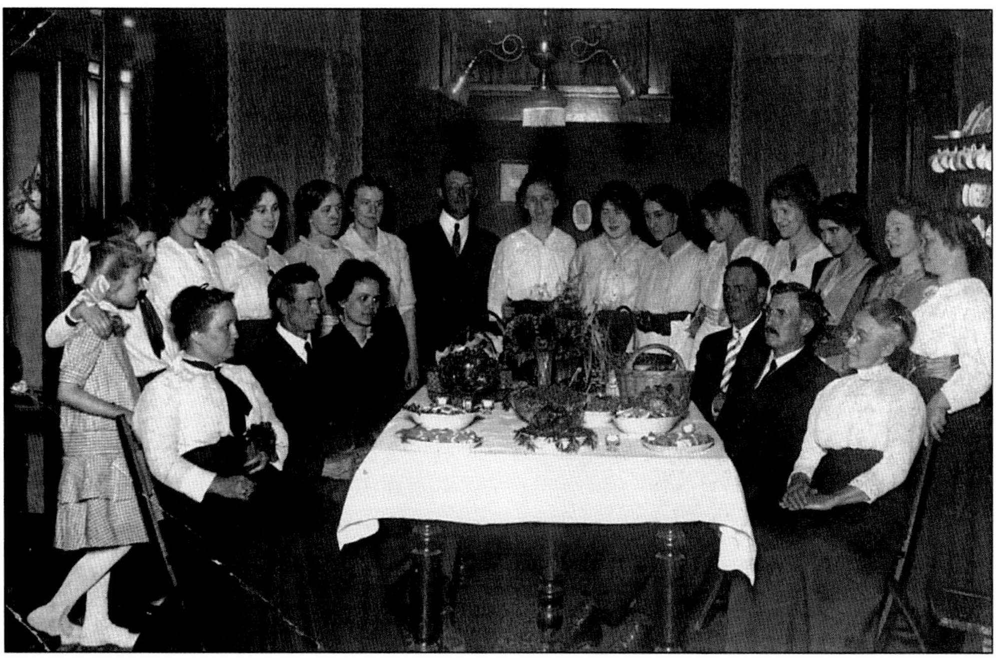

The Cletus Stripe family gathered for this early 1900s card. Cletus, his brother Emmett, and father Elmer worked together as Stripe and Sons, General Contractors. The company built many masonry and brick buildings and bridges throughout the county. Cletus and his wife Norma (née Gribler) raised their family in Van Wert. (Ken Cripe collection.)

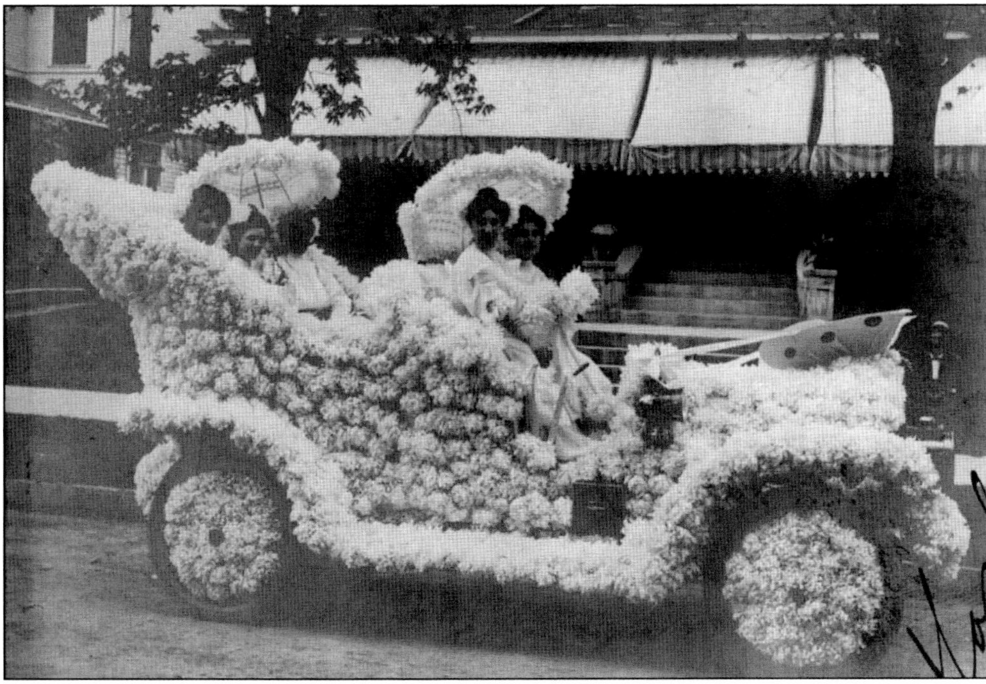

Van Wert County history books tell of the local women's many charitable endeavors including caring for the needy, raising funds to build churches, starting the public library, and supporting medical care for residents. These five unidentified ladies decorated their car with flowers for a Hospital Fund Festival in early August 1905. The photograph was taken on South Washington Street in Van Wert. (Ken Cripe collection.)

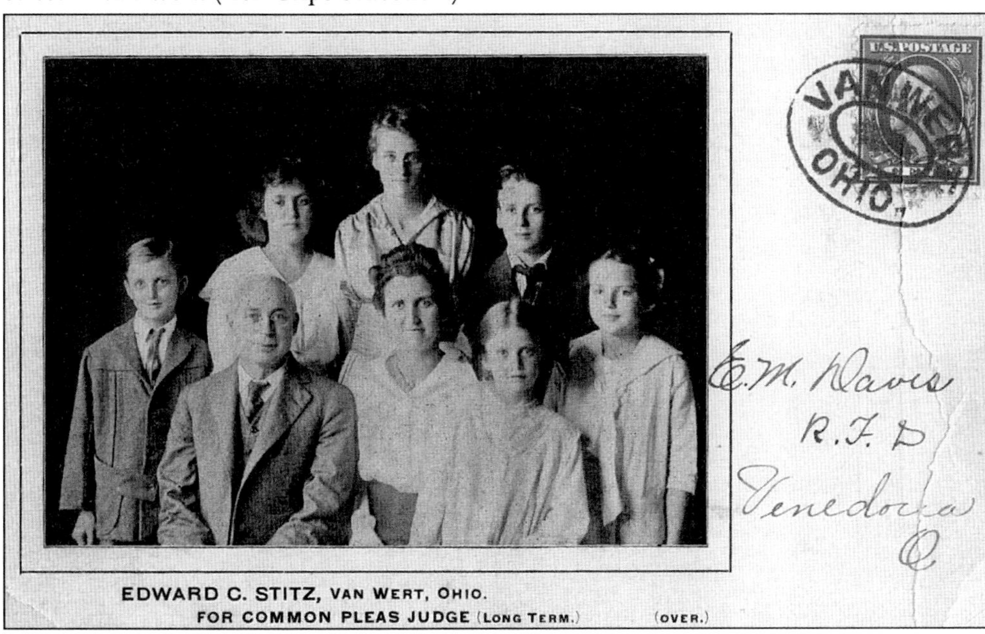

Van Wert solicitor Edward G. Stitz showed off his family in 1916 when he made a bid for Common Pleas Court judge. Stitz, a Republican, had 25 years of experience as an attorney when he ran for judge. (Ken Cripe collection.)

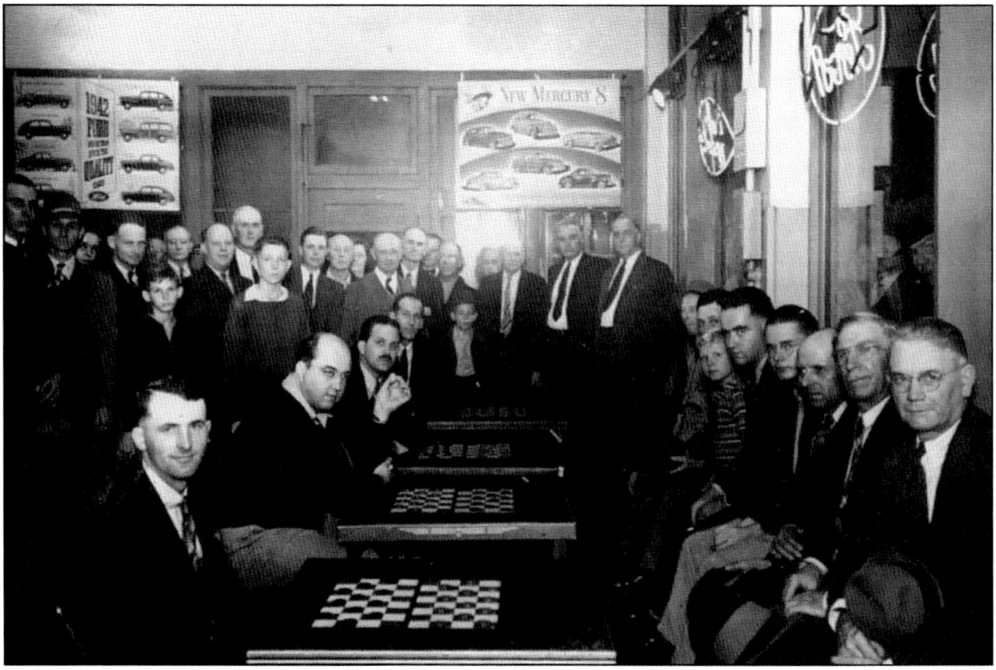

A group of men gather in an unidentified Van Wert automobile dealership to play chess in this postcard from the early 1940s. The Mercury advertisements on the wall point to the date. (Ken Cripe collection.)

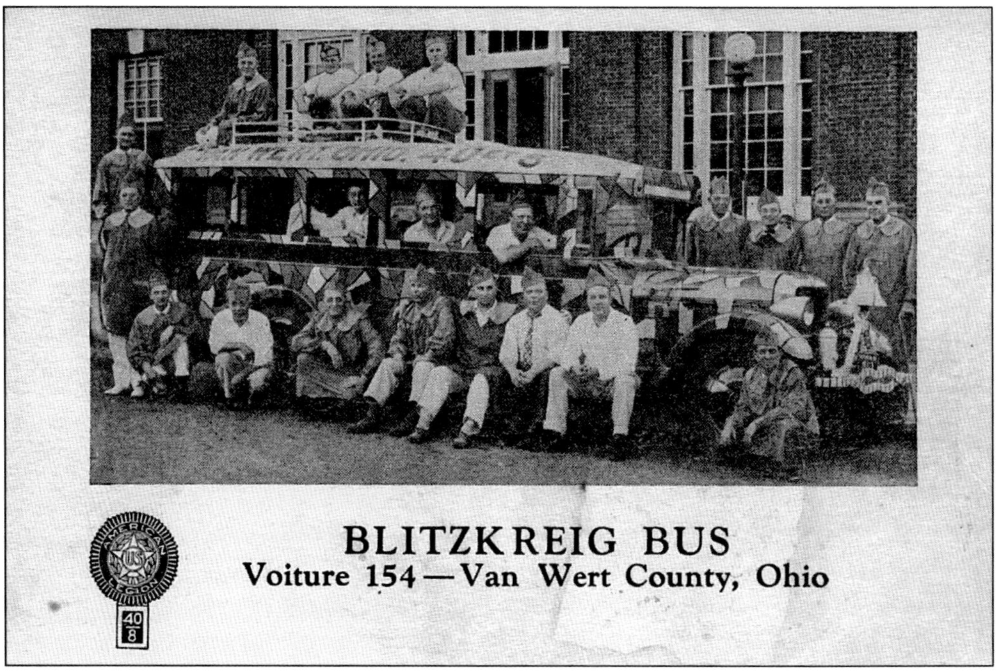

They have been dubbed as America's "Greatest Generation" for good reason. The members of American Legion Voiture 154 in this World War II era postcard represented the sacrifice and commitment of thousands of Van Wert County men and women to provide a promising future for the next generation. (Ken Cripe collection.)

Bibliography

Amstutz, Jim and Kent McMillen, editors. *Van Wert County Sesquicentennial, 1821–1971: Out of a Wilderness.* Van Wert, 1971.

Complete Directory of Van Wert County, O. Portland, Indiana: Prillman Directory, 1909–1910.

Convoy Centennial Committee. *Let's Hear It For Convoy: Convoy Centennial, 1874–1974.*

Dineen, Jeanne, editor. *Van Wert, Ohio, Sesquicentennial, 1835–1985.* Van Wert, 1985.

History of Van Wert and Mercer Counties, Ohio. Mt. Vernon, Indiana: Windmill Publications, 1991.

History of Van Wert County, Ohio. Van Wert County Historical Society, 1981.

Howe, Henry. *Historical Collections of Ohio. Vol. II.* Cincinnati: C. J. Krehbiel and Company, 1888.

McNutt, Randy. *Lost Ohio: More Travels Through Haunted Landscapes, Ghost Towns, and Forgotten Lives.* Kent State University Press, 2006.

O'Daffer, Floyd C. *History of Van Wert County.* Lima: Fairway Press, 1990.

Photo Star: Convoy Centennial Edition. Willshire, Ohio. July 16, 1975.

Portrait and Biographical Records of Mercer and Van Wert Counties, Ohio. Chicago: A. W. Bowen and Company, 1896.

Prill, Helen White. *Van Wert County Fairs, 1855–1996.* Van Wert County Historical Society and Van Wert County Agricultural Society, 1996.

Willshire Sesquicentennial Committee. *And I Have Laid Out a Town.* 1972.

Wren Historical Society. *From Greenwood to Wren.* 1976.

Information was also gathered from interviews with Ken Cripe from August through December 2005, and from Web sites posted by individuals, groups, businesses, and municipalities discussed in the book.